Motif v 3
ALL THE LIVELONG DAY

an anthology *of* writings about work

~

edited by

MARIANNE WORTHINGTON

All the Livelong Day
an Anthology of Writings about Work

Volume 3 in the Motif anthology series

Marianne Worthington, editor

ISBN 978-1-934894-46-0
anthology

Book Design
EYE.K

Cover Photo
"Two American Workers" © Toby J Larkins

Back Cover Photo
"Drugstore Lunch" © Jackie White Rogers.

Photos used with permission of the photographers.

Published by
Motes Books
Louisville, Kentucky

www.MotesBooks.com

For my father, Thomas Andrew Worthington, in memoriam,
who defined himself through work,

and

For my father-in-law, David Caskie Semmel, in memoriam,
whose favorite expression was "Shut up, and get to work."

—mw

Contents

I. Day Shift

II. Swing Shift

III. Night Shift

Introduction

Song for Atlantic Avenue

The workingmen come walking
They lean across the stone
Huddled up in hats and coats
They take themselves toward home
A journey that each day
Begins anew on Atlantic Avenue

The puddles in the parking lot
Reflecting the sky
As the evening rain lets up
In the glow of twilight
The crack between two worlds
Comes into view on Atlantic Avenue

Darkness falls forever
On broken wheels and dreams
Alley cats and night birds play
In the shadows and machines
A signal from the streetlamp
Breaking through on Atlantic Avenue

Windows in old houses
Glowing rosy in the night
Lost within exhausted sleep
Sheltered in the life
And the stars above twinkle out
Of the blue on Atlantic Avenue

— R B Morris

The wistful song that begins this anthology has a particular appeal for me because it is about the working lives of residents in a Knoxville neighborhood. Like the songwriter, RB Morris, I grew up in Knoxville, Tennessee, in a working-class family in a working-class district (not too far from Atlantic Avenue) in a primarily working-class town. Of course there were families in other, diverse economic situations in Knoxville, but not in my neighborhood. My father was a washer and dryer repairman for the city utility company—a steady job with decent benefits—but the work required making house calls all over town, repairing broken-down laundry equipment in tight spaces, and it exhausted him. My mother worked, too; first as a tailor in our home and later as a bookkeeper for a mechanical contracting firm. My aunts and uncles all had similar professions: cafeteria workers, telephone operators, linemen, mechanics, secretaries, welders, and small farmers. Now that I'm looking back on their working lives, I'm astonished to remember that they never stopped working, even after they left their jobs each day. The overwhelming responsibilities of family and home never ended. As the song states, "A journey that each day / Begins anew . . . "

I mention these personal characteristics of my own upbringing because I discovered how universal they seem when I began reading submissions to this anthology on the theme of work, the third in the *Motif* anthology series. The working experiences recorded by the 130 writers included in this anthology are as routine as the work day yet as varied as the work force.

One pattern that emerged quickly is how we tend to hold our ancestors' working lives in higher esteem than our own. We never seem to work as hard as our parents worked, as poet Lucia Cherciu reminds us:

> How many times
> have we thought ourselves buried in work
> only to remember the toil of our parents?

And while some sense of accomplishment may have resulted in the hard work of our foreparents, it was usually accompanied by some injustice or loss of dignity. The subtext of inequality and discrimination in the working-class world is obvious in the writings here, as well. A second pattern that defines these pages is that all work involves some kind of peril, either literally or metaphorically. Some of the prose and poetry in this anthology chronicles the particular injuries that befall the dangerous occupations of the coal miner, butcher, carpenter, farmer, uranium processor, or steel worker. Other writers detail the psychological risks in the work of health care providers, family caregivers, clerks, artists, activists, and unrequited lovers. A final pattern in these works is how often we tend to avoid working, or how we will occupy ourselves with one kind of work in order to evade another kind. We clean the house instead of repairing interpersonal relationships, or we tear apart a machine instead of facing grief or loss. Or as some writers suggest here, we write one thing because we cannot find or cannot face the thing we really should be writing. Earning a living as a writer is a topic addressed frequently in these pages, despite what that work might look like to others (as Jennifer Horne says in her poem about working as a poet: "I admit it looks a lot like goofing off").

These universal themes circling around the routines of work, however, make up only one side of this versatile volume. Many of the voices in this anthology are marked by a sense of diversity and uniqueness. Some writers tell the stories of those with unusual occupations: circus clown, methamphetamine maker, entomologist, film projectionist, car hop, faith healer, and prison guard. Others tell the often harrowing stories of unemployment and the resulting wounds that joblessness inflicts on families. Some writers comment on the creative ways that workers soothe the ennui of office work. Finally, there are pieces here that are written from the perspective of the worker in unusual situations: A physician dealing with the drug-seeking behavior of a favorite patient; a Peace Corps volunteer in a small village in the vast transcontinental country of Kazakhstan; an activist at a union strike in eastern Kentucky; and the farmer who imagines that heaven will be just as segregated by economic status as life on earth is now. The late Lee Howard predicted injustice for the working person even in heaven in her poem "Celestial Farmer":

> I'll die and be living in a shanty on Heaven's dirt road
> while the rich folks are sitting pretty
> in them many mansions on those streets paved with gold.

The short fiction, creative nonfiction, song lyrics, and poems contained in this volume have been arranged to reflect a common characteristic of the American work force: shift work. Readers can begin this journey in the morning with the day shift, travel through the working day with the swing shift, and proceed into the hoot-owl hours with the night shift. As with previous *Motif* anthologies, our goal has been to provide a varied and colorful reading experience on a particular theme. In this third volume on the familiar theme of work, I hope readers will find the dedicated efforts of these 130 contributors as challenging and rewarding as a good day's labor.

—*mw*

Day Shift

Exhausted

I've done my best to live the right way
I get up every morning and go to work each day
—Bruce Springsteen

Five a.m. My father rises, shuffles his callused feet to the bathroom and slides open the pocket door. A brief coughing fit, hocks into the sink. The exhaust fan rattles above him. A fart kick-starts his long piss, then several quick, hard blasts into his handkerchief. Pocket door slides open, down the stairs, wood creaking and popping, sandpaper hands rubbing along the banister. Muted Weather Channel's blue glow, silverware drawer, running water, coffee pot. Back up stairs, bathroom, mug placed on permanent coffee ring on the sink. Shower. Sparks a Winston, lets it burn like incense on the wicker shelf, scrapes his neck with a razor, slaps Old Spice into his cheeks. Stairs, checks weather, coffee cup thunks in the sink. Blue Nissan truck. First gear, second, third, and I won't see him again until four in the afternoon, when he coasts the Nissan back into the driveway, tosses his bloody white apron over his shoulder, and embraces me with a lifetime of tobacco and coffee and cold cuts.

Seven a.m. My mother officially rises, though she's been awake for hours, tossing, turning, mumbling incoherently. Zombies out of bed in her pink nightgown. Into the bathroom for an unproductive bout with IBS, expelling yesterday's swallowed air. A sigh. Tosses my father's burnt Winston filter into the trash, down the same stairs, same Weather Channel, same coffee pot. Sparks a Marlboro Light. If she's cleaning houses, she takes her rags from the dryer in the basement, packs them into a canvas tote, then collects the rest of her supplies: Windex, Lysol, an all-purpose spray called Simple Green, which she swears by.

Perhaps these are her yacht club years, and instead of Windex and rags, she loads a rectangular plastic bin full of restaurant checks, an enormous printing calculator balanced on top. Or she's a secretary for a dermatologist, so she's been up since six, showering, blow-drying, ironing, heels clicking on wood, then tile, wood, then tile. Perhaps arts and crafts, wedding albums with thick cotton covers and lace trim, or something she called *Poofs*: little, flower-shaped puffs of satin with a metal clip glue-gunned to the back that one could attach to shoes or blouses or use to cinch a pony tail.

Beauty parlor in the basement fully equipped with hair-washing station and spaceman dome, which she assured me was for drying the hair of the strange women who entered our home and not for transforming them into a *Jetsons* character and blasting them into another galaxy.

Maybe this day she works two or three jobs, loads all of her equipment into the car, takes a final sip of coffee and bursts out of the porch as if it were a phone booth, returns hours later for a quick costume change, then back out into the world again. A different role. A different identity.

When I was in elementary school, I often joined my father at 5 a.m., sipping the bitter coffee in his mug while he shaved. The residual shower steam swirled with his cigarette smoke like offshore storms we glimpsed on the Weather Channel. As he splashed water on his face, I watched the exhaust fan suck the tiny hurricane through its golden grate and wondered what happened to the storms off the coast of Florida or Cuba that never touched land.

"Chilly willy, today, boy," he said, tossing me one of his wool hats, which smelled like everything else he owned – Winstons, coffee, gasoline, a hint of Old Spice, a whiff of bologna. I picture him now on a billboard, straddling a dusty horse, cowboy hat tipped over his face, leather reins clenched in his left fist and in his right a small bottle of amber cologne. *Work* by My Father.

As he finished his routine, I watched the thick exhaust pouring out of his truck in the driveway. He paced the house, searching for socks, then dug his old sneakers out from beneath the couch. He held his shoelaces between his callused fingertips, and as he tied I could almost feel the smooth dead skin guiding a heavy hammer in my hands. The deli took a piece of nearly all his fingers, the slivers ending up "in somebody's ham sandwich, I guess." He glanced at me through the smoke, slapped both hands on top of his thighs and said he'd see me later.

Once, in fifth grade, an overzealous guest speaker came to our class to teach us about fingerprints. I believed the man to be a private investigator or secret agent, but most likely was a criminal justice major from Farmingdale Community College. He distributed inkpads and pieces of paper which had a box for each one of our prints. Fighting the urge to smear each other's faces or leave a permanent high-five on a friend's back, we listened to the man indentify the loops and whorls and arches, explaining that each one of us has a unique print unlike any other person in the entire world. He told us about desperate criminals slicing off their fingertips in hopes of eluding the law.

"But," he said, holding up an inky finger, "they always grow back."

"How long does it take?" We nodded, anticipating an expert's response.

The man paused. "Not as long as you'd think."

I wanted to ask more questions, but, as usual, I kept quiet, my face burning for answers. How many times can you slice your fingers before you alter your prints? What if this guy was wrong? What if my father's whorls have become loops, arches into whorls, or if now there's nothing at all, no unique markings, the skin as smooth and common as sausage casing?

At an early age, I learned that mornings were pain. Stretching, groaning, shuffling, showering, shot of caffeine, sigh after sigh after sigh – all in preparation for leaving the place you loved, the place you felt comfortable and venturing out into a dreadful world. I watched television shows where the mothers and fathers sat around a marble island of pancakes and eggs and bacon and fresh-squeezed orange juice, chatting about their plans for the day. None of them swore beneath their breath or paced the house searching for a missing shoe. While I knew these shows were fake, there were parts that felt very real: a science teacher who acted just like mine or a kid who said the same things I did. I second-guessed myself: Perhaps I'm wrong. Perhaps all of it could be true.

A lot was required to break my parents' routine. When it was temporarily broken for a long weekend or a trip to visit relatives, the first day was spent leaving the routine, the last day was devoted to reentering the routine, and much of the time in between was spent in limbo, neither one sure what to do or how to act. So my mother scrubbed Simple Green on her sister's stove while everyone slept and my father took long walks to 7-Eleven, returning with his 12 oz. coffee cup clutched in his hand.

Our home was an integral component in my parent's routine. They seemed unable to operate at full capacity without first loading themselves inside our home, as if the floors of our house were circuit boards, their morning rituals a computer's processes. While they seemed to need their routines in order to function, I never noticed them deriving any pleasure from these essential habits. Perhaps in my mind I lump together their preparation for work with the work itself, envisioning my mother pacing and sighing through the dermatologist's office or my father breathing Winston after Winston as his fingers work a ham across the slicer. But it's hard not to. I can not remember my parents ever saying anything positive about their jobs. Work sucks. Work is life.

I once asked my father what he wanted to be when he was younger. He looked at me, a bit confused.

"What do you mean?" he asked.

"I mean is there anything you wanted to do."

He paused. Chewed the inside of his cheek a few times, then raised his eyebrows.

"Not that I can think of."

The Butcher's Daughter

Cow and *pig*, she learns from the inside.
Papering the stone wall:
Hock, Snout, Jowl—This is a sow.
He lifts her to the cardboard lamb,
each section she kisses.
His hands have stained her dress again,
so he lets her touch the scar
that fences his thumb.

Familiar, the knife to his grip.
Juice from a hind shank
dribbles to the wooden floor,
where crayons lose color between planks.
It speckles a storybook,
whose chickens circle Farmer Brown
as he sends them to school,
a kernel of corn for their lunch.
Like other things she knows to be true:
a chicken can't go to school.

The tiny table furnishes her corner,
wobbles to the door's bell and steady chop.
His steel blade draws across cuts,
bringing pink out of mutton, loin or rump.
The pieces he positions on ice
and scoops slush that runs dark—
The customers don't like to see blood.
Come Back, he smiles, nods.
The wrapped packages like gifts—
in her studious eyes—
he gives too much.

Pitting Cherries

I dig my thumb into firm flesh,
release the pit. The skin sucks
a sigh of relief. The juice, deeply
red on my fingers, splatters
the cutting board in patterns
so like my own blood in perfect
polka dots on the floor. It came in a gush
at lunchtime, a crimson line laced
the toilet. My floral skirt
transformed to a thick velvet
curtain over the show.
Somehow the baby's heart beats on,
though my own hangs silent,
a stony vessel ripe for the picking.

Still Life

(excerpted from *This Labor*, a novel-in-progress)

Estelle Dunn has been called home to Carthage (a small town outside Lexington, Kentucky) to care for her ailing father. Unmarried at 39, she has lived away from Kentucky for twenty years, after being forced by her mother to leave home and give up her twins, born out of wedlock. As this chapter opens, it is late October, 1989. She has been home for eight months, working at the Safeway, caring for her father until his death and then for her mother, who has just been diagnosed with pancreatic cancer. Her estranged sister, Lula, also lives in Carthage, with her husband, Herman. They own and run an auto parts store.

The faucet dripped in the cold kitchen. Estelle, in flannel gown and worn terry scuffs, moved toward the sound, a metallic pling-plink, pling-plink. The shushing of her steps sounded a percussion counterpoint, like a feather stick on a snare drum. Exhausted from being up with Mama all night, she leaned into the counter, listening. Outside, the sky whitened. White sky, white sink, cold plink, she thought, then wondered, what note could that be?

Pling-plink, pling-plink. Plang. Pling-plink. It did make something like a melody. But how could anyone know the notes out of all the sounds in the world? She tried an experimental hum, to match the pitch, but her voice was thick, and she couldn't get a pure tone from her throat. Hadn't she heard a radio show about how people with perfect pitch could hear what note even a drip like this was hitting? Amazing to think that each sound in the world (even the vacuum cleaner they'd said) had its own pitch—a note, a name behind its everyday name.

She ran water for her pot of coffee, turning the faucet hard to shut it off. And heard the singing.

It floated from somewhere behind the back wall. A man's voice singing "Oh What a Beautiful Morning." And not just humming or singing to himself, but belting it out, as if *Oklahoma* were being staged in her own back yard. Who'd he think he was? Coming into a private yard like that? She glanced up to the ceiling. She'd left Mama sleeping a jerky, moaning sleep. All she needed was another round of trying to ease her. She had to work today.

"The corn is as high as an elephant's eye . . ." came loud and clear through the closed window, the voice full and vibrant. Estelle could feel July in it.

She stepped onto the enclosed back porch and opened the outside door, shivering on the stoop as she scanned the yard. Trees, bushes, fences stitched patchwork of backyards, familiar as her own feet, and as foreign when she stopped to really look. She leaned out into the cold and strained to locate the voice. Where *was* it coming from?

"I've got a beautiful feeling . . ." The singing stopped mid-line. "Good morning!"

Off-balance, she nearly fell off the stoop—

"What?" She swung her head back and forth.

"Hope I didn't startle you."

Her gaze seized the source of the voice—a face in the lilac bush at the back corner of the house. "You certainly did!" She straightened, pulling in her chin to look down at him. He had a very large head – or maybe it was just that mop of curly black hair that made his head seem too big. As he walked toward her, she noticed that he was a generously built man – large all over, though not particularly tall. She gripped the top of her gown, pressing her elbows into her breasts. "What are you doing . . ."

"In your yard?" he finished for her with a grin, walking toward her. How dare he be so casual? "Mr. Dunn hired me to take out these bushes back here –"

"Mr. Dunn? Papa did what? You must be at the wrong house. When was this?" Estelle asked.

"Back last spring," the man pulled off his glove and extended a hand, which she ignored. "I'm Tom Reed," he went on without missing a beat. "Reed's Restoration—We Repair and Restore From Your Yard to Your Doors," he intoned, pushing his hand back into the glove. "I told Mr. Dunn that it would be fall before I could get to it. Anyway, this is a good time for taking out bushes, if you don't want to replace them, and he said he definitely didn't. Said he wanted the house secure and didn't like the thought of all the bushes where a prowler might hide."

Papa must have made the call on one of his better days, Estelle thought. "Better" meaning that he could sound like he knew what he was doing.

"Mr. Dunn is dead," she said. The words still felt new, though they fell from her mouth cold and certain as stones. Her body sagged with their weight. "I'm afraid you've come over here for nothing." She craned to see around him without stepping into the yard. "You haven't taken any bushes out yet, have you? My father was not quite himself last spring. He died June 19."

"Oh. Well, I'm awfully sorry to hear that. No, ma'am," Tom Reed answered. "I did take some dead branches off the lilac. It's a lovely old bush," he added, looking back at its ragged silhouette.

She had begun to shiver. It'd turned cold overnight, she realized.

"Yes. I used to love playing under that bush. The smell of the blossoms . . ." She stopped, rubbing her crossed arms. "Look, I'll be happy to pay you for your trouble. Could you come back later today? I'll ask Mama if she wants the bushes out." Backing up, she grabbed the door handle behind her.

"Sure." Tom Reed took a small notebook from his shirt pocket. Despite the cool morning, he was not wearing a jacket, just a flannel shirt. Estelle could see the black hair curling on his chest in the neckline's vee. He stood at ease, studying the creased pages.

"I have another job here in town today. What about 2 o'clock?" he said.

When he looked up at her expectantly, she looked away.

"I'll be at work then," Estelle said, her face hot. Her body shook as if it would fly apart. "Can you come by the Safeway? Just ask for Estelle."

She stepped back through the door as Tom answered.

"Safeway. Estelle Dunn. Sure." He gave a little salute. A comically cheerful man in his khaki and flannel, she thought, as she fled into the back hall.

She went straight to the divan and curled up with an afghan. It was a good ten minutes before she lost the quivery feeling in her stomach.

Under the buzzing fluorescence of the produce department, Estelle pulled at the tight waistband of her uniform and settled the bulky walkie-talkie more comfortably against her hip. She reached into the crate for two more handfuls of lemons, stacking them in a pyramid display. The produce manager had called in sick for the second day in a row, and the fruits and vegetables wouldn't wait for him to get over the flu. Everyone seemed to have it except her. She couldn't afford to get sick, no matter if she did feel tired and achy all the time.

The lemons were cool ovals between her fingers. Their dappled skins with their pin-prick pores, shed light from their curves as she balanced them in place. She loved the sharp scent of their peels, the feel of them in her hands, and how they shone, each one. They made her think of a still life, of fruit glowing on a rumpled tablecloth, perhaps the rich plush of a dead rabbit stretched next to an orange, an egg, a vase of mixed flowers, impossibly alive-looking.

Memento mori, she thought. Remember death. That's what she'd read in that *Smithsonian* magazine article about Dutch painters. She had never realized that the lovely arrangements of fruit and flowers in the paintings she'd admired were about brevity rather than abundance. She emptied the crate of lemons, puzzling over the thought, as she pictured the boxes of produce in the back growing limp, heading into rot if they didn't sell quickly enough. She hated going back there—the slick ooze of overripe meat, the smell of slimy vegetables, waiting to be carried to the dumpster out back.

She glanced at her watch. Time pressed on her everywhere–even on her wrist. It was 1:50 already and none of *her* work accomplished, thanks to the absent produce manager. She'd have to get Joanie onto this job. Her lunch break was coming up. Damn! and it was almost time to meet with that gardening guy.

She felt someone approaching and steeled herself to deal with a customer.

"Miss Dunn?" It was that voice again—deep, melodious, a radio voice.

Estelle spun about. "Hi. Just give me a minute here. I have some things . . ."

Tom Reed's eyes widened. He reached toward her. Estelle inched backward and stepped into a cascade of lemons. Lemons tumbled down her backside and rolled between her feet. A flood of lemons spread out in an arc, releasing their clean scent.

A few customers stopped their carts, staring at the stream of lemons on the floor. One started picking up lemons as they reached her. The rest turned away and went about their business.

"Get them! Someone might fall," Estelle said. She reached for her walkie-talkie and pressed the button. "Maintenance," she said. "I need maintenance!"

But Tom was already on his knees gathering up the fruit, reaching discreetly between her legs and turning in place to grab the lemons rolling toward the center of the floor. He was quick, she noticed, graceful for a large person.

"Here," she said crouching down herself. "I can get these." She turned in a tight circle, grabbing every lemon she could get to.

"You ought to put up avalanche warnings!" he said, grinning, as he came up. He stacked lemons and stopped the pyramid's dissolving, while

Estelle bobbed up and down, running from place to place to pick up the farthest fruit.

I yelled *I need maintenance*, was all she could think. I know it's true, but why advertise it, she moaned to herself.

"Clumsy!" she muttered aloud. Some days she completely lost track of her body. As she pushed lemons onto the pile, others rolled out from under. She was too embarrassed to call for maintenance again and couldn't remember who was on that day. "Oh dear!"

"Whoa, now. You grab and I'll stack," Tom said. He was focused on the pyramid – or what would be a pyramid again, once she got away from it.

"I'm sorry," Estelle said.

"It's not you, it's the lemons."

Estelle stopped her frantic cramming and watched him. His thick hands moved in a deliberate rhythm, tucking each lemon into its place. In a moment he looked at her. She looked away, scanning the floor. She took a step and picked up three last lemons, aware of how tight her uniform had become. She teetered and huffed, trying to squat with a measure of grace as she retrieved them.

"Okay?" Tom said.

"Yes. Thank you." Estelle handed him the lemons.

His face seemed very near, very distinct. Broad forehead, deep-set eyes, the abundant black hair curling around the edges of his ears. She wanted to tuck it away. She took a step back and realized she was light-headed. Maybe she *was* coming down with something. She couldn't seem to get her breath.

"I'll just be a minute," she said. "Need to clock out." She turned toward the office cubicle. "I'll get my coat and meet you at the door."

At the cafe down on the corner they found a booth away from the door. It was going on 2:30, and they had the place to themselves. Her breathing had finally settled.

Tom Reed ordered a cup of black coffee, and she asked for a bowl of tomato soup with a grilled cheese sandwich that arrived garnished with a slice of orange and a sprig of droopy parsley.

Tom glanced at this watch. She realized then he'd already spent thirty minutes of his time and they hadn't even talked about his work yet.

"My mother doesn't care about the lilacs or other bushes, but I'd prefer to keep them," she said. "How much do I owe you from this morning?"

"It's a ninety dollar fee to come out from Lexington, which usually also covers the first hour of work. I'd really just gotten there."

Ninety dollars? Had Papa known that? "Well," she said, "I want to be fair. After all, you did make a trip in good faith. But things are really tight now, with Papa's death and now Mama being sick." Might as well be straight with him.

"Yes, Ma'm. I understand. But I have to bill you anyway." He sat, his only motion one index finger that circled the rim of the cup he held. "Maybe you have other work – to fill out the hour?"

"Nothing in the yard," she said. Stopped. What was it he'd said that morning? "from yard to door?" Something like that. "You said you do repair work?"

"Yes – well, restoration mostly and some remodeling in addition to landscape design," he said. He cradled the cup, tilting his head. His eyes were hazel, she noticed. Too pale to be arresting and too dark to be strikingly pale.

She wiped a rim of soup from her mouth, still a bit dizzy and feeling not quite there. She didn't have the energy to supervise his work. But then, she didn't have the energy to fix things at the house, either. Herman didn't have the time—or the tools for that matter—to fix things, and she couldn't get by with a chair wedged against the front door forever.

"Okay," she said. "I need the front door repaired – or replaced. That's top of the list." She took a deep breath and met his eyes, made a quick decision and plunged ahead. "And there are loose boards in the front porch. Someone could get hurt there." She stopped again. "I'm worried about winter – some of the windows seem ready to fall out of the frames." This tumbled out in a rush between the last bites of her grilled cheese. She chewed and swallowed, now. Dropped her hands back to her lap, suddenly self-conscious.

"Anything else you can think of?"

Except for that index finger circling, circling, he sat self-contained as a cat. She, on the other hand, felt all jiggly inside, apt to spring up at any unexpected movement. "Nervous as a cat," her papa would say. How is it that cats are both, she wondered, irritated at herself for this train of thought. She picked up the orange section from her plate and popped it in her mouth for something to do. Juice dribbled down her chin.

"Well," she dabbed at her face and neck, "do you sing in some kind of group or organization?" Where had that come from? Her cheeks burned. She busied herself with the napkin, glancing up at him.

Tom leaned back and gave her an appraising look. "I used to – back in the dark ages."

"You mean high school?" Estelle said, relaxing into a grin.

"How'd you guess?"

"Oh, I remember high school," she said. "But you didn't go here did you?"

"No. I grew up in Lexington." He paused and looked down at his hands, loosely wrapped around the mug he'd set on the table. She noticed his wedding band half-hidden in the nest of his fingers. He looked up then.

"Anything else — about the job?" he said.

"There — there may be. I can't afford much more than the minimum. The front door won't close at all. I do need that fixed."

Tom pulled a spiral top notebook from his shirt pocket and jotted some notes. He looked at her quizzically. "That all?"

"I'm sorry," she said. What was wrong with her? She didn't have to prove she needed his help. But if she had to pay him anyway, she wanted her money's worth. Maybe this was just too much trouble, though, for both of them. She gripped the table's edge and leaned forward. "I'm sorry if I've wasted your time. I'll get the check – and you can bill me for your visit today." She stood and rummaged in her purse, waving the waitress over.

Tom waved the waitress back. "Now hold on. What makes you think you've wasted my time?" He looked at his watch again. "I have to get to a job in Lexington. I don't want to cut this short," he said, easing out of the booth. "I *am* interested in the job. I don't intend to take ninety dollars for nothing." He put the notebook back in his pocket and pulled out a card. "Here's my number. I'm over here about once a week lately. Call me if you think of anything else. I'll come by your house to work on the door and take a look at the boards on the porch. I'll need to look at the windows, too, to see about resealing the beading. They're the original windows, if I remember." He seemed to be talking to himself now. From the pocket of his jacket he brought out his battered datebook and flipped the pages. "I'll be over here next Wednesday for another job. Does that work?"

Estelle thought a minute. She could have sworn he was brushing her off just a few minutes ago. She swayed slightly as if she'd just come off a carnival ride.

"Wednesday?" She thought for a moment. "It's my day off, I think. Yes. That should be okay. If it's not too much trouble." She flinched. Wasn't she the boss here?

"Course not. My job to be there," he said. His face opened into a grin. "You're giving me the business, so to speak."

Estelle stared at him.
"So, Wednesday, then?" he added.
"Sure," Estelle said. "Wednesday. What time?"
"High noon?" he said.

Worker

Like towering cumuli
Big white houses
Float on razor-cut lawns
Amid seasonal flower beds
Gardeners change
In the night like sheets.
At curbside this early morning
Sits a battered Chevy wagon,
On its hood arranged
To catch some rays
A canning jar of sun tea,
Eight fat tomatoes;
Clasp knife and salt shaker
Laid out beside them.
Down the wide clean street
A woman in a gray uniform
Walks a cocker spaniel.
A lone hammer rings
Steady as a clock
Insistent as a telephone
No one was hired to answer.

Roofing

"I'm different now," you said that summer,
knowing that's what I'd always wanted
to hear firsthand, not from Nanny
or some court-appointed suit and tie.
And for those two weeks atop the roof
we were never more exposed. Working
with you again, it seemed like I
was five or six, almost clinging to
your pants leg, trailing like a shadow
from door frame to window pane—
mindful of stray nails and wet paint.

I spent eight days on Nanny's roof
consumed by our infrequent, distant
past, while watching you—the way you kept
your balance driving nails in asphalt
into faithful overlapping rows,
or how you sidearmed the shreds
in the truck bed below. I tried
to mimic all your moves: chose hammer
over nail gun, made perfect cuts
and worked without ceasing. All this
with Grandpa's legacy on the line.

Striking the sun-scalded surface
in unison with you, I sopped up
your new monologue: you'd stick around
to keep a roof over my head,
pay the mountain of child support,
attend more of my games. Vows
hammering infinite nails into
remaining holes of reservation,
shatterproof shingles casing my life's
yearning for a perfect dad—or just
a dad at all.

Wallpaper

Working with four or five neighbor women
after I moved north, I learned to hang wallpaper.
We'd move from one house to the next
pooling our tools and skills, helping each other out.
First, we'd scrub down the walls, if we didn't strip them,
counting all the layers, then prep all the cracks
in the lath and plaster—all those houses
were old, not historical; some like mamma's
had log frames. I never got the hang of papering ceilings,
which required two pair of hands in unison; more than once
the whole run fell, draping heads and shoulders
in paste—I'd paint my ceilings from then on, like mama

who'd roll wet color every spring,
cheap paint, last in stock or custom mix
that hadn't matched—why was there so much
of that green? Not a healthy or a sunny green
but that kitchen green none of us girls
would ever use. It covered even the ceilings and slanted
walls in our bedrooms upstairs. When asked
she said *Maybe, maybe it matched*
the linoleum on the bottom half of the kitchen walls.
I don't remember. I was making do.

It was a different story up north among women
with kitchen knives removing switch
and plug plates—laughing, gossiping and cutting up
rolls of paper, just so; we'd paste, plumb, and hang
to make crooked walls look straight, overlapping
designs lost in corners. I was good at patching
in the tough spots no one else wanted to touch—
under stair-steps, around windows, over doorways.
Get your stuff they'd say—scissors, paste, brush,
scrap strips of paper—*this is your job*. They didn't know
I merely tore the paper along the pattern so no edges
show, blotting with a wet rag, making do.

Clean

The scuffs on our white walls call out to me, first one, then another a few yards away. A splotch of dried juice on the kitchen floor, smudges on the bathroom mirror draw my eyes to them like magnets, shrieking for attention. I see them, and I see more: the frenzy of newspapers on our coffee table, the fuzzy lint accumulated along the top edges of our cabinets, the never-ending cat hair attached to all our cloth surfaces like hatch marks gone awry.

I am possessed by this disarray. It has slithered inside me and tightened my forehead, pushed down the edges of my eyes. I feel it clutching me below the ribs. My reality is wrinkles and bedlam. I am gripped by the need to clean.

Clean, as in scour, disinfect, as in behind and inside and underneath. Need, as in driven from within, beyond choice. I stack and align, sweep and wipe. I kneel with a scouring pad to rub at something imbedded in the grout between the pantry tiles. I unload the refrigerator shelves, unhook them from their brackets, bring them one by one to the sink. I push appliances away from the wall and remove dust balls that cling to their sides.

A sparkling home, however, is not my goal. I have always been tidy; I take pleasure in order and keep my house clean. I learned from my father, who lived by the credo that everything has its place. I knew early that anything left in the wrong spot would provoke his ire, and so became adept at scanning a room before I left it to ensure nothing was amiss.

I have, however, failed to impart my standards to any member of my family. In our home, lights are left on, drawers left open, and possessions left where they are deposited rather than where they were found. Neither my husband nor my two daughters are troubled by dirty dishes or counter crumbs. It is I who straightens up, because it is only I who cares.

But days like this are different. I am both oppressed and exhilarated. I dress for the job — sweat pants, a stained t-shirt, and hot pink, extra durable rubber gloves. I spray geranium-scented cleanser over every surface, wipe it away with a sponge. I wash not only the dishes, but the dish drainer where they dry. I wash salt and pepper shakers, the telephone receiver, the small glass plate that holds the oil and vinegar cruet. I wash the prisms that catch the sunlight on the kitchen windowsill, and then I wash the windowsill, too. I open the door below the sink to toss out some garbage, and moments later

I am squatting, surrounded by household cleaners and dry rags, scrubbing the floor and rearranging bottles.

I am taut, alert, a robot programmed to find and obliterate filth, to create straight lines from piles and carelessness. My senses guide me: my eyes rove, my nose catches odors, my fingers, even gloved, feel the roughness of crusty matter that doesn't belong. I have become a slave.

And I have become a master. My slavery empowers me. It is, today, my means out of the mire. In my cleaning, I control my world.

I am pleased by the results of my efforts, but this is not why I work. Unlike the demands of the aftermath of a dinner party or the departure of overnight guests, my spells are not necessarily connected to actual mess. If I think to wonder later, I might find the bridge: a squabble with my husband, an unexpectedly large bill, my aging mother's growing fatigue. But until then, I am simply overtaken by a force that pushes me. I work for relief, for release; I clean until my eyes can breathe and I can once again feel quiet in my own surroundings. Only then can I walk blithely past a used tea mug left on the table, or wipe away my husband's shaven whiskers with a sweep of the bathroom sink and go about the rest of my day.

In Defense of Dirt

I belong to the dirty desk brigade.
Not so bad as my friend Clara who raises
great garbage heaps of paper, notebooks,
clippings, jars of jam, ticking clocks and mail
rising into mini-mountains. Guys hide
open cans of tuna beneath and wait
for the odor to offend the office.
I grow respectable piles of debris.

One day, in lowering mode, I pitched
paper and uncovered a miracle.
A bug—not to get technical—that moved
somersault after somersault across
my desk. No legs, no tail, no antennae.
A circular, see-through being, all muscle,
that curved into each step with such sublime
skill. I have never seen its likes again.

Virginia Green

She knows her way around an adding machine
Been keeping books since she was nineteen
A more efficient worker they have never seen
Not much gets past Virginia Green

She's been around here since before the union came
She's seen them come and go and play their games
She sees them swagger, brag, accuse, and shift the blame
To her, they're all about the same

Virginia simply has her job to do
Has to hope the company makes it through
When times are lean
Numbers are easy for her, figures speak true
Her balanced books are always clean
And they all trust Virginia Green

What they don't know about her life would fill a book
But they'd learn a lot if they could learn to look
Beyond the corner where her little office nook
Marks the last turn her journey took

She doesn't think about romance much anymore
Her one love took care of that in '64
Still way down deep she keeps the suffering that she bore
And leaves the fit to fight that war

But Virginia has this smile she wears
She believes her heart won't rip and tear
Like some she's seen
Counting is easy for her, errors are rare
Her balanced life is always clean
But no one knows Virginia Green

Ah, Virginia has this smile to wear
Has to believe her heart won't rip and tear
Like some she's seen
Marking the seasons passing helps her not care
Her balanced life is very clean
But no one loves Virginia Green

No heart keeps Virginia Green

Rapture

It's five a.m. on the day Larry might get fired, and he's lying in bed, hoping that Keith will get fired instead, and then hating himself for hoping such a thing. But it'll be Keith or him, one or the other.

His stomach churns. He hasn't slept well, hasn't felt well, in weeks.

He adjusts his pillow. Sue doesn't move. The king-sized bed towers above the hardwood floor and makes Larry feel like he is rising toward Heaven. Sleep deprivation, maybe, or idle hope. So much to do before that reward, and then it comes back to him, his recurring dream. In it, he is running through the neighborhood of his childhood, among the half-constructed houses, fronted by piles of dirt and gravel. The bulldozers are idle, the hammers and saws quiet. His neighborhood is empty. Jesus has lifted the believers to Heaven and left Larry behind.

Sue is drawing in long, deep breaths, occasionally rattling out a snore. Hoping to relax, Larry tries to match her breathing, but his lungs stiffen. He sighs. The room appears in the half light: the armoire, the dresser with its big, dark mirror, the 46-inch LCD television mounted on the wall. Monroe, their golden retriever, is snoring on the expensive rug near the bathroom door. Nothing, except the dog, is completely paid for, and they cannot afford the payments even now. The thought makes him hate Keith.

He rolls over to face Sue, flat on her back, lips parted. Married for eight years. Eight years of pencil pushing. His whole adult life. He rubs his stomach and prays: *Jesus, please don't leave me behind.*

Monroe starts whining, so Larry gets up to let her outside. She scurries about the yard for a long time, sniffing, searching for some perfect place to defecate. When finally she returns, Larry showers her with praise.

Though sick to his stomach, he pours a bowl of cornflakes. He eats two spoonfuls before giving the rest to Monroe, who slurps greedily, her tail wagging, keeping time for the whole world's happiness.

Out of the shower and dressed, he leans over the bed to kiss Sue, who doesn't move, though he knows she's awake.

So she's still upset. Great.

Downstairs, Monroe follows him to the door. He leans down and kisses the top of her wet nose. "Be a good girl," he says, and wonders who she'll live with after things fall apart.

In contrast to the cheery Retail Fashion Brand stores all over the country, the company's headquarters are black and low slung against this morning's gray sky. Three revolving doors front the building. A long sidewalk spills outward, like a giant tongue, to the spacious parking lot.

Late winter, and the snow has melted except for some dirty piles at the back of the lot. Larry parks against the largest pile, far from the building, though many closer spaces are available. He sits there, his hands on the wheel, and recalls playing king of the hill once as a child. Snotty-nosed, all bundled up in his winter coat, the hood tied tightly, he charged up the hill only to be shoved back down. His head thumped against a large stone. Teary-eyed and dizzy, he screamed and ran up the hill with renewed determination. He played that day past dark.

At home, his mother inspected his coat's yellow lining, streaked with blood. She shook him and screamed about his recklessness. Would she be proud of him now?

He trudges up the long sidewalk, between the bushes and flowerbeds that will soon reek of mulch. At the revolving doors, he pauses to look at the sky. Maybe the sun will come out, he considers, and then pushes his way inside. Two guards sit at a long security desk; on the wall above them are five clocks, displaying the time in Los Angeles, New York, London, Paris, and Hong Kong.

Eight years ago, waiting for his interview, the clocks scared him. A small town kid, he'd gone to a small state school, and suddenly, holy shit, he was interviewing at a place where they knew the time all over the world. He pauses to remember the fear he'd felt then, but cannot, though he knows now his fear was real: his department has been outsourced to India.

Up the two flights of stairs he climbs, pulling himself along with the handrail. His lungs feel like granite. He enters a corridor that leads to the payables department. The lights above the cubicles pop on as he passes. He used to raise his arms and snap his fingers as each light illuminated, as if he were some minor god instead of a mid-level manager for Retail Fashion Brands. Today he plods along, barely noticing.

With Keith he shares a small, windowless office, where they sit with their backs to each other. Between them, on a small table, are a printer and a phone. Gray fabric pads the walls, for soundproofing, though the outsourcings have made soundproofing unnecessary.

Yesterday morning, his willpower gone, Larry rooted through Keith's desk. To find what? A clue, maybe. Instead, he found the same things he had in his desk: staples, paperclips, pens, a calculator, a notebook.

In bed that night, he confessed to Sue. "It's like Keith and I are the same person."

She turned to face him. She stroked his shoulder and said, "You worry too much, Larry. You work harder than Keith does. You're not out all night chasing girls. They'll keep you. And if they don't?" She shrugged. "If they don't, you'll get another job."

Her hand felt nice on his shoulder. He reached to feel her waist, taut and smooth. "I suppose I will."

"Of course you will. You should have been looking already."

"But you just said you thought Seth would keep me."

"And I do. But just in case."

"So I haven't been worrying enough?"

"That's not worrying, Larry. It's preparing. Shit happens. Adults prepare." She removed her hand, then his, and turned her back again. "I swear, Larry, I can see it now, if Seth does let you go, you'll say, 'Well, thanks for letting me work here, sir. It was fun.'" She huffed and went quiet.

Monroe, on the floor, shuffled and groaned. "And what if I'd found a job?" Larry asked. "And then they keep me?"

She sighed. "What I don't understand, Larry, is why you'd stay. You've known for weeks you might get fired. And what have you done? You've gone in earlier, you've stayed later. Why?"

"They still pay me, don't they? Was I supposed to just give up?"

"Whatever. You're right. I'm going to sleep."

His heart thumped against her indifference. He drew a long breath and slowly exhaled. "None of this is easy, you know."

She moaned as if she had already fallen asleep. "No shit. But what is? I'm tired."

"Me too," he whispered so low he could barely hear himself. He lay there for a long time, listening to Sue and Monroe sleep, watching the clock as the night wore on. When finally he slept, he dreamed his rapture dream, then woke around five a.m. on the day he might get fired.

Sue's right, Larry thinks as he turns on his computer and takes a pen from his top drawer. He works harder than Keith. That should count for something. For a lot. Only it doesn't, not since Roger was fired. If Roger were here, Larry wouldn't be worried. Roger valued hard work. What Seth values is a complete mystery.

Seth's assistant, Eva, slips into his office and closes the door. "I knew you'd be here," she whispers. "I brought you this." She sets a toasted bagel, all slathered with cream cheese, on his desk.

"I'm here," he says. "So far. Thanks." The pungent smell of the cream cheese twists his stomach, which he holds with one hand. She is wearing a black skirt and tall black boots, with a cranberry blouse and a black jacket. Her pale hands are marbled red in a way that tells him they're cold. Her brown curly hair is pulled back to expose the soft flesh of her neck.

"Are you okay?" she asks.

"Mostly."

She sits on the edge of his desk. "I could get fired for this, but oh well."

He feels dizzy. "Don't get yourself in trouble."

She waves a hand dismissively and leans toward him. "Fuck it," she says. "I can get another job." She puts her hand on his. It's the first time she's touched him since the night a year back when they kissed behind Eddie's Grille. "I'm calling you in to Seth's office at ten." She looks down at her lap. "I'm sorry."

He nods. "I should have known. Thanks for telling me."

She looks up at him. "What are you going to do?"

"Do? Get another job. Start over."

She pulls her hand away to scratch her nose, then rests it back on her lap. "I mean when you talk to Seth."

He shrugs. "Just hear him out, I guess."

She is quiet for a time and then says, "Larry?"

"Yeah?"

"That night. In the parking lot. You've never said anything about it."

His face warms. "I'm sorry."

"No. Don't be sorry. You're married. I'm married." She snorts. "What can you really do about anything?"

He thinks and says, "Not much."

She gets up slowly and goes to the door. Her hand is on the knob. For a long moment, she stares at him. "It's a thing that happened, isn't it?" She looks down to the floor. "It happened, and I wanted you to know how nice it was."

Without looking at him again, or waiting for his reply, she opens the door and leaves.

Long after nine, Keith bursts into the office reeking of cologne. His hair's wet, his tie's loose. His blue eyes are bloodshot.

"What a fucking day," he says. He closes the door and pulls off his jacket. "I overslept. Killer traffic. A mad rush to get here, and for what?"

Larry holds his breath and shrugs.

"Chop 'em up day, Larry. You or me. A mad rush to lose my job or watch you lose yours. Why? So Retail Fascist Brands can make more money. Scan the invoices! Transfer them to India! Fucking Internet. I liked it better when it was just for porn."

"It's going to be me, Keith," Larry says. "I know for sure."

"You? Are you kidding me? You?" He pulls a bar napkin from his pocket. "My speech is all prepared. You? Shit. I don't know what to say. I've always considered you a friend. But the last few weeks—I hate to say this—but the last few weeks it's been hard to like you."

"I know. I've felt the same way. It's weird."

"Weird?" Keith lets out an exasperated laugh. "It's not weird. It's capitalism. It's me vs. you as much as it's Google vs. Microsoft. We all want to win so badly we forget about the losers. Not that you're a loser." He shakes his head. "I don't mean that at all. Who told you?"

"It doesn't matter."

"Eva?"

"It doesn't matter."

"Okay, Eva. She likes you. You know that, right? I know you're married, but she is too, and she likes you."

"We're friends, I guess."

Keith sits against the edge of his desk. "You should just go for it."

"For what? Eva? I'm married, Keith." Larry's irritation is making his stomach rage all the more. Or is it the bagel? He ate more than half of it after Eva left.

"So what are you going to do?"

"About what?"

"Seth. When he tells you."

"Puke, maybe. My stomach's not right. But other than that? Just listen to what he has to say and then get escorted out. The same as everyone else."

"That's it?" Keith uses the bar napkin to wipe away the sweat of his convictions, then looks at his notes there. "I got fucked up last night," he says. "Looks like I wanted to tell Seth that we don't almost have the same name. Did I tell you he said that to me the other day?"

"You told me."

"Seth and Keith. Are they close?"

"Not really."

"I was going to call him a dumbass. Which he is, no doubt. Don't you think?"

"Have you been looking for a job, Keith?"

He huffs. "For months. Since the chopping started. But nothing. It's hard to match the salary here."

"I haven't looked. Sue's pissed." He rubs his stomach. "I kept pretending everything would be okay."

Keith shrugs. "So what? What else can you do? A lot of life is pretending everything's okay. You'll get another job."

"Sue says that, too. That I'll get another job."

"You will. A better job, maybe."

Larry suppresses a belch. Now that he knows he'll lose his job today, and he knows it with near certainty—he still harbors a small hope that Seth, upon seeing his dedicated, hardworking employee, will change his mind—he is filled with a sickening nostalgia. "I was lucky to get this job."

"Lucky? Bullshit."

"I was. I worked hard in college just to earn mediocre grades. I couldn't pass the CPA exam. I'll get another job, maybe, and start over. I feel too tired for that."

Keith runs a hand through his hair, which is all but dry now. "You've always worked harder than me."

"But you get your work done."

"I think so."

"Things just come easier to you."

Keith moves into his chair. "Shit, your last day. It's sad. I'll come in Monday and you won't be here to listen to me talk about all the stupid shit I did all weekend. No one to say to me, when I'm done, "I cleaned out the basement." It'll just be me and all those people in India—people who are nothing but computer files to me."

Larry imagines it all as Keith describes it, but doesn't say anything. It's 9:45, so he starts filling a large envelope with his belongings—a picture of Sue and Monroe, a *Word-a-Day* calendar, his copy of *The Seven Habits of Highly Effective People*, and a blue rubber ball he squeezes to fight stress. The desk drawers screech as he opens and closes them.

Finished, he leans back and closes his eyes. Keith is still talking, though Larry isn't listening. He holds his stomach. He waits.

Eva calls just after ten. In her most professional voice, she says, "Seth would like to see you." Larry manages to say, "I'll be right there." He grabs his personal belongings and shakes Keith's hand.

Eva isn't at her desk. Seth's door is closed. Larry knocks and goes in. The sun is pouring all its light and heat through the large window behind Seth's desk. The office is hot. Larry can barely see.

"Sit, Lawrence, please," Seth, a dark silhouette, says. "You know Sandy?"

"Hi." Larry sits down, still blinded. His stomach has reached the brink of collapse.

"Sandy brought me your file. You've worked here a long time, Lawrence. Are you okay?"

Larry peeks up at him. "Yeah. It's just the sun."

"I know. It's hot, but nice. Anyway, we have to chat. First, you listen, then you can speak." A desk drawer opens and closes. "At Retail Fashion Brands, our mission is to deliver great fashions at competitive prices. As you know, we've outsourced most non-strategic jobs overseas. That outsourcing has reduced the need for management and, sorry to say, your job. We know that's not easy. But we care, so we're prepared to give you eight weeks' pay in exchange for a release."

Head bowed toward the desk, Larry sees an envelope move toward him. He squeezes the large envelope that contains his belongings. The sun is baking the top of his head.

"Read and sign that," Seth says. "We just need it before the next payroll. Okay, your turn."

Larry hears Sue's mocking words from last night. He tries to look up at Seth, but the sun is too bright. He is suddenly and acutely aware of the metallic smell of Sandy's perfume. His stomach churns and renders him speechless.

"Okay, then," Seth says. His chair squeaks. Larry sees his hand reach across the desk. He rises and looks right at the man, at the hot yellow sun behind him, then grabs his hand, which is putridly soft and clammy. Saliva fills Larry's mouth. He tightens his grip.

"Good luck," Seth says.

Larry's stomach heaves. An otherworldly sound escapes his throat. Seth tugs to get away, but Larry has him in a death grip. Vomit splashes on the polished desk, then all over Seth. Sandy cries, "Oh my heavens," and rushes out the door.

Larry releases Seth's hand and says, "I don't feel well, I guess."

Outside, the wind is whistling across the sidewalk.

"I can find my way from here," Larry says to his escort. The sun doesn't bother him now. Empty, his stomach feels fine.

Without speaking, the guard motions Larry forward and follows him to his car. Larry tosses his personal belongings onto the passenger seat, followed by the severance agreement. The guard, ten yards away, watches. "Don't worry," Larry says. "I'm leaving."

Behind the wheel he stares at the huge snow pile. He considers getting out and rushing to the top of it, but then laughs.

Right now, he imagines, the people inside, those left behind, are telling the story about his vomiting on Seth. Keith is claiming that he would have pissed on him, too. Larry starts the car and says, "Don't be afraid." And though he has said it many times, this time it feels different. Everything is lost, or will soon be lost, he thinks. He takes his foot from the brake and eases backward, feeling nothing but relief.

The New Shepherd's Staff

If you please him, you please me,
he said, as if his primal order
should be the first thing on our minds
as it is in his.

The new boss presented at staff
by his new boss, both eager
to shepherd in the new order
but the lambs are unimpressed
and do not slaughter themselves
nor even crawl onto the altar.

Western Medicine

Talking faces on TV assure me
that our air strikes on Baghdad are surgically
precise. My dentist Thelma
dons her mask and leans
into my mouth. Innocents are not
the target, they say, which appeases me

as I think of my daughter, fair-skinned,
blonde, and feel the pinch, precisely sharpened
steel entering my gums as Thelma
numbs me. Into the mouth of Baghdad
stealthy bombers swarm like blackbirds.
The only sound — Thelma's howling drill.

Relax, I tell myself and fold my hands
like prayer, this will soon be over. Our missiles
strike like matches flashing into flame
while the blue-eyed commander, a jaw
settled on destruction, says *Good*
against Evil. Thelma reaches for a scraping

tool. After you say these words, *Good,*
Evil, where do they go? Do they rise
in the smoke from charred bones?
Is it lucky to die and not see? They don't
ask that on TV. Above her mask
Thelma's trained eyes peer into my mouth.

I close my eyes and picture calm blue sea,
azure blaze of sky. I want this to be over.
A woman on TV, glossy lips moving —
such white teeth. *Surgical. Precise.* Words
like anesthetizing vapor drift and dissipate
in soft pillows of cloud while worlds

away, a busy marketplace in Baghdad,
                    a young woman, dark eyes, jet black
hair, inspects an avocado. Silence
          roars. She's not my daughter. Thelma
drops her mask, smiles, says We're done.
                    I spit blood and rinse as if it's over.

Weekly Letters

Every week the letters come,
words choked with steel, noise,
molten gun metal.
She calls her new friends sisters,
works men's work—
lifts, shoves, slams,
pushes heavy carts through treacherous aisles.

The children's minds jumble
thinking of their pretty aunt's
blonde curls bound in course kerchiefs,
fancy skirt replaced with coveralls,
painted nails hidden in asbestos gloves,
long eyelashes singed in a Baltimore armory.

Handsome fly-boy groom
flies deadly missions over dark waters,
dreams of his bride wearing lace,
hair perfumed, lips parted in passion,
eager for his return.

Week after week the letters come—
Mama's voice caresses every word;
the children listen, willing her sweet syllables
to soften the foreign sounds of war.

My Land is Calling

My land is calling
Making space for my skin
Making space for my bones

Earthworms
From my land
Are lining up
To race one another
From one of my hip bones
To the other

My land is calling
For the frog in my heart
To jump
On the streets of my childhood
To jump
On the water lilies of my former hopes
To jump
On the shoulders of the men I loved

My land is calling
For my fingers
To trace the names on freshly chiseled headstones

My land is calling
On my cell phone
Long
Long
Long distance

My land is calling
To collect me

My land is calling
To ask hard questions:

"Would you be mine
In sickness and in health
Death cannot take us apart"

But I have worked so hard
But I have worked so long
But I have worked so much

I have put in all the extra hours
I have worked
Days and nights
I have worked weekends
And every
Single
One
Of
The
Holidays

I have worked so hard
To make
This land my land

This land
That is your land
From California
To the New York Islands

Answering the Call

My cell phone rang one Saturday morning as I was shopping at Tractor Supply with my husband. "Mom, I just spent an hour and a half with the Marine Corps recruiter, and I'm shaking so hard I can barely think."

Ah, so it goes when one has lurched headlong into the thing that resides at the core of their being. I remember that feeling the first night I sat in a creative writing class at Carl Sandburg College. I was among a smattering of students gathered in the school's theater waiting for class to begin. I'd enrolled because I needed a break from life. My four children were elementary and preschool ages, and my husband was recovering from brain surgery. I had begun working in a grant-funded program that allowed me one benefit, free tuition at the community college.

The path that led to that dark theatre on a cold January night had been uphill the entire way, and as I waited for the instructor to appear I tried to suppress the feeling that I was wasting my time. I liked to write, but I wasn't sure that I was a writer. Maybe I was fooling myself. Then Dr. Pazereskis walked onto the stage in gum-soled loafers and greeted us with a wave of his hand. He was on the down-side of middle age, wearing a tweed jacket with leather patches at the elbows and an ascot. His sentences sounded memorized.

He told us we were brave for enrolling – not because we were now under his tutelage, but because we were willing to expose ourselves through our work. He told us we were a rare breed, the kind who wanted to go deeper into the craft. Maybe we wanted to write better or maybe we wanted to be the best; that was for us to decide. Maybe amongst us was a playwright, or a poet, or a Pulitzer Prize winner. What was beautiful was that he entertained the possibility, and by doing so, gave us all permission to do the same. His words were verbatim recitation for the umpteenth semester, but it was the first I'd ever heard anyone imagine me capable of reaching such daring heights. I sat in that dark theatre listening, my eyes brimming with tears, feeling as though I was at the mercy of an awesome force. It would have been no less powerful an experience if a shaft of light had shown down from heaven. I was exactly where I was supposed to be, and I knew it.

That's how I knew what Robb was feeling. He asked me to meet him in an hour to discuss a few details with the recruiter. "I'm going to be a Marine, Mom," he said, his voice quavering.

Having served in the Marines, my husband's knee-jerk response was that Robb wasn't going to be able to cut it. He would screw it up. He had a long way to go from holding an MP3 player to holding an eagle, globe and anchor in his hand.

"I went to college to become a Hemingway, not because I already was one," I told him, feeling defensive and protective. He sank into that thought as I drove toward home where I left him to dwell on it while I headed back out the driveway to meet Robb.

I wanted Ted's support, and I'm sure Robb would have liked it too, but we would be OK without it. Time would bring him around. Robb would have a tough road ahead of him, but no way would I question his ability to accomplish the task. Regardless of the fear I feel for Robb, I choose to support him, because I believe that's the crucial element to his success.

In the recruiter's office, a sergeant in dress blues introduced himself, shook my hand, and then proceeded to tell me why Robb was a good fit for the Marines. I looked at my son, all 18 years of him, and felt an enormous sense of pride. Through the long hair, funky clothes, and boyish insecurities, I saw remnants of my mischievous little boy, but I also saw a young man whose heart was pounding with promise. We asked questions that the sergeant carefully answered. He made plans for Robb to go for a physical the following week. If he passed all of the pre-qualification requirements he would have the opportunity to enlist.

Suddenly, my husband burst through the door, smiling. He extended his hand toward the young sergeant. "Semper fi," he said.

"This is my husband," I explained, in shock. "Robb's stepdad."

The sergeant smiled. "You a Marine?" he asked.

"Yes sir," Ted said, and they were off on the familiar banter I've heard exchanged among Marines around the country. There's an impressive bond that I've witnessed from coast to coast, across generations. But more than the friendly exchange taking place between my husband and the recruiter was the effect it had on Robb. They included him in the conversation, and Robb grew flush with the realization that Ted's presence in the office that day was a blessing. A vote of confidence. A passing of the torch.

The next week he went away for his physical. I should have known that if he passed all of the preliminary requirements they weren't going to let a live one get away. And they didn't. He called me, collect. Caller ID said, "U.S. Government."

"I did it Mom," he sounded like a kid who'd just ridden a bicycle for the first time. "I swore in about five minutes ago. A General did the ceremony. I wish you could have seen him."

What was there to say? I plopped on the bed, where I'd been folding laundry, and began to cry. It's hard to articulate these moments in a parent's life, the ones in which their child makes an unmistakable passage out of their youth, into the wild blue yonder. I think my tears were a combination of pride and fear and grief, but mostly pride. That's what I told Robb anyway. "I'm so proud of you, son."

"Thanks Mom," he said. "Are you crying?"

"I'm fine, kiddo," I said, boning up my voice. "I'll see you tomorrow, and we'll celebrate."

After I hung up I let myself sob into the pillow for a minute. Then I collected my composure, went back to folding laundry and thought about my brave son, sitting in a Des Moines, Iowa military recruitment depot, bathed in a shaft of possibility.

MSCI 1217: Physical Fitness (Basic)

By 6:35, we run
because Master Sergeant Brown
wants two miles in our best time.
Cadets push themselves, urgent,
strong, younger than me
and encouraging, not sure
why I am here. I could say
I want more control, but I don't.
I like one sweet hour a day
when I do not have to think.
I want someone to say, "Run,"
and I will, panting, hurting,
but running until my mind
accepts the creaky ride
my body provides, gauging
my breath, acknowledging
when I veer to the left,
and putting aside class prep,
administrative duties,
a son near ready to leave
for university life.

Homework

Third grade seemed destined to sameness,
predictable as white anklet socks
worn by every girl even though
humid summer moaned relentless as math,
multiplied misery of returning to a school
without air-conditioning, every window
stuck like we left them in spring.

When the new boy introduced himself,
said, "Your mother knows my mother,"
pointed to where they stood talking,
I do not know which I worshiped first,
her coal-colored hair piled high
like cotton candy, or his skin,
muddy river brown, eyes green
tree leaves spackled with gloaming.

And, he who confessed being dizzied
by my mother's constellation of freckles,
began counting mine, lost track, started over,
marveled how they matched his tan flesh
and the leather straps of my sandals where
each toe gripped hard my first lesson in grammar
noun and verb of his name, *Jimmy Chance*,
teaching me sweet prying open of luck.

Memorial Day

I had no idea why I took up with the man. He quickly became my occupation. My job at a college didn't seem to be my real work anymore. *He* was.

I began writing about John Brown of Harpers Ferry fame in 2008, but I didn't understand my obsession with him for several years. I just kept writing, kept reading, kept visiting archives and taking notes.

He persisted in calling me out into the field whenever I tried to rest, or tried to give him up. And I went! I let it happen. I don't generally let men I know take over my life—much less historical ones I don't know—but I found him irresistible.

I'm still writing about him, but, since Meadville, I've begun to know what this is really about.

John Brown grew up in Hudson, Ohio, and I've lived in his town for thirty years. One block from my house his original cabin stood. Around the corner from me is the Free Congregational Church—still standing—the pure abolitionist church financed and erected by John Brown's father, Owen. Two blocks away from me, Owen Brown had his tannery. It was built beside a creek—old Brandywine. It's a tiny trickle now and draws no attention to itself, flowing modestly, quietly under the road. If you walk up the hill on Main Street, and turn right on Chapel, you'll come to the Old Hudson Township Burying Ground. Here, John Brown's mother, Ruth Mills Brown, was buried in 1808, when John Brown was only eight years old.

In the time of innocence, before John Brown, I would sit on my porch swing and just read or watch the black-capped chickadees and mourning doves peck at the magnolia tree that presses close to our house on Church Street. Then one day I noticed, kitty-corner from my home, a bronze plaque that marks the location where John Brown first publicly vowed to destroy slavery in 1837. It took me five years to spot the sign. After I read it, I wasn't able to see my town the same way again. John Brown was always in it. Every year that passed, he became more real to me and sometimes, even at night, when almost everything disappeared, I would think I saw the brightness of his gray-blue eyes punching through the dark, or his black coat flapping like a moonlit bat.

I still sometimes imagine him like that, or, as a boy, walking up the hill behind his cabin to sit by his mother's tombstone. Did the firm lines of his mouth, which we see in photographs, set as he spoke to her in this old cemetery no one visits anymore? Did he make promises to Ruth long before the ones he made in the meetinghouse that stood on the corner of my street? Was it beside her grave that he planned to do something so important with his life that even stone would notice him?

I've traveled to places I can't even pronounce because he's led me there. Osawatomie, Kansas. Pottawatomie Creek.

I've sometimes given up holidays for him. This past Memorial Day I talked my husband into driving to Meadville, Pennsylvania, to visit the tannery John Brown built in nearby New Richmond. My husband didn't mind. He wanted to go.

The truth is that we always leave town on Memorial Day anymore. We've found it's better that way. Sometimes I stay for the parade, but this year I didn't even do that.

It's impossible not to think about our own son on Memorial Day. John Brown had twenty children, but we have only one son. That son loved coming downtown to watch the parade. But he's been gone from Hudson a long time now. You're not supposed to miss your children this way when they're all grown up, but when you have just one child . . . we can't help how we feel. It's not every day we long for him like this. Just special days, mainly, and a few we can't anticipate that take us by surprise. We've learned to cope. We leave town and go for drives.

It never feels lonely in the car on Memorial Day traveling with my husband down an unfamiliar road, but it does if we stand in the driveway together beside the grill with aprons on and spatulas and tongs in our hands. Something's always missing. Our son isn't there. We know it's impossible to wish him here, but the scene is unfinished without him, and we can't pretend it's not. *Memorial Day* is a tableau vivant that has a boy in it, and that boy has disappeared.

I need our son in the group. I don't know how to position myself on Memorial Day anymore when I stand in the place I used to occupy. I'm fine if I'm still, but when I blink and come to life and the scene advances, I don't know what to say or even how to move my feet.

So we don't wheel the grill out of the garage any longer on Memorial Day but get in the car and drive away. When we return, usually late at night, the holiday is over.

On Memorial Day this year, we programmed our GPS and drove to

Crawford County, Pennsylvania, where John Brown bought 200 acres and moved with his wife, Dianthe, and their three children in 1826. There, in New Richmond (located just outside Meadville), he built a tannery, a log house, a barn.

For a few hours I could escape the small, private sorrow of my own life and lose myself in research about a man whose life had nothing whatsoever to do with my own.

In this small place, John Brown held the position of postmaster for many years, surveyed for roads, built a free-standing schoolhouse, organized wrestling matches, served as a lay minister, became the region's librarian, and entered into political debates.

But the New Richmond years also held deep sadness for him. His son Frederick, who was always a sick child, died at the age of just four. The next year, John Brown's wife, Dianthe, died after childbirth. Her newborn child died as well. A baby boy. In June of 1833, after all the deaths, John Brown married a sixteen-year-old spinner named Mary Day and moved back to Ohio. She would bear him thirteen more children, and watch nine of them die.

I knew all this before I got in the car. But I didn't know what physical evidence remained of John Brown's property in Pennsylvania. I packed up my camera, my paper and pencils, my binoculars—became a veritable detective moving securely toward the clues.

But there was a second story in New Richmond that I hadn't expected to find. It was the story of the two people who managed the John Brown property—Donna and Gary Coburn. The point of intersection between those two stories—John Brown's and Donna Coburn's—changed me, and my work, forever, once I noticed it. It would have been impossible to photograph something as intricate and nearly invisible as that intersection point, so my camera was no good to me. Neither was my pen. The point was too tangled, too complicated to unravel in a simple note I tried to take that day. But I sensed it, nonetheless. I somehow knew it would alter my work in a lasting way.

We drove up a long driveway of a house on John Brown Drive, a country road twelve miles from Meadville. A woman shouting about running out of mustard moved toward our car.

"Is this the house mentioned on the sign?" I asked her.

" Oh, no, none of it was here."

"The sign said—" She cut me off before I had a chance to tell her I'd seen a marker in a gulley at the side of the road that identified the house on the hill as John Brown's.

"I know, but it's wrong. Don't read the signs." She motioned to a man standing with some Amish workmen.

Gary, her husband, came over to us with tools in hand and told us about his grandfather's purchase of the property and how it eventually ended up being Gary's.

"All that's left of the original property is the wall," Gary said, pointing across the road to the foundation stones of the tannery on the other side. He and Donna then led us across a prickly field toward a small building, and we followed.

"We're getting ready for Freedom Weekend. Just a few days away, and I have a lot to do," Donna explained as she and my husband hauled a set of long newly-painted steps toward the door of the museum so we could go inside.

"We don't charge any fees," Gary said as we all entered. "My grandfather never thought it was right to teach people about the Civil War and slavery for money."

Inside was Donna and Gary's collection of everything they had gathered about John Brown. In a glass case there was a ceramic statue of the abolitionist holding the hands of two black children. There were shackles. There were sleigh bells *found on John Brown's farm*, a little sign said, and there was Dianthe's purse.

"I have a hundred eighth graders coming on Thursday," Donna said. And then, almost as if we weren't even there, she began to tell the story of how she came to this place.

"I was a mess," she said. She and her first husband had separated, she was in counseling, her children were young. She had always been told she had no knack for school and wouldn't amount to much. She had jobs that never seemed to matter. And then in 1992 Gary asked this Idaho girl, this waitress who was running from everything, running from state to state like some common felon, to move to Pennsylvania and live on top of a high hill.

Donna locked the museum and pointed us toward a narrow path that led into deep and beautiful woods behind us. We followed her.

She kept talking. I don't remember saying a single word. She had cleared it herself, she told us. It was a glorious path, with giant pine trees edging both sides—the lower branches cleanly trimmed, little fresh cuts all along the bark climbing high into the air.

I saw a wooden sign in the shape of a thin arrow nailed to a tree. It read, "Cemetery." We followed it and soon were in an open area that had recently been mowed. The ground cover was low, but full of wildflowers, weeds, and grass. In the center were two headstones and two footstones.

In memory of Frederick, Son of John and Dianthe Brown. He died March 31st, 1831. Beside him was Dianthe's stone. *In memory of Dianthe. Wife of John Brown. She died Aug. 10th 1832. Aged 31 years. Farewell Earth.*

"So I moved here with Gary when I married him. For eight years I didn't care about John Brown. I'd see angry people wandering around our property looking for something. Mostly, I just tolerated them. They were intruders to me. And then in 1999," she said, slowing down a little, "my sixteen-year-old son went to Washington to live with his dad."

She looked at the trees, at the graves, at us. "He had a horrible accident. His brain was damaged. And—"

"Oh—" I said. I wanted to fold her in my arms, but I knew the story wasn't over yet. I could see that she was just pausing. We weren't there, anyway. Just her boy was, with John Brown's dead.

"In 2000 I had a breakdown," she said. "I would lie in the house all day. I couldn't function. Couldn't get out of bed. I saw no reason to do anything. But one day in spring I heard people outside and something happened. I don't remember leaving my bed, don't remember my body even moving, but I was at the door. Something pulled me toward it, through it, and then I was saying to the people, 'You're looking for the cemetery, aren't you?' And they were. There was no path, so we had to walk around all Gary's construction to find those graves. I led them there as if I'd done it all my life."

Her granddaughter came down the path and joined us.

Not much taller than the child, Donna touched her granddaughter's back, held her close, and continued. "I knew when they left that I had to open the cemetery to the public. I don't know how I knew—no one made me, no one asked—but I knew. I paced for four or five days. I took a typing stand I saw in the room and placed a guest book on it, for signatures. This was part of what I had to do. It was as real as any job I'd ever had, only so much better. Every day after that, I got up early and built the trail. I chopped through the difficult brush and trees, yelling at God, singing 'Amazing Grace,' and then praying about my son because of the accident. Six weeks later, it was cleared."

Donna's own son, and maybe her own former life were buried in this meadow, along with John Brown's wife and his son Frederick. I was mixing everything up, and not getting my facts straight. I knew I had to concentrate on *history*, on the lives of the Browns. My work depended on it, I thought.

"The ladies of New Richmond dressed her in her wedding dress on her burial day. Her baby boy is in her arms. She was strewn with lavender, and placed in an oak casket," Donna said, returning to the story of Dianthe Brown as suddenly as she had left it.

It began to rain. We said goodbye, thanked Donna, waved to Gary, and drove down the hill. We parked at the side of the road and crossed the street to look at the foundation of the tannery. We stood inside its walls and let the rain soak our hair and necks. The structure once had held eighteen tanning vats. It was both the place where some of John Brown's children had slept at night, and where animals had been stripped of their hides. A place of sleep and blood. I could hear the rain on the stones of the foundation, but as I closed my eyes, I was quite sure I could also hear sleigh bells and then a deep cry coming from the meadow where we had so recently stood. From a different time, I thought I heard my son's bicycle bell and a hollow howl filling the chapel of the funeral home where we eulogized my aunt.

It was there, in the rain, that I knew for the first time I would have to stop thinking of John Brown as an elusive shadow in front of me. He was not a specimen on a cold glass plate, but my neighbor. We lived in the same town. There were intersections between our lives. I had family, too, with tombstones and loss everywhere in my life, with issues of conscience and race and mortality and courage and democracy on my mind, with a terrible fierceness in myself that I recognized in him. Donna told her story and the story of John Brown as if they were a single thing, and I would have to do that too.

My thoughts did not all arrive that day in the rain, but I knew, even then, that John Brown would force from me matters I hadn't written about before. He was a dangerous man, and dangerous friends force the truth out of you.

I would have to tell the story of the day a .30 caliber machine gun was pointed at my head; of a dangerous protest (with our son at the center, and me on the periphery) of the firing of a prominent African-American musician from a school in Hudson that Owen Brown helped to found; of small and sometimes great secrets of family life that I'd kept hidden even from myself; of the futility and unnaturalness of trying to pretend we know how to exit our children's lives; of the deep worry I have for this democracy of ours; of the fear I face about how I'll meet my death—and whether eloquence and strength, as they did for John Brown, will play any role in it.

It was more comfortable, and so easy, to remain separate from him—from a man who lived in my town, after all, over two hundred years ago. To study him from afar instead of letting him get too close to me. More comfortable and so easy to distance myself from a son or a husband or a friend who forces me—without words or deliberate intent—to see something in myself that I'd hidden in a private cave, or never known was there.

But that *is* our true work. To find intersections with others that finally let us understand ourselves, and them. A son and a mother. A father and a son. Two lovers. Two strangers. An American icon and a neighbor woman from another time. We can't run away—not even across the centuries.

On summer mornings, I walk up the hill in town to visit the family plot of Owen Brown. I pull the weeds around the grave of Ruth Mills Brown and pick a sprig of trumpet-creeper from a fence that borders the cemetery. I lay the long orange blossom, funnel-shaped, on the stone of John Brown's father. Sometimes I even feel that John Brown visits me. He arrives in the stories of Donna Coburn and in the dark of night when nothing else is visible. He comes, most rapidly, when I find the courage to let my work explore the dangerous intersections between our lives.

The Burn-Off

Should you go out in the fields
and pitch-in at the spring burn-off
ahead of the plow and planting
(planning death for bad memories
in the meadowgrass cut and dried
and forked on smoking stubblefield
pyres), you will feel an intensity
of cleansing fires.
                Awash in stench
you may smile to see ghost-funnels
vanquished by big gusts onrushing
till a greasy smolder runnels.
                        Still
on the perimeter, and past, lie
ubiquitous and random the seeds
of ragweed and joe-pye weed, wild
strawberry and wild carrot—raw
materials a poet needs.
                    Never forget,
these too must you learn to cultivate.

December

Frozen mud crunches like glass shards beneath
my boots. Cold's sharp kisses cut at my chapped
sleep-drunk face. Five dark muscled shadows
lumber along the fence row at cockcrow.
A thin red strip of sky rides their backs as pin
pricks of stars cleave to the last of night.
They hear the coffee can scrape and shovel
molasses and corn. Hear the sweet feed
hale down into troughs. Thousands of pounds
gather, gear up, threaten, ears pinned flat,
thick chests shoving, heads slinging, shod
hooves stamping. Their broad asses swing,
their eyes huge and liquid in the last drop of dark. Mean
dances across the thick black grass
until safe in their stalls, alone, hungry,
their thick lips reaching toward what they count on.

I make my hurried way back to the square
of creamy lamp light fading into
dawn in a rush to write the lines
that came to my cold mind in the crisp
dark walk to the feedlot. They ride my spine
to my cold toes and back again to
brittle fingers already pushing off
gloves and coat and hat to reach for that old
sweater, tea cup, afghan, notebook, cheap pen.
We all rush at what we're given.

Water Bearer

His hand to hoe,
foot to row,
my bare feet fit
into the toe of his boot print;
I'd have followed him far
past any field.
Sun a blister,
I lugged a dented
bucket of water,
banging against my shins.
I shared one dipper-full
with each plant, two with Daddy,
only taking my own drink
on return trips to the spring.

Then the day the baby died,
my newborn only brother,
my father's hard brow softened
and water fell from his eyes
making muddy spots on the ground
to mark the way for mine.

Locking the Gate

The sunrise is staring through fog,
is stretching vulture wings across pine limbs.
My father is mixing some pesticide and ashes
for the bean rows. Then he laughs at his hands
slathered in poison, or a strange hour fighting
insects then hauling some calves to Remington.

He says nothing really bodes well that sees
sunlight sneaking through the river mist, herons
squawking along a flood road, and bees clumped
in a willow snag, swarming like the crazy face
of heaven buzzing out beyond creation.
He tells me to lock the gate, starts laughing again.

Ars poetica for the working class poet; Eviction Officer by day

Define the following

a) Onomatopoeia:

Click a padlock
displacing people
precise as a pen

b) Irony:

A woman unceremoniously
humiliated, displaced
formal attire in-tact

c) Dissonance:

Surveying former residents'
children, stuttering synonyms
for... for ...Foreclosure Crisis

d) Post-modern Existentialism:

Working class poet
salaried only
to be

Biplane

Right now a yellow
biplane is performing
aerobatic maneuvers
over my house. My wife
is in the other room
sweeping the floor.
She has her headphones on
and is singing "Tomorrow"
from "Annie." She sounds more
like a drunken Ms. Hannigan
than the kinky haired orphan.
I believe in prosperity, but have
no more means of supporting
my family than I did at twenty-one.
She is sweeping and I'm
writing poems about what to do
when it is summer
and you are unemployed.
Walk in the woods
at least once a day,
recite Yeats to the trees.
Take the kids to the pool.
Read fairy tales at night by flashlight.
Listen to Eddie Cleanhead Vinson
sing the blues on old scratchy records.
Attempt Bach on the cello.
Break out the old fishing poles.
Dig for night crawlers.
Walk to an abandoned pasture
at midnight and bathe in the sea
of fireflies. My trust in serendipity
has dissolved. I am catching up
on the classics: *Don Quixote,*
Moby Dick, Ulysses, Bleak House,
Lear. I already feel guilty

for not working and for
suggesting that my wife
can't sing. The yellow biplane
climbs up into the sky
then doubles back.
The pilot cuts the engine
and the plane falls straight
toward earth.

Getting Ahead

I was working real hard
Ten years on the line
I felt a tap on my shoulder
They said boy it's time
Time to step up
Time to join the team
Time to be a leader
Time to …
Follow the dream

So they gave me a title
And a corner cube
A quarter an hour
And a new set of rules
Then all of the bosses
Who never looked at me twice
Came over to offer
Their own …
Twisted advice

To grab the brass ring
You've got to play their game
Take comfort in knowing
The only constant is change
When opportunity knocks
Jump on it quick
Cause a moving target
Is …
Too hard to hit

Take special assignments
Make your own breaks
Stay one step ahead
Of your latest mistake
The key to success

I'll let you know now son
Is to kiss all the asses
You're sure to ...
Hit the right one

You need a global perspective
Be a big picture guy
Pay all your dues
And never ask why
Move to HQ
Start a new life
Your kids will adjust
And you can ...
Get a new wife

These days you'll find me
Back on the line
Flying under the radar
And biding my time
You see that dream wasn't worth it
And I'm doing fine
If that's getting ahead
Then I don't mind ....
I don't mind ...
No I don't mind ...
Falling behind

Oxymoron
From An Office Window

The buzzer sounds at eight o'clock.
I will not write one poem today,
nor with elbows propped on the window sill
ponder the uncommon sense of crows,
or how spring has come
on the wings of the swallow.

Unlike Schiller's drawer of rotting apples
my Macintosh leaves me wordless
before the sweet lyre of Apollo
and the squeal
of nine dry joints in a coal pile track.

The muse tarries
like a beggar on the doorstep
while I answer "Code Red" on a 992G
front end loader stalled in the rubble of
Laurel Mountain,
squalling like a wildcat for a new Y-pin.

I dare not try the iambic pentameter
with a cam bearing knocking on a D9T.
I put away Whitman, Eliot and Rimbaud
to open Cat Service Updates
user friendly on InfoCast.

With hands by ink unstained
I bar the door
against the teeth of the west wind.
I close my ears
to the "trumpet of prophesy."

Aching with carpal tunnel
I compose an order on DBS

to remove the green top of
Laurel Mountain
and the nests of a million smart birds.

Fireflies

In the pre-dawn gloom
The glow of the carbide lamp
Prepared to pierce the ebony darkness
Deep within the earth
Rumbling in the man-car
Into the depths of the mine
Shining from the hardhats
The army of Cyclops
Swarming into the bed of coal
Laboring in the pitch blackness
Like fireflies.

Dusk comes.
The cluster of lights emerge
From the hole in the mountain
Sunlight but a distant memory
From childhood
And another way of life
Human and earth
In symbiosis
In rhythm with sun and moon
Human gave care
Earth gave food

Lights extinguished
Men as black as the coal
In which they labored
To pay their debt
To the company store
Continually returning
Like Sisyphus
The stone ever rolling
Down upon them
In their labors
As Cyclops

De rerum domesticae

What can, what cannot come to be
— Lucretius

I can't really say I like getting up in this killing cold,
watching my breath escape towards the midnight constellations,
as vapor from the stream arcing onto the ground
also rises hours before the sun starts turning
the sky over the Chiricahuas that luminous blue-
pink-lavender and the full old ivory moon
slips down behind the low mountains we call the Mules.
Back inside, something else four-footed is moving
— slowly, purposefully — behind the curtains along
the sill outside the south window, brushing the glass

To the north an owl calls in the voice of a dove.
I light a small fire, noting as I wait
the fitness of this familiar rehearsal: metal
crystals recalling the forge and hammer. One thing
leads to another. The liquid makes itself known by sound.
A hand reaches out. Hot water swells dry leaves.
The smell of sage from the garden last summer fills the room.

Jezebel Makes Your Doris Day

Let's start with a housewife
mashing white sausage on percale
with an intensity so admirable
some call it absence of craft

who's in love with a guy
whose wonderful spine is a metaphor
for why Shylock should lean on a cane.
A leg of lamb is a new leaf

deserving her rubdown, mint smells
like the tassled go-ahead beret
she wears to stream flags
from her clothesline in rain.

Adorn this bare hour
too far from the time
Cupid may take her
east of the doghouse and shoot her.

Crazytown

This is how it worked: the crazies, they came in, and they went out. We didn't get attached; they were usually gone in 72 hours.

But we had our repeat customers—regulars, we called them—just like they were customers at Starbucks or Krispy Kreme. To them, sometimes we did get attached—especially if they weren't *too* crazy.

That's how I met Jimmy. I hate the name Jimmy, so it's a wonder that I even spoke to him, I hate it that much. He was a regular, and he would sometimes try to score nicotine patches off of the staff. They were free to us so staff would quit smoking, and they weren't counted by the nurses.

The weird thing was Jimmy didn't smoke. He used them to trade with the other crazies for time on the phone. I thought he was a druggie, but turned out he had a sick mama and he was calling her. After that I gave him time on the phone whenever he wanted.

I had lost my mama the year before Jimmy started coming around, so Jimmy and I got to talking about it. We got close, but never took it too far, though we did go into his room and talk all night quite often, which was against the rules.

One day Jimmy stopped coming. He had been pretty regular—every two or three weeks. A few weeks went by, then six months. Then Norton cut the psyche ward. I moved to another hospital, but before leaving I looked up Jimmy's number.

It took me three months to call. I was sure he'd be nuts, but he wasn't. His mama had died, and he wasn't depressed anymore, so hadn't needed to come back. We decided to meet and talk about losing our moms.

I didn't know what to expect, but when I saw him I knew I wanted him. Him, as a boyfriend, as a man. That's what I got, too.

Once we were all talked out about our mamas, and had been together long enough that the sex wasn't boiling hot anymore, Jimmy disappeared. Fell away like a dropped call. His apartment was cleared, and someone new moved in. I thought he was dead, and grieved the loss.

I was working in a different hospital when he showed up. His hair was long and matted. He had a beard. He was dirty. And he didn't even know me.

Before I got to see if he'd remember me with meds, his doctor ordered electroshock therapy.

It's hard to work with him now, hard to look at him. He got straightened up, but never has remembered me. He comes in, and he's polite and kind, but it's like we never existed. Like I never existed. Like I've been erased from the planet.

I say we never get attached, but I am as stuck to him as lint on the nonslip booties we give him each time he comes in.

The Balancing ACTT: A Letter to Gurney Norman

Writer's block? Well, when you can't write a word,
just write a letter—write a letter to me.
–Gurney Norman

Close to where you spent summers with relatives in western North Carolina, I pull over where a dirt-worn crescent serves as the placeholder for stopping and breathing in the view of titrated blues. I roll down the window and the wind jumps in like a stray dog starving to be petted. Toward the left, the Sugar Top condo shoots up high enough to be giving the world the finger—but the Appalachian people are the ones to feel the insult of a ridge remodeled. Farther, Grandfather is distinguishable even from this angle. Straight ahead, I recognize the Roan of my own birthplace. I cannot discern the Black Brothers range that must be among the farthest waves of blue ringing from this vantage point. They're out there, though, with Mt. Mitchell, the background of my childhood that every south-facing cabin window framed.

When I was born, a fairy milkweed seed must have landed on my cradle and tagged my fate with its blessing or curse: "I wish for you a job requiring a poet's creativity, a psychiatric nurse's skill along with an understanding hard wrought from experience." Thus, this job was made for me. I work as a nurse for ACTT, Assertive Community Treatment Team. A job description in a nutshell might be that I assist with medication compliance and therapeutic monitoring and offer a weekly Wellness Group to promote exercise and to educate on health issues. I work with a team consisting of a psychiatrist, two therapists—one of which is our team leader—a substance abuse counselor, a peer support person diagnosed with Bipolar Disorder, a case manager, and a secretary (who inadvertently serves as each team member's therapist as we file back into the office, ready to vent). Our goal is to keep people with a mental illness or dual diagnosis out of the hospital and to facilitate their ability to function in the community. Despite all our specializations, we all share many of the same tasks from providing transportation to the grocery store and dentist to tons of documentation. Sometimes, we make home visits in pairs for safety, and our conversations backed up by mountain scenery are worth it all.

In our joint office, humor helps us work with a population that is under duress. One stress relief is the creativity we're allowed. The Wellness Group prepared, planted, and raised a garden this summer. With the zucchini harvest, the clients made bread while learning the nutritional value of the ingredients. Then, we froze bags with grated zucchini for bread making and solace during the winter. I enjoy the same freedom as my job of teaching in the college classroom affords—except I'm not alone. My team and I make decisions together in staffing each morning, prioritizing and planning according to clients' needs.

Our clients represent the misunderstood. As a shy person, I know what it is like to be misunderstood as speech spills into sand. They need someone to be honest but not hurtful—that's where my writing confessional poetry comes in handy I hope. Some clients with borderline personalities or substance abuse are more challenging than others. They keep us in a balancing ACTT.

We have to trust ourselves to safeguard against staff splitting, lean on one another for advice, and understand beyond our own understanding. When awakened at 4:30 a.m. on the Crisis Line because someone has run out of cigarettes, we have to remember that a crisis is what the client thinks is a crisis. We often face the wall of frustration. How do we motivate clients? Sometimes, we question if we are helping or enabling.

Today, I have seen twelve clients in their homes and drawn blood work and given two injections at the office. On my way home, I fit in another client, one I have known since her first schizophrenic break when I was working on an inpatient unit. Even this client would call me odd for my reflection on her chickens grubbing along the road – their necks and legs with the mechanical rhythm of oilrigs. Noncompliant with taking pills, she will decompensate quickly without timely antipsychotic injections. Unchecked, she will escalate into active participation with hallucinations. We want to prevent a psychotic break not only for the obvious reasons of her not becoming dangerous to herself or others, but also because she will lose brain cells and never function this well again. While I take notes of her vital signs and slightly pressured speech, she writes frantically. Some might assume she is mocking me; however, as I leave, she hands over her scrap of paper complete with an apple butter recipe, wanting to give me something, anything I could use, as is the local custom to offer visitors a gift.

My car flows down the mountainside, the road parallel to the natural road of Beech Creek, both starting to collect darkness now. I marvel at the sides of the mountain with maple, poplar, and beech offered like huge ice cream cones dripping red, orange, and sweet yellow. So many times, I have corrected a comma, or lack thereof, teaching grammar instead of poetry and looked up to hear the seconds of my life ticking away. All I want to do is write—except for, of course, this writer's block. A golden leaf pats me on the back when I arrive home, and there's no way that I deserve such an image. Have I really made someone's life better in the way I hope my poetry would serve—not taking on the whole world but starting at home? Here in the mountains I love—fully alive, one day at a time, one letter at a time—my soul babbles on, tumbling the edges smooth, until I can write again.

Two Peasant Women Digging in a Snow-Covered Field at Sunset

On a winter day of grays and blues
two women bent from the waist
are digging into the hard, frozen field
looking for carrots, turnips, potatoes.
The houses on the right
are themselves running into the ground,
crouching under the cold.

Every morning
Van Gogh went to his easel
and recreated
the toil of the workers
sowing in the fields, shoulders hunched—
he understood the stubborn hold
of that iced sod,
the sweetness of those turnips.

How many times
have we thought ourselves buried in work
only to remember the toil of our parents?
Even after my father passed away,
it took my mother years till she learned
to give up planting corn crops,
digging in the harsh sun
lest the land were left fallow
lest people said she let the plot go.

The Eastern Shore

Wander east with me. Arc high
above the tide-swept Bay, beyond
wispy sails, barges cutting wakes.
Cross tender-shooted fields, fingertips of land to reach the Wye.

An ancient cherry weeps beside
the groan of splintered boats,
the shuffle of rubber-booted men
whose cheeks show signs of squalls.
Weathered hands restitch snagged

nets as bodies balanced like great
blue herons sort each catch.
Silent as crustaceans, they scrape
and scoop, toss a too-tight carapace
out to sea. Linger here where damp

air smells of salt and centuries,
where bibbed men trust the tide,
the call of geese. Leave *terra firma*
and city streets for piney banks
where the sun bronzes a coastal

shoulder where watermen leave
no wake, where swan and cygnet
glide, where cove meets fresh-mown
lawn. Come to the Eastern Shore
and yawn and smile and rest.

What Is Not There

Every day for four hours she shucks oysters
on the back table of the bar kitchen
claims to be older than what she is
but tells the truth about being a cutter
has to, can't hide the scar-stars on her hands

the owner pays her by the plate, replies
of course she can keep any pearl she finds
although there are no pearls in these oysters
makes a point to tell her what is not there

with the quiet vigor of a downstairs maid
she rearranges mollusks in their slippery half shells
creates platters of tiny forks and half a dozen oysters
to be swallowed with lemon, hot sauce, beer, white wine

to a heartbeat rhythm, she inserts and re-inserts the blade
in a steady sort of expectation, a calcite quest—
for if there is a pearl, you can bet she'll find it

sometimes the knife slips and stabs her cold palms
sometimes there's no slip, it's a sharp shell that slices
the embroidered web between thumb and forefinger
sometimes it's on purpose to remind herself she's alive

she always rinses off the blood quickly, needs to do this
to allow the cutting, the relief its certainty brings

every day she opens doors to homes being vacated
again and again, oyster after oyster, holds herself
in devoted readiness, works her faith and bleeds
for what the man who pays her says is not there.

The Fisherman's Daughter

She is not a problem
or a creature of pity.
She is his daughter,
born with a lack
of oxygen in her brain.

He refused institutions
and takes his girl to work—
ties the wheels of her chair
so she will not roll
on their little shrimp boat.

She is his captain.
Her green eyes tell him
where currents swell.
She does not need speech
to warn of hidden shoals
and gathering storms.

He can feel her stories
in the palms of her hands.
A moonlit leap of dolphins.
The smell of salt laced marsh.
Bright falling stars in August.

There is no beginning or end
to water and air—only him,
only her, working, living
an abundance of wind.

They know this breath
of blood cannot be broken
as old nets lower slowly,
blooming in the ocean.
Forever open, always full.

My Work: Discerning Lies, White Lies and the Truth

Slats of golden light fell on Sally's hands as she held out her short and plump, pink fingers. A simple gold band encircled her fourth finger. Fingers as knotty as the gnarled roots of an oak tree would come later in her arthritic illness. "You know how much I need the pills," she pouted. Twenty something with lots of kids, she had endless household chores.

I sat across from her on my stool, mentally preparing myself for her reaction to the accusatory news I needed to deliver. Turning the computer screen toward her, I began. "Your urine drug screen shows no evidence of narcotics. In fact, it shows that you are taking something I am not giving you. That's a violation of your narcotic contract."

Tears welled, tumbled down her cheeks as she shook her head.

"Where are you getting a medication like Valium?" I asked.

I liked Sally; she'd been my patient for almost three years. She had a rough life: six young children, poverty, depression and pain, but she had a tenacity and resourcefulness I admired. Her husband worked out of town, so much of the time she was a single mom. She scraped the money together to join the Y. In the evenings she took yoga classes while her kids participated in other activities. Her son with behavior problems loved his dance class; his behavior had improved. Early on, child protection had been involved, but eventually they closed her case. When her children accompanied her to clinic, she seemed to be an attentive mother. She had rheumatoid arthritis and asked me to prescribe Oxycontin. I did.

I am a seasoned physician. When a patient wants narcotics, I request and review old records and make sure that non-narcotic pain medications have been tried. I have patients sign a contract. I grow suspicious if the patient loses prescriptions, forgets appointments, or asks for additional pills before the designated refill date.

I skimmed Sally's visits to her previous physician. Our narcotic contract limited her to sixty 40mg tablets a month, one in the morning and one in the evening. I scheduled an appointment for her with a rheumatologist a few months out. I did not grow suspicious when Sally asked for the smaller 20mg tablets; she got better results if she staggered them throughout the day. I did not question her when she told me the rheumatologist suggested increasing her dose to five 20mg tablets daily; although, despite requests, I never received documentation from the rheumatologist. I celebrated with her when Child Protection rewarded her family with a trip to Disney World.

She always called to cancel an appointment if she could not make it. I only interrogated her briefly when she told me her problem son had dumped all the medications in the house down the toilet. He was, after all, a difficult child. I gave her extra Oxycontin for the month. She had only made a request like this once before when she had left her medications at her sister's over the holidays. I was honored when she brought her brother-in-law to see me. But I declined to prescribe Oxycontin for his back pain; his reasons for needing narcotics were unclear and there were no old records documenting his problem.

Two years into my relationship with Sally, the clinic received a fax with details about the Oxycontin prescribed to her address for the past few months. Not only had she paid cash for her last month of her Oxycontin, but two other adults in her household were receiving Oxycontin from other physicians. One was the brother-in-law for whom I had refused to prescribe narcotics. She had laid out over $800. How did someone on medical assistance pay $800 cash?

I started doing random urine screens to confirm that Sally was indeed taking her meds. The first screen was positive for Oxycontin, but the second came back negative. After that I confronted Sally, but her excuse seemed believable—she'd run out when she was visiting her Dad in Texas. I gave her the benefit of the doubt. But two months later her second urine drug screen was negative. I could not ignore those results.

"I can't give you the Oxycontin anymore, Sally." I stared at her, setting my jaw.

"But I hurt," Sally blubbered; elephant tears continued to slide down her face.

"Drug tests don't lie," I stated. "You are *not* taking the Oxycontin." I pushed the box of tissue toward her and swallowed my anger. "Let's talk about your depression. Depression hurts too. I can't give you the narcotics, but I can still take care of you." I made an appointment two months out with the new rheumatologist who had started seeing patients at my clinic. "We will see what he says." In the meantime, I rearranged her depression medications and told her to use her Celebrex (a non-narcotic pain medicine) which I had also prescribed for her. She left the clinic crying, but returned to her scheduled appointment a month later and asked if I'd reconsider giving her the Oxycontin. I declined. We talked about her hectic life and her pain.

I had grown fond of Sally and always enjoyed seeing her. I had been proud of her tenacity and had boasted about her success—my patient with chronic pain who had learned the value of yoga and meditation. I pictured her in the family van, filled with kids, driving to the Y in the evenings after dinner. Or at least that was what she had told me. Was that a lie as well?

Now, embarrassed that she had bamboozled me, I felt stupid. How much of what she had told me were lies? Twenty years in practice and I'd missed the clues. For three years.

I flagellated myself with *shoulds*: I should have reviewed the old visits to her previous physicians more carefully. I did after the fact and clearly saw the clues I'd missed. I should have insisted on receiving a copy of the report from the rheumatologist who recommended increasing her dose. I should have done urine screens from the beginning.

Sally served as a reminder to slow down, be more thorough, spend the additional time with patient records in the evenings after clinic to make sure that all was in order. Always check random urines on patients taking narcotics. My Catholic upbringing had schooled me in *shoulds* and sin.

The chalk squealed on the blackboard as Sister Saint Joseph wrote *right and wrong*. The folds of her black veil and floor-length habit swished as she turned to face the class. She brushed white chalk dust from her hands. Only her eyes, mouth and hands seemed alive; the rest, hidden in the pleats and folds of her black habit. "You will be making your first Confession. You are old enough to know the difference." Then beneath *wrong* she printed *sin: mortal, venial.* "Who can tell me the difference?"

Having done my homework, my bony arm shot up, stretching out of the short-sleeve of my white Peter Pan collared uniform blouse. Around the family dinner table the evening before I had reviewed my homework questions with my mother and father. My five younger siblings listened with interest to our conversation. I was ready.

Sr. Saint Joseph stepped toward the class and scanned the forty squirming second graders. A large rosary swung from the thick black belt at her waist. The beads clinked as she called, "Therese?"

"Venial is little like telling a lie or pinching my sister. And mortal is big like murdering someone," I said, with confidence, but not too much confidence. Pride was not a good thing. Pride was one of the seven deadly sins.

"Very good, Therese. Thank you. Now class, close your eyes and think about what sins you have committed."

I covered my eyes and tallied them up: I'd argued with and pinched my sister. What else? Someone behind me farted; several students giggled. Through my fingers I saw Sr. Saint Joseph frown in their direction.

We learned that there was right and wrong, big wrongs and little wrongs. Behaviors and thoughts were either good or bad. Sin was doing or thinking bad things. It separated us from God. If we confessed our sins, we could be forgiven and reconnected with God's grace. Simple as that. We should always try to do what Jesus would do. Sr. Saint Joseph did not lecture us on the subtle gradations of gray.

I was seven years old when I made the sacrament of First Confession, designated the "age of reason." I entered the confessional, a closet-sized space off the side aisle of the church and knelt down on the hard wooden kneeler. Amidst the smell of oiled wood and darkness, the priest slid back a little door. Although screen separated us, I could see his shadow.

"Tell me your sins, my dear." He had stale breath.

I swallowed hard, squeezed my folded hands. I recalled my list. "Fighting with my sister. Sassed back to my mother..." There were others, but did I need to confess them? Were they sins? Already I'd begun to wrestle with the gradations of gray.

"Anything else?" the priest queried.

"No Father."

"Say ten Hail Marys and listen to your parents." Then he rattled off a prayer too fast for me to understand and finished with, "I absolve you..."

I touched my fingers to my forehead and down, around, the sign of the cross. The wooden door squeaked and the priest's shadow disappeared. I found the doorknob, scrambled out of the confessional and into a nearby pew. I pressed my hands together, bowed my head and recited the prayers of my penance. *Hail Mary full of grace... Holy Mary Mother of God pray for us sinners...*

Sins? What about the gradations between black and white? The white lies, some version of the truth? A misrepresentation to spare another's feelings?

I can't come to play with Veronica because I have a sore throat. Of course, I didn't have a sore throat. I didn't like Veronica. She smelled and her house was messy, but I couldn't tell her that. A sin? A lie, but a little lie, a shade of the truth.

∾

In my own dealings with people I have come to prefer the truth. Just tell me what you are thinking. Don't protect me. Lay your cards on the table. But even now, I am not sure I could say to Veronica: I don't want to come over because you and your house smell.

At work, I know that patients tell me shades of the truth, doll out portions of the truth. Perhaps it is what they think I want to hear. Or the reality is too complicated to explain?

Joe told me he was taking his blood pressure medicine. But I was growing convinced that he was not. He was on too many meds and his blood pressure should have been under better control. Instead of believing him and increasing his dose, I poked around for the truth. "Joe, is it a money problem?" At least he had insurance, but maybe the co-pays were too high? Or "are you having trouble remembering?" He was disorganized; there were competing demands, perhaps a lower blood pressure just wasn't a priority? He could not feel the impact of his high blood pressure? Maybe there were side effects Joe was too embarrassed to tell me about? "Joe are you worried about your erection?" He stared at his brown work boots. Maybe that was it. If I knew the whole truth, we could figure out how to proceed. I am not a mind reader, but I am skilled at asking the right questions to get at the truth.

Patients drop clues like bread crumbs. If am paying attention, they lead me to the unvarnished truth. But with Sally I wasn't paying full attention and my affection for her clouded my judgment.

After the confrontation, Sally checked in with me periodically, but missed many of her scheduled appointments. She kept her appointment with the rheumatologist who diagnosed her with fibromyalgia and declined her request for narcotics. She was angry with him, "He did not spend much time with me." Reports from her insurance company indicated that she'd visited other physicians in the area requesting Oxycontin. Since I was her designated primary care physician, I denied payment for those claims. I talked with Child Protection about reopening her case. They considered and declined; I did not have evidence that she was a bad mother.

I talked with the clinic lawyer to see If I could report to the police my suspicions about her selling, but due to HIPAA (Health Insurance Portability and Accountability Act) I could not.

Four months later an article in the local paper confirmed my suspicions: Sally and her husband were charged with drug prescription fraud. I had no doubt that Sally was guilty; I'd seen the evidence, but I'd missed the early clues. Partly too busy, partly biased by my affection for Sally. I had trusted her.

In my work, I am both the confessor and the accuser. Sometimes I hear the whole truth, every detail as if he/she must confess the transgressions. The infidelities, the excesses, the poor judgments that hurt the patient as well as their loved ones. There is a relief that follows laying bare one's soul. *Here I am and here it is—the awful truth*. As the listener, I accept it without judgment. Personally, I've known that relief, like the clear air after a dramatic summer thunderstorm, I am washed clean, I breathe easier, the humidity, vanished.

But I can set patients up to lie. "Joe you are taking your meds, aren't you?" How could he say no?

It is better to poke around the white lies, to discover the unspoken truth, to ask in a nonjudgmental manner to get at the truth. Sometimes it is embarrassing to admit the facts—I could not bring myself to tell Veronica she smelled as a child. Could I, as an adult, a doctor? *Veronica, I like you. Here is a gift of soap. You'll smell better if you use it. Maybe your mother did not teach you about bathing regularly?* As her physician I could do that, but could I as her friend?

And then, with patients like Sally I missed the clues, perhaps lied to myself for a myriad of reasons. After the fax from the pharmacy the truth could not be avoided: $800 in cash paid when she had insurance? All the other excuses were now evidence: Social services paid for Disney World? Did her son really flush her pills down the toilet? How could she run out of her medications and not go through withdrawal?

I became the accuser. I have no choice but to be the accuser.

To be honest, I prefer the role of confessor. It suits my personality more. But in my work as a physician, I must be capable of both.

Performance Review

It's not New York but still a big town for her small
town sense of self. She's packing change for the bus.
Gulps down shyness. Pretends her job is old hat.

Her industrious ancestors, dead but loud, encourage
a quickstep through downtown traffic: Anticipate
every light that changes! Don't get caught napping!

She needs community real bad but can't quite leave
herself to find those folks she yearns for. She's all
backward to the bone but bleeding for liberation.

There's a geyser of fear bubbling up in her chest.
She's real cool about not acting cool. Her heat
is more than a bus ride home on a summer's day.

She's studying the procedure manual. Knows
the salesman wants to take her back to his room
to ratchet things up. But she has work to do.

Drugs would surely pull her under so she relies on
the endorphins of books, orgasms, real conversation.
There's lots of room left in her homespun briefcase.
She's packing carefully, unpacking more carefully.
She's puzzled about what to put on her résumé.
Plugs in a calculator. Starts adding things up.

Looking back some forty years out now, I watch her
navigate the jungle in her bell-bottoms, boots and beret.
I offer her the peace sign. A meal. A place to stay.

After receiving the entire presentation on paper

I speed read while the speaker drones on,
clicking from slide 2 to slide 3. I stare at
the woman in front of me. She knits,
needles flash, yarn snakes. I wonder,
is it a winter scarf or baby booties?
How many speakers will she stitch through
before she's done? I take out my evaluation
and write: *PowerPoint works best*
when it complements the presentation,
as opposed to listing items verbatim.
I feel smug, knowing the difference
between *complement* and *compliment*,
but I berate myself for not knowing
if Dante's *Inferno* has a circle in hell
for those who exist in a state of ennui,
for I am surely in that liminal state now,
with the only thing to look forward to
in my dismal future being a cold sandwich lunch
(drinks are *complimentary)* in the exhibit hall
with the vendors. That is, until the gray suit
next to me leans over the empty seat between us
and, with gusto, says the most engaging thing
I've heard yet: *Great shoes.*

Walk Fast, Look Worried

There is a stain of ranch dressing, white and speckled as an egg, on my apron. I pour some coffee on a bar rag and rub the spot out quickly, before JC sees that I haven't washed my uniform, that I have two creases down my sleeve from ironing it again after wearing it last shift. I tuck my shirt tightly in the waistband of my miniskirt and run my hand along my stomach, feeling the slight bulge. Yesterday I knocked into one of the girls as we tried to pass each other, unaware of my own changing dimensions, and I watched as silverware slid off the plate she carried and onto the runner. I bent over for the forks, feeling too full, as though I'd just eaten Thanksgiving dinner. I had to grab the counter to pull myself up.

Everything has its place here in the restaurant. I crave the monotony of setting out the glasses, filling the boxes of Sweet 'n' Low, opening the matchbooks in the ashtrays so the restaurant's logo can be seen. JC will turn on the lights and start some music soon, but for the moment, all I can hear is muted sounds from behind the kitchen door: pans skidding against the round open mouths of the gas burners, knives tapping against cutting boards. The chefs speak quietly now, while they are able to and can still be heard. The dining room is lit only by the neon that stretches along one wall, coating everything with a soft pink glow. It should always be this way, but the lunch crowd is already starting to fill up the parking lot. I see them through the windows, chatting on cell phones in their company cars.

My section is almost full by 11:15—a four-top of bored women with perfect manicures; a couple sitting on the same side of the booth so the man can hold the woman's thigh; two younger boys in cowboy boots and backward baseball caps who suck in their breath when they see the prices on the menu. Sticker shock.

One of my regulars comes in—Paul Noonan, the attorney general. He has this salt and pepper hair that seems to curl just a bit out of control around his ears, a handlebar moustache, and a slightly crooked front tooth. He looks whimsical—disarming, even—but he's great at his job, and has the reputation to prove it. There's something I like about knowing him personally, as if he could protect me from mail fraud or identity theft. When I see that he is seated in my section, I bring out his iced tea without him having to ask.

Yesterday I did a head count then estimated a dollar tip from each person. It makes it easier to be friendly, to ignore the feeling in my gut that something is eating me inside, taking all my energy away from me and growing stronger by doing so. I just keep telling myself to remember to breathe, to focus.

The new hostess comes up and tells me table twenty has two, then spins and walks back up front. She's named after a spice—it's Ginger, or Cinnamon, or Saffron, or something. She won't last long here. On Friday she paged "Craven Morehead" three times before someone finally told her it was a joke, probably a businessman on his cell, probably someone in our own bar laughing at his cleverness. I give her two weeks, max. She's just another paper doll with hair that adds two inches to her height and a skirt that reaches the exact point on her thighs that my small apron reaches on mine.

I grab the water pitcher and head for twenty, walking fast and looking worried. It makes people tip better, and I don't find it difficult.

At the table, expecting to get a drink order from the woman and her partner, I instead get a ten-minute list of allergens that cannot be allowed near her faux-Fiesta plate. I say to her, "Yes, Ma'am," when what I really mean is, Jesus if you're allergic to half of the ingredients used in common dishes, why are you eating out? Order a salad!

This woman is about eighty or so, and I happen to believe that people shouldn't live that long anyway. The younger generation should be given a chance to build a home, find a well-paying, stable job that ends at the same time my dinner shift begins. Instead, people like this lady are hanging around, stealing air and making sure the money I put into Social Security will never come back to me. She looks at me like I'm some slave and not just trying to put myself through college on the two-dollar tips that her type leave me. I've always believed that anyone who wants to eat out in a restaurant should have to work in one for at least a week. Then things would be different; they'd see that we all earn our fifteen percent. I know I have—I go through a pair of decent walking shoes, the white leather ones, once a month. By the end of thirty days, fifty-two shifts, I have either worn out the soles on the paisley carpet or the leather tops have melted from the grease in the kitchen.

But the fossil doesn't know this and she goes on to tell me that the customer is always right, that the kitchen must surely have the ingredients to make her a good meal out of things that won't make her lethargic after eating. I tell her the cooks will do what they can, but they aren't trained dieticians. What I don't tell her is that they aren't trained in anything, really. Three of them used to be down at Fort Selcar in minimum security. We got them on work release to wash dishes, then put them on the cold line to make sandwiches after awhile. Now they're running the hot lines, and I keep my purse up front and have a manager walk me to my car if I close.

Slinger is at the grill, sweating from the heat, his brown hair long, covering one eye, though I can see the other and it is squinting fiercely, the pupil permanently dilated and cat-like. I don't know if his name is a reference to how he puts the food on the plate or his list of priors with a weapon. He screams at me when I tell him about the old woman's order. He tells me that it's the middle of the lunch rush, as if I didn't know. I have five other tables: two eating meals which I haven't had time to check on; one whose bill is still sitting face down, waiting for the first person to grab an expense on their corporate card, two who've laid their menus in a pile at the end of the table so I will know they are ready to order and I'd better hurry.

From where I am in the kitchen I can see seven empty water glasses in my section. A man with a fuchsia tie and a black suit is tipping his glass back, trying to get another drop, when the ice shifts and bursts over the rim into his lap. He jumps out of his chair, brushes the cubes off himself in quick downward slaps as if they were flames.

"Just do it, all right?" I say to Slinger, who rolls his eye and mouths the word—the word that starts with "c" that you never call a female. By now I don't care if the woman at table twenty puffs up and explodes from what she eats here. This isn't a geriatric ward, and I don't have time.

I send Larry out to water my section. He is partially deaf and wears a hearing aid the size of a golf ball behind his left ear. He doesn't have any front teeth, and I've heard that he freebases cocaine and uses LSD to come down. He has two kids by different women. I have no idea what kind of woman would let him come near her, but I have to admit he's a fast busser, and he gets the job done. We tip out two percent of our sales to the bussers and hostess, and this guy earns that tax-free bonus.

Last night, a table left me a five-dollar tip on a hundred-dollar tab, and I thought about the fact that I truly paid to wait on them—after tip out and claiming the eight percent mandatory for our government. Three of my friends have been audited after working in restaurants, and made to prove that they had been tipped only the money they claimed, and not thousands more. Why do you have to prove you're innocent?

JC comes in the kitchen wearing hundred-dollar gym shoes with cuffed pants and a shirt stiff from the drycleaners. He looks at me, raises his eyebrows and parts his lips for just a second, then reconsiders and looks toward Slinger, who is still cursing and raising his arms. They are hairless from sautéing and flipping steaks above flames, and he has baby hands, plump fingers and skin pinkish from grease burns. JC has that look on his face—the one that says that everything is under control. I know better. I know him well enough to know that he is going to make this all my fault. I've seen him lose his cool, scream at the assistant managers when he finds out one of them has been doing blow back in the liquor room or drinking on the job.

It's a rule here that the management can't date the wait staff or bartenders; it says so in the employee manual. I know. I wrote it. It says clearly, "No sportfucking." But every one of the married managers—and even the owner—met their wives here. This place is the microcosm of the universe. There are the scurves—the Slingers and Larrys; there are the preps, like JC and rest of the managers, and even most of the wait staff. Hell, two of the best servers here are in their third year of medical school. We probably have the highest collective IQ of any restaurant in town.

You couldn't tell that, however, by the way the kitchen is reacting to my special order. I feel a little sick—the doctor had told me this would happen—and I reach over to the basket of crackers by the soup tureen. The whole kitchen gets quiet, watching JC for some sort of reaction. We aren't allowed to eat anything when we are on shift, not even dead food, the mistakes made by the chefs or wrong orders by the servers. I know this, and I don't care. JC looks at me as I put the whole cracker in my mouth, washing it down with the 7-Up and bitters I've been nursing during my shift. He huffs and walks out to the bar.

I follow him out, past the framed picture of a woman's spread legs sticking out from beneath a Porsche, the license plate demanding, "Go For It." He turns to me and points his finger at my chest. "You," he says. He pulls his hand across his head. He got a haircut the day after I told him. I can see the moles on his scalp. "You know better!"

"Yeah," I say. "I do." But there are practical matters to tend to. And I have things that need to get done.

I run through my section while I'm waiting for my meals to come up. Two tables have finally decided on who gets to pay, and they each hand me their bill and credit card. I stop at the old woman's table and tell her it will be a couple of minutes before her food is up. If you warn people, they seem to take it better.

One of the newbies brushes by me, a plate of linguini in one hand and three iced teas in the other, and tells me that I have food up in the window. I head from the dimly lit dining room to the bright lights of the kitchen. JC is expediting, and I load my arms with the grilled chicken breast and rice pilaf for the woman in twenty, and blackened catfish for her partner. JC places the parsley at ten o'clock on each of the plates while I'm turning, then he smiles at me, naturally—as if he really means it. I can see the slight space between his front teeth, and the laugh lines at the edge of his eyes. For a moment I remember everything I saw in him, and I remember looking down at him, the way he brushed my hair away from my cheeks and pulled me to his chest. But then I think, it's his job to keep us happy, and when I smile in return, reflexively, I feel it spread across my face like a crack.

"We didn't use butter," he says. "She's the kind that will ask, so tell her *no lubricants*."

I nod and walk back out with the plates balanced on my left arm, my right arm free to serve. The woman looks pleased as I set down the meals.

"Now," she says, "there's no butter or garlic in here."

"No ma'am."

"Wonderful. Thank you," she says. "You don't know how hard it is to deal with these kinds of allergies."

She seems to melt in front of my eyes, the folds in her skin looking less like leather and more like sheer cloth. I have the urge to touch her, softly, as if she were my grandmother.

On my way back to the kitchen, I take an order from a young couple that mispronounces "fajitas," making the word sound like some part of the female anatomy. I say it back to them in correct Spanish, quietly enough that it won't affect my tip. A middle-aged lady with a Dooney & Bourke purse that would be checked as luggage at an airport asks me who chooses the music we play and if I have any idea who Mozart was. I smile and nod. The goat-ropers in twenty-two discuss a murder on the other side of town last year, the one where the killer was identified by the ejaculate in the victim's stab wounds.

I try not to hear.

Club Paradise

He bids the job based on aerial photos.
The easiest 10 acres ever, he predicts
not knowing that a tornado took out the old home place
and filled a hidden ravine with rusty sheet metal,
trees piled like Lincoln logs, now tangled with vines and briers.

He leads with a machete. I follow far enough back to avoid his swing
tying a trail of pink ribbons as we climb down the bank,
over and under, around the impenetrable. On the adjoining hillside,
we discover an old cemetery, stones from the 1800s.
The last people who ventured through the valley of doom, we joke.

On the way home he stops so I can take pictures of the neon sign
at the old Club Paradise, now shuttered and grown up with weeds
on the wet side of a dry county line.

Looking for Mount Fuji in the Japanese Tea Garden

Because nothing
permanent,
evokes the present.
Language key
and maze.

Keep hands ajar
counsel the trees
wind will blow through.
The gardener says *watch*
and prune.

What you seek
undeniably
iconographic,
conical
in the corner
squaring off
against distance
and larger
than in the woodblock prints
you had as mentors.

The present
Mount Fuji, deliberate
and vegetal. Dark,
with a lighter crown.
Perhaps, a gesture
of snow?

You seek energy
in word and symbol.
The gardener looks
for meaning in the shape
of her work, what illusion has
wrought.

The Bird

"Aw Jesus Tom!" I gasped with my palm flattened against my chest. I wondered how long he'd been standing there beside my desk. He was always doing that, sneaking into my office, pausing silently behind me and then looking surprised when I turned around and flinched.

He frowned and shrugged his heavy shoulders.

"My bad, Kelly."

"You really startled me," I told him. I did not tell him that my name wasn't Kelly. Suddenly, I was in a very foul mood.

"Kelly," he said again, "I need you to run to Jessamine County. Pick up some films. Oh, and you've been scheduling for Otis Phillips? Well, I need you to cancel what you got and do letters. Guy's daughter just called. He's dead."

I spun back around and stared into his face. I hadn't ever noticed his eyes were green. I waited for him to say something else about Otis but instead we stared dumbly at each other until it became uncomfortable. Tom turned to leave then stopped at the door, turned and smiled. "Hey, it's one less problem for us," he shrugged.

Alone again, I closed down my solitaire game out of respect for Otis. It wasn't as if I'd known him. I'd never met the guy or even seen a picture of him. I did, however, know his birth date and his social security number. And I had, in fact, seen a picture of his marriage license. I also knew things about him. I knew that he didn't like doctors. I had scheduled four different appointments for him. He hadn't showed for a single one, costing our office two grand in cancellation fees. I knew that he was poor, that he couldn't afford an attorney of his own to fight our attorneys over his federal black lung claim. And now I knew that he was dead, at age 63, that he'd left behind a wife of forty years and a daughter who was willing to tie up his legal loose ends on the very morning of his passing.

For awhile, I sat very still at my desk and stared out the window. I could hear Shannon and Todd whispering in the office next to mine. They were always over there, giggling and whispering but I never could hear what they said. I never had noticed the color of their eyes. I took a deep breath. I thought about Otis again. Outside, the sky was like the ocean, infinitely gray.

I took another long inhale and held it. Shannon and Todd fell silent.

A salesman had snuck into the reception area. He was spieling to Anne about some sort of golf package. Anne was gently insisting that she didn't golf but the man didn't seem to believe her. I grabbed my purse and scarf and headed out to the parking lot.

I took the back roads to Jessamine County where last week's winter storm still slushed across the roadways and pastures and the treetops were so heavy with ice that they bent over like old men and scratched the top of my car. I pulled my car off the road and shut off the engine. I knew that Otis and his wife owned some land and some chickens out in Harlan County and I thought about his chickens now. I wondered if they had felt his passing. I imagined the frozen farm had trembled a bit beneath their cold claws this morning when Otis never showed for their sunup feeding. I could almost feel it trembling now, and I could hear the low groan in their bellies as the morning broke and they went without breakfast. And then I heard something else.

"Honey? Hey honey, you stuck?" Behind me was a large two-toned diesel truck, trembling and groaning, thick white exhaust curling in its wake like a ghost. I sighed and I started up my engine. When I hit the gas, snow and ice and mud kicked up and sprayed against my windows. I tried again. I got out of my car, turned to the truck and nodded.

Two old and skinny men slid out and a small boy stayed inside the cab, peering out with an amused expression. "I appreciate you stopping," I lied. The men just smiled and went around to their truck bed, fetched out two snow shovels and still without a word, began shoveling snow and ice out from beneath my tires. I stood on the road and watched. I dug my heels into the slush and felt embarrassed. I fidgeted with a low hanging tree branch and the little boy stepped out of the truck and walked over beside me.

I looked down at him. "Hi," I said. He shoved his fists into his jacket pockets and looked at his feet. "No school today?" I tried again. He bent down and scooped up a handful of snow. "A friend of mine died this morning," I told him. The boy looked up at me and I wished I hadn't said it.

"I had a dog that died once," he finally told me. "His name was Lucky."

Now I looked at my feet. "Oh," I said, "I'm sorry."

"It's okay," he told me, "he grew hisself some wings and turned into a bird and now he gets to fly wherever he travels." The kid smiled. "Lucky likes being a bird," he said.

Once my car was unstuck I called into work and said the roads were too icy, that I was just going to take the afternoon off. When I got back to my apartment I put on my mother's old Stravinsky album and turned the volume way up. I grabbed a half-eaten bag of unsalted sunflower seeds and took them to my back porch step. For the rest of the afternoon, I tossed out handfuls of the seed to the wintering robins and cardinals and sparrows and I decided that I did believe in second chances. I decided that when I went into the office in the morning I would tell Tom that Kelly is not my name.

Work Till Jesus Comes

(monologue excerpted from the play, *The Gifts of the Spirit*)

LIZZIE: Most people nowadays don't want to work. Always expecting something. People expects too much. Got their hand out from the word *go.*

I was a girl on the farm the first time I put my hand out. Daddy gave me one end of a cross-cut saw to pull and I went to the logwoods and stayed all day.

They was twelve of us, and we all had a job the year round. I've shot coal out of coal banks, waded snow a foot deep feeding cattle, grubbed sprouts, laid off ground, follered Dad all day carrying a corn planter. Stop to get your breath, he'd holler — Git busy!

Now they talk about this women's lib. They wasn't much to be done on the farm us girls couldn't do. Worked side by side with the boys and the men. And had house chores, too.

After I married Harold it was hit the ground running ever day. And you better never think we was running to get ahead. We was running a step in front of starvation. I done housework and washing for people for fifty cents a day. And hit was a long day, too. Harold drove a truck, worked in the logwoods and the coal mines, these little dog hole mines. Flunkeyed around at whatever he could to make a dollar. Now Harold's gone, been dead twenty year. My children's grown and gone off. Grandchildren's even grown. I got one great-grandbaby. Aye, Lord, things changes.

But now I ain't one of these that wishes things would go back how they used to be. Most of them is young people that don't remember. I believe in working, but buddy when no matter how hard you're at it you're still barely hanging on— that's a different story.

But what worries me, my grandchildren don't know how to work nor play neither one. Take Sandy, Gene's girl. Come in from Covington last summer and stayed with me two weeks. Wanted to help put up the garden. I didn't need no help, what little bit I had. But I went along with her, I knowed she was trying. Well we gathered corn to put in the deep freeze and I give her a paring knife and put her out on the porch to cut it off the cob. I went out there twenty minutes later and name of God if she wasn't still on the first ear. And had gouged the cob so bad, what little dab she had in the dishpan was about all fodder.

That got me to thinking. I've not got one granddaughter that could kill a chicken if her life depended on it. And the boys is just as bad. Can't hunt nor fish. Petey? Raymond's boy that's thirteen? Why he won't even ride the lawn mower. Stays in the house all the time, playing video games and reading funny books. You just have to drive him outdoors and once he gets there he don't know how to play. Walks the fence line with his hands in his pockets.

We're raising a generation that can't do nothing for theirselves. Not make their living nor make their fun. All they know how to do: sail up to a drive-in winder and order what they want. Someday them winders'll all be boarded up. What are they gonna do then? Now you tell me. What're they gonna do? People used to tell their kids, "I don't want you to have to work like I did." Well, they don't.

Hard work can be a fine thing. Can teach you, besides, how to play hard. And play's a fine thing, too. If the Lord hadn't a meant for us to enjoy life, He'd a took us straight to heaven and skipped over it.

We're born into this world with nothing, and we die the self-same way. We've got to make the most of what's in the middle.

Work in the Fields of the Lord

A hymn to be sung following the monologue "Work Till Jesus Comes" by Belinda Ann Mason (excerpted from Shelby's play *Passing Through the Garden: The Work of Belinda Mason*).

Help Wanted, the sign says, the job starts today
There is work in the fields, in the fields of the Lord
No job applications, no one's turned away
There is work in the fields of the Lord

Chorus:
There's brothers and sisters in need day and night
There's beauty to find and there's wrongs to make right
Until Jesus comes and it's time to go home
We will work in the fields of the Lord

There's no competition, no pressure, no greed
When you work (in the fields) in the fields (of the Lord)
And job satisfaction can be guaranteed
When you work in the fields of the Lord

Chorus:
There's brothers and sisters in need day and night
There's beauty to find and there's wrongs to make right
Until Jesus comes and it's time to go home
We will work in the fields of the Lord

A Sense of Accomplishment

7:30 a.m.

I wake with the alarm and stumble sleepily into the kitchen, filling the yellowed ceramic tea kettle with water from a bucket near the stove, punching through the sheen of ice that grew overnight on the surface with a sound like breaking glass. Two scoops is usually enough. Like Raisin Bran, my sleepy mind thinks, and I smile at the memory of breakfast cereal. Singe-ing my fingertips, I light all three burners of the gas stove with a match to help warm up the kitchen.

That's not safe! screams the American part of my mind, remembering warnings of carbon monoxide poisoning, but the part of me that has become almost entirely Kazakh after joining the Peace Corps just grunts and hits mute. The temperature for the last week has hovered around -35 degrees Celsius; any extra warmth is welcome.

Gritting my teeth, I slide on thick boots and fight my way outside. A fresh six inches of snow carpets the ground, and now the snowdrift encasing the outhouse is nearly as high as the wooden door itself. It takes me a minute of pushing and pulling, but I eventually force the door open wide enough for me to sneak inside then spend the next minute kicking at the ring of snow around the triangle opening in the floor away so that I have room to squat. The pee stalagmite reaching up from the depths of the outhouse is now almost to the opening, and I do my best to melt it a little.

7:47 a.m.

Aigerim, my sixteen-year-old host sister, is awake now and has finished putting out the dishes of pickles, bread, jam, cookies, and chocolates for tea. It has been just the two of us for a while – her mother, Sara Apai, is very ill and staying at a hospital in the city – and we have an easy routine.

"Good morning," I say as I grab my precious jar of peanut butter from the cupboard and pour myself some tea. "How did you sleep?"

"I slept well," she answers, her English now almost perfect. Even though I know Russian near fluently, I make it a habit to only speak with her in English to help her practice. "I think you will not have lessons today. It's too cold."

"Maybe," I answer, making myself a pb&j. I momentarily miss sliced bread. "What about you?"

"Yes, I must go. We have to prepare for the national tests."

The Kazakh Gymnasium where she studies is the best school in the region, and her test scores at the end of her senior year will determine what universities she gets into and whether her widowed mother will have to sell their house to pay for it. She will do well on the tests, I know; my students at the Russian School, however, with only two hours of English study a week will fare much worse. I sigh.

8:37 a.m.

My eyelids have begun to freeze shut.

Three layers of clothing and a thick jacket are not enough to keep me warm against the bitter cold. The streets are practically empty, and I think seriously about turning around and walking back home. Although it's only a half-mile to school, when I'm plowing my way through waist-deep snow, it feels like running a marathon. No one would blame me or say anything. I'm their American and as such get special privileges. Not that I want them.

In the distance I see Maya Ivanovna struggling through the snow. At 62, she is a pensioner and teaches only a few English classes for some extra income; she is also one of my favorite people. With a bad heart, she shouldn't be walking in the snow like that.

I call out for her to wait.

Her smile when she sees me is enough to melt ice. I walk in front of her to act like a plow, clearing a path.

By the time I reach the school, I have a small following of students and teachers.

10:07 a.m.

A handful of students in the older forms have shown up for class, but the school is vacant for the most part. I sit in the teacher's lounge reading *Harry Potter and the Sorcerer's Stone* in Russian. I've been on page 4 for about an hour.

Maya Ivanovna is sitting next to me for company, grading some of our students' notebooks. One or two other teachers are sitting in the Teacher's Lounge; the rest have the good sense to stay home. After the fourth time I ask her for a translation of something that I can't find in the dictionary, she smiles and says in Russian: "You'll be reading that chapter for the rest of your life."

I shoot her an affronted look that makes her smile more.

"We'll see."

10:52 a.m.

Tea time has come early, and we are sitting on cold metal chairs in the back of the school cafeteria, Maya Ivanovna, her two sisters, and myself. A cup of dark, toxic tea steam warms my hands. In the center of the table rests some wrapped candies and chunks of fresh bread. One of the women brought a jar of homemade winter salad – ground up tomatoes, garlic, and onions – to share. It tastes delicious. I miss vegetables.

"Do school girls in America have sex?"

They look at me expectantly, curious what I'll say to this question, and I hide behind my cup for a long second to think of an appropriate reply. All these women – and, realistically, everyone else in the village – know about America is what they've learned from Brittney Spears, David Hasslehoff, and *Sex in the City*. As a volunteer, I spend most of my time countering these pop-culture-born myths. Yes, there are poor people in America; I am one of them. No, people don't just have sex with strangers they met in the bar; it happens, of course, but not as frequently as television would make you think. No, everyone in America isn't fat; just me.

The time for hiding behind tea is over. "Yes, of course school girls in America have sex. I was a school girl; I had sex." They nod their heads as though I've given them the answer they expected to hear, a look in their eyes that oscillates somewhere between envy and distaste. "Not everyone does, though. I know plenty of boys and girls that didn't have sex in school."

"Here, good girls don't have sex before they're married. But I think boys are the same anywhere. They only want one thing, so girls will do it to keep them from leaving," Maya Ivanovna says; the other women nod in agreement.

In Kazakhstan, the ratio of men to women is about 1:2, making it difficult for girls and women alike knowing they have only a fifty percent chance of getting married. There is a traditional belief that if a girl hasn't married by the time she's 25, she never will. To avoid that fate and have a chance at stability and a family, girls will go a long way. It's considered okay for a young man to date and sleep with multiple girls at one time since it's the girl's job to catch a man and a man's job not to be caught.

We spend the rest of tea time gossiping about which of our students has and hasn't had sex.

12:15 p.m.

Shutting the door behind me, I enter the kitchen and take off my boots and jacket, relishing in the relative warmth of my house compared to outside. My host sister will be home from school soon, so I need to start making lunch.

The chicken leg – I'm no longer surprised that they actually look like the calf and thigh of what had once been a walking, squawking chicken – is thawed and ready for boiling. When I go to dip some water from the bucket by the stove to start boiling the meat, however, I'm forced to acknowledge that we are out of water. Just in case, I check the other two buckets but find nothing.

I could wait, I know, for Aigerim to come home; if I asked, she would go get water and think nothing of it. Sigh. I grab the buckets, don the requisite boots, coat, scarf, and two pairs of gloves, and trudge outside and over to the intersection where the nearest deep-water well is located. Most people, my family included, have a well dug in their yard somewhere, but these shallower wells can't withstand the cold of the winter and freeze up, forcing residents to use the deeper wells maintained by the village itself.

There are about ten people waiting in the closest thing to a line that happens in Kazakhstan. Usually, people will just surround counters at local stores and offices, clamoring for service and pushing their way in front of other people. This amorphous line is one of the legacies of the Soviet Union, but when it comes to waiting at the well people will actually line up for the most part and are strict in policing the order.

As I find my place, I look around and can't help but be impressed at the ingenuity of homemade sleds and carts that will carry the volumes of metal canisters, buckets, and basins needed to supply a family. I'll be carrying my three buckets by hand, but then I don't live far from the well. Some people have walked nearly a quarter mile to use this well, and carrying water by hand over that distance isn't feasible.

12:50 p.m.

I've lost sensation in my toes and fingers. Stamping my feet on the ground and hitting my hands against my side, I try to return circulation as stories of frostbite march relentlessly across my mind. There are only three people in front of me, but they all have several big, metal containers to fill.

The spring before, I was in a taxi that got stuck in a large puddle of melted snow. Water had seeped in the car from the cracks around the door and rusted holes of the floor, soaking my feet in cold water before I had had a chance to get them free. It had taken the driver over an hour to get the taxi free, and in that time my toes felt like they had turned into ice cubes. That pain was nothing compared to the fear I feel now that I've stopped being able to feel my feet. I consider, seriously, going inside and forgetting about the water. But we need it. There has to be water for me to make lunch for Aigerim, and there is no way I can ask her to do it now, not knowing what it's like.

Ten more minutes, I tell my feet. Hold out ten more minutes.

1:09 p.m.

It's finally my turn. Grabbing the metal pump for support, I manage to negotiate the five foot wide hill of ice surrounding the well and hook my first bucket over the nozzle. The splash and gurgle of water would be music to my ears if I could still feel them. I let the bucket fill to the top, thinking to get the most out of standing in this line. Muscling the heavy bucket off the nozzle, however, water splashes everywhere as I try to slide off the ice to sit it somewhere safer in the snow.

For the second and third bucket, I'm smarter and leave a two-inch gap between the water and the top of the bucket. The downward slope of the ice ramp around the well makes getting the water safely to the snow difficult, but I manage without spilling too much.

I carry the buckets carefully back to the house, not wasting a drop of the water. If I'm lucky, I might be able to go two more days without needing to fill them again.

2:15 p.m.

Covering the leftover pot of soup with a lid, I put it in the entranceway to keep until dinner, not wanting to waste my host mother's money by putting it in the refrigerator when the temperature outside is plenty cold enough. The dishes are easy, and I use the largest bowl as a makeshift basin to wash the other bowl, spoons, and cups from the meal, pouring the waste water into a bucket that I notice will sadly be needed to be emptied soon.

As quiet settles around the house – Aigerim has already gone back for her afternoon tutoring – I wrap up in an extra blanket and sit in the warm kitchen, futilely trying to make heads or tails of *Harry Potter*. Most days, like Aigerim, I would go back to school after lunch to teach my afternoon classes, but I had already been told not to show up. Instead, I return to my bedroom to read and take a nap.

4: 50 p.m.

Waking up, I pet my cat, Quanish, who has decided to sleep curled up on my neck, then stand and stretch. My host sister should be home in an hour, and I need to see about preparing something extra for dinner because the leftover soup isn't enough. Pizza sounds good, so I go into the kitchen and mix the ingredients for the dough, sitting it covered on top of the furnace so that the yeast will rise.

When I have finished that, I wash my hands and remember that the bucket needs dumped, but there's no way I can get to the back fence with it through all the snow. I put back on my five layers of clothing – especially the two pairs of gloves – and grab the snow shovel to clear a path back outside. Looking out the window, I see that it's snowing again. I sigh.

5:30 p.m.

I've managed to clear a path to the outhouse and dumped the waste water inside for the lack of a better place. It's nearly dark, but I walk up to the front of the house, through our big gate, and look up and down the street. The neighbor boys, I guess them to be about eight and ten years old, are shoveling a path to the road.

Careful so as not to be seen, I squat down as much as possible and quickly shape four snowballs. I peek up over the snow bank and throw my first missile and then another. Twin squeaks tell me that I hit my targets, and I stand up to get a better look, earning myself a face full of snow for the effort. Thus begins the war.

Only a few casualties have been claimed when my site mate, Tom, walks by and notices the action. Having another volunteer working in the village with me is a blessing, especially at moments like these. He joins in the attack as we launch countermeasures determined to destroy the quickly-erected snow barrier of our enemy. Another squeak of terror confirms my hit, and I laugh triumphantly. When I stand up to look, I'm pelted by a half dozen more snowballs; I let them do it, I consoled myself, so that they wouldn't feel bad that they were losing. Yeah, that was it.

5:45 p.m.

The neighbor kids' mom, my own host mother's friend Saulema, calls the boys inside, ending our battle. Looking at Tom, I smile and thank him for helping me. Most of the kids in the village don't get to have a lot of fun, and it's part of our personal mission to create it whenever and wherever possible.

Exercise and movement have kept us relatively warm, so we decide to build a snowman on top of the small mountain of snow in my front yard. Although the snow worked well for snowballs, it wasn't the best packing snow, and our snowman – standing over six feet tall – looked more like a bunch of square snow bricks stacked on top of each other than the traditional rounded snowman.

Tom found a couple of sticks to use for arms and I took off my scarf, wrapping it around what I hoped was the snowman's neck.

7:00 p.m.

Aigerim takes her pizza into her bedroom and eats while she's studying, a bad habit I taught her. Tom and I sit in the kitchen, eating and playing a card game called Set. We each win about half the games.

9:30 p.m.

Tom has gone to his house and my host sister is finally finished with her homework. Sitting on her bed, we play with my cat and talk about this boy she's been dating, the brother of one of my worst students. I know this boy to be a hooligan, and he has a reputation for having a lot of girlfriends.

Aigerim is sweet and unbelievably innocent; I worry about her terribly. Remembering how I was at that age, I knew I couldn't tell her not to date him as a good big sister would. Instead, I did the next best thing and talked about sex and using protection. She looked shocked that I had suggested it as a possibility, which made my heart feel a little better, but I still made her promise to ask me for some condoms should the relationship move that direction.

She agrees.

Lying in bed, I look absently at the ceiling as I try to figure out what we would do for meals the next day and whether the water would last. A realization, like stepping out of my skin, made me sit upright. Even a year ago, a day like this would have left me feeling frustrated, like I was wasting my time.

Work should involve measurable achievements, gain and loss and bottom lines; that's what my American mind believed, at least. The part of me that was irrevocably Kazakh, however, savored the relationships that had strengthened, even if just a little, by sharing a cup of tea or throwing a snowball.

Swing Shift

Waiting

for Beth

Yes, we are waiting,
pacing between chair and window,
staring down our cell phones or
kneeling, heads bowed.

We are restless.
We have such questions.
We have lost the sense to get good work done
but we are busy with tasks.

Hauling the laundry basket,
weeding the garden, sweeping the floor,
we check things off our lists, but really
we are waiting.

We want to be ready.
The kitchen should be clean, the dishes washed
when life shows up, asks for tea,
finally tells us what's going on.

Meanwhile, we sit behind the window
shades drawn, unseen,
frightened beyond reason
of who or what we may become.

Aerie

(She

You bailed your boyfriend out of jail, because you're one
of those girls that needs a man to feel her own nakedness.
Now his tongue is the only syringe you crave.

You chose to meet this morning dehydrated and persistent.
Lips wrinkle from expired kisses without moisture, leaving
your mouth sun-sucked and water robbed like dried tomatoes.

was born with

I can hear stitches dissolve into moist skin. A drunk driver
hit you while you were walking across the street. The scars
on your knees are blistered banjos reminding me that I need
to be gentle with you, bird lady.

You bleach your hair with color-stripping chemicals, during
your lunch breaks you fly to Italy, climb on trellises and porch
gardens until your fingers can find a scorching tile roof.

white plumes for arms)

Perched like the heron you are inside, you'll bake until all of
your hair is naturally blonde. Your body, like an overused
teat, is left cracked and shriveled by the afternoon sun,

which is really the tanning salon that is closest to our restaurant
where we work the same lunch shift on Friday.

Saturday at F. W. Woolworth's

Steam rose from a silver crescent hood
sterilizing plates and swallowing cutlery.
The silver goose-necked fountain honked
and caged canaries sang. Hair-netted,
I crated and emptied, crated and emptied
then nickel-and-dimed BLTs:
one strip broken into four bits,
a tomato slither, a pinch of mayo,
lettuce laid on rye toast dipped in
grease served with coffee, cherry coke,
or an egg cream to my boss, Mr. D'Amboise,
whom we dubbed *Fang,* leering from the edge
of the counter, and to neighborhood
shoppers who gossiped and left small tips.

I loved the small talk, the girls' scarfed hair
set in bobby-pin grids of perfect Xs,
the teenage boys swiping
dog chains, the ache in my lower back,
the mustard-clogged funnels, loved
even my father who tipped
his tweed cap after eats, *'Twas grand,* he'd say
then stiffed me as he spun from his red leather stool.

Husbands

My mother likes a man who works. She likes
my husband's muddy knees, grass stains on the cuffs.
She loved my father, though when weekends came
he'd sleep till nine and would not lift his
eyes up from the page to move the feet
she'd vacuum under. On Saturdays my husband
digs the holes for her new roses,
softening the clay with peat and compost.
He changes bulbs she can no longer reach
and understands the inside of her toaster.
My father's feet would carry him from chair
to bookshelf, back again till Monday came.
          My mother likes to tell my husband
          sit down in this chair and put your feet up.

Ada and the Epileptic

(excerpted from *Fire Is Your Water,* a novel-in-progress)

Ada watches out the window from the shadows of the kitchen. She just had sat down after putting away the dishes and had hoped for a quiet Sunday afternoon nap. But now the muffled sound of car doors shuts away that hope of rest. She peeks once more to see a well-dressed couple and a young girl step out of a shiny, new Buick. The strangers walk by the daffodils and forsythia and ignore the bright yellow of so many blooms.

The man takes off his bowler when Ada greets them at the door. He has a round face, black hair parted in the middle, and a trimmed mustache. The woman and daughter both wear dresses and feathered hats, and they both glance at Ada and then away to the yard as the man introduces them. Ada listens, but the feathered hats keep distracting her. She has seen those in catalogs, knows how expensive they are, knows she'll never be able to afford one.

"Are you Ada Shuman, the healer?" the man who calls himself Walter Stottimeir asks.

"Yes, I am," Ada answers. She is used to strangers coming to her door, but not wealthy ones. So she tries to focus on the man's face. Still she keeps glancing at the women and their hats, especially the daughter's. She is probably twelve or thirteen, Ada thinks, and her hat has pheasant feathers streaming out, their rich tans matching the tan of the felt hat.

"We've driven over an hour to come see you," Mr. Stottimeir says, and then asks, "May we come in?" Ada says, of course, and opens the door.

They sit on the sofa while Ada makes tea. The man rests his cap on his knee and tells Ada that his daughter, Isabella, has epilepsy. "She started out having a seizure maybe once a month, then once a week. Now we can expect at least one fit a day." He pauses, braces his hands on his thighs. "I'm a banker," he continues. "We have taken our Izzie to some of the best doctors in the country, in Baltimore and Boston and Colorado. We've given her some of the most advanced medicines and treatments, and none of them have healed her."

The mother and daughter watch Ada setting out the cups and saucers, and Ada tries not to rattle this, her mother's china that normally is only used at Thanksgiving and Christmas. When she looks at them, the mother smiles, a pleasant smile, while the daughter looks out the window at the chickens. They both sit upright, more poised than even Mrs. Hartman, the preacher's wife.

As he takes the cup of tea from Ada, Mr. Stottimeir looks her in the eye and asks, "Do you think you can help us?"

Ada waits to answer. She takes her cup and sits across from them.

"I don't know," she finally replies. "I've never dealt with epilepsy. I've heard of other healers stopping seizures, but never have seen it myself. But the Lord is a powerful God. He can do anything if we just invite him." She sips her tea and then adds, "Let me go upstairs and look in my books and see what they say." The family waits in silence and listens to the creaking steps as this tall, thin woman disappears.

Later, their tea cups empty, they finally hear movement from the floor above, and soon Ada appears. She pulls two chairs from the kitchen table and asks Isabella to sit in one while she sits across from her in the other. The young woman is hesitant, until her mother reassures her, places her hand behind her daughter's back to gently press her forward.

"I looked in my books, and they told me two different cures," Ada keeps her eyes on the young woman's face, but directs her words across the room to her parents. "Then I turned to the Bible and found what I needed."

Ada softens her voice and talks just to the girl. "I'm going to say this chant for you, Isabella. OK?"

Isabella nods.

"We need to take that hat off." At these words, Mrs. Stottimeir hurries over to unpin the hat. She squeezes her daughter's shoulder and then sits back down.

"I'm going to hold your head while I say it three times. You just close your eyes and don't worry none."

Isabella closes her eyes as she feels Ada's knees bump against hers, and then Ada's hands touch the sides of her face. They are rougher than she expected, but also warmer. Ada's fingers gently press on her cheeks, her forehead, and then settle on her temples. Isabella peeks and sees Ada's eyes pinched shut in concentration, her smooth forehead now wrinkled. Then the woman starts mumbling words, and all that Isabella can understand is "Holy Father" and "healing fire." It is a long chant, and as Ada repeats it, Isabella feels these hands on her temples grow hotter and begin to sweat. Then Isabella, too, realizes that her own hands have started to warm, her whole body suddenly heating up. And she knows this flash of heat as that one sensation she always feels just before she blacks out, before her body disappears into someone else's, someone who gets laughed at by her schoolmates and who is told later that she jerks and shakes on the ground ("like an electrocuted snake," one boy once said). Then this foreign body grows quiet and rigid.

Isabella tenses even more, afraid of another seizure here in a stranger's house. She no longer hears the healer's words, just feels Ada's hands pressing harder into her temples. And suddenly, instead of a black-out, the young woman senses a fire in her body, sees red on the back of her eyelids, and she shakes, one violent tremor. It's not the long, tensed-up jerks of a seizure, but a quaking that starts in her feet and shivers up her spine in one long shudder of release. Her fear melts, and then she feels nothing but cool blue.

Ada's hands are no longer touching her, and Isabella opens her eyes to see the healer sitting back in her chair, watching her. She hears a voice, faraway, but growing closer, and turns to see her mother by her side, asking, "Are you all right? Isabella, are you all right?" Her father is there, too, both of them touching her shoulders.

She nods, looks down at her lap, then grabs their hands with her own, and wipes her tears on her mother's dress.

Then she looks up, smiling, and says, "Yes, Mama, I'm fine."

As they leave, Mr. Stottimeir offers again to pay Ada. And again, she refuses. "I can't take money for God's gift," she explains as she watches the other women walking toward their car. In the kitchen, they had thanked her repeatedly, and Isabella and Mrs. Stottimeir both hugged her at the door.

"But I would like to hear from you," Ada adds. "Will you let me know how Isabella does?"

The man nods and puts on his hat as he turns to drive them away.

A month later, Tucker Shaeffer, the mailman, stops his car at the mailbox and honks his horn. When Ada runs out to greet him, he hands her a square package. "This wouldn't fit in your box, so I wanted to make sure you got it," he tells her and watches her face. She knows he's curious, but she has no idea of the contents, so she thanks him and Tucker pulls away to finish his route.

Back in the house, Ada opens the box to find a fancy tan hat with pheasant feathers, much like Isabella's. She gasps with pleasure as she turns it in her hands and then snugs it onto her head. Her mother watches, smiles, and says that it fits just right.

In the accompanying letter, Mr. Stottimeir's fancy penmanship writes that this hat is a small thank you for healing Isabella who has had no seizures since their visit with Ada. He ends his note: "Our life has truly become a miracle, thanks to you, Ada. Thank you so much."

"That's high praise, Ada," her mother comments.

Ada only looks out the window for a moment, and then reads the letter again.

In her bedroom, Ada and Kate admire her new hat in the mirror. "This will go just right with the new Easter dress you made me, Mama." Ada looks at her mother in the mirror, who nods in agreement. Then Ada says, "I don't know that I've ever felt anything so soft."

As Ada turns her head back and forth, they both notice one of the feathers jiggling loose. "That's a surprise," her mother says as she holds her daughter's head and tries to push the quill back into place. When Ada takes off the headpiece, she too tries to push the feather back into its special slit. But then she notices a piece of paper in the way. She finds tweezers and carefully pinches something from inside the hat's lining. At first the opening is too small for the tweezers, but eventually Ada pulls out a tightly-rolled green coil. It is a twenty-dollar bill.

"Mama, look," Ada says, holding up the bill. "That Mr. Stottimeir thinks he's clever, but I can't keep this." In her lap, she stretches the green print between her fingers, admires the portrait of Grant.

"Why not, Ada? A reward for all of your work. A way to buy those shoes you've been wanting."

"Oh, it's the Lord's work, not mine. Plus if I keep it, Isabella's seizures might return. No, I can't keep it." She places the bill on her dresser, next to the hat.

That Sunday, Ada wears the hat to church and glows in the compliments from her friends. "It just matches your new dress perfect," Delores praises, her lipstick just right. Ada tries to hold on to these warm words, but she also tries not to think about the scuff marks on her best pair of dress shoes. When the offering plate comes down her pew, she closes her eyes and quietly gives the twenty-dollar bill to God.

House/Tree/Person

The first time he comes
I hand him paper and pencil
saying, *Please draw me a house*
and the boy draws his house
without hesitation
or a door or window.
His head shakes "No" when I ask
Is anyone home?

Now draw me a tree
and he faintly sketches
a leafless tree
with a scribbled bird's nest
fallen on the ground
and branches shaped like spears.
He shrugs when I ask
What lives there?

Now draw me a person
and we'll be done.
And in slow motion
he makes torso and legs,
feet, arms, and hands,
scant clothing. He will come

each week of his boyhood
to someone like me
who is sad for this riddle
of a child who does not seem sad,
for this boy with the echoless eyes
which may never see
that the picture he's drawn of his body
has no head.

Local Knowledge

Tomorrow, Ednitza Santiago walks out of Family Court holding her seven-year-old daughter's hand for the first time in three years. She will bring her home to live with her boyfriend, Eddie Roman, a man who spent time in prison for sexually molesting two little girls.

There isn't a damn thing I can do about it.

I don't know Ednitza personally, but I do know her by sight. I pass through the methadone maintenance center often enough to know just about everybody there by sight. The center is run by the medical school, which also runs the hospital where I work as a research assistant. This is a common and cozy arrangement, but I can't complain because it makes my job, recruiting HIV-positive people for clinical studies, a little easier. They had their shooting galleries and now I have mine.

I don't know Eddie Roman, personally, either, and I never saw him at the methadone pick-up window though I did find out that he went to get his fix every day. Ednitza went in only once a week, a privilege she earned because, unlike Eddie, she didn't sell her dose on the street to get cash for coke or smoke or something else to get high with.

I show up at the methadone center trolling for research participants two, three times a week. On Tuesdays around 9 in the morning, Ednitza is just ahead of me, her dark hair pulled tight into a pony tail bouncing back and forth as she gingerly picks her way through the corridor, wearing stretchy black tights, high top sneakers, and a bright bubble vest, looking like she is just dropping by for an aerobics class or a tai chi session. We were both there to see Louise De Souza, the counselor in charge of family life programs at the center. This was a euphemism for recovering drug-addicted mothers desperately trying to get their kids back from foster care. Louise, a petite beautiful black woman with a wardrobe of classy business suits, is one hell of a taskmaster and facilitator with her family groups.

"Hey, Ednitza, thanks for coming early. Can you set up the chairs in the group room? Terrific, see you there in a few minutes." Then Louise would steer me into her tiny office and we'd run through a list of her clients who had appointments at my clinic this week and those who hadn't shown for their appointments at my clinic last week. We communicate in code, one we developed because she isn't supposed to tell me who was HIV positive and I'm not supposed to let her know that I know who was HIV positive.

This works because we need each other to make it work.

Like I said, I don't know Ednitza, not personally, but I know the mother of two of the little girls Eddie Roman molested. Her name is Clara.

Clara is dying on the AIDS ward and I can't do a thing about that, either.

Everyone at the hospital knows Clara. She is a celebrity patient. Before I met her, she was famous for her accusatory rages, for her demonic cursing streaks, and for the two little girls molested by her husband, now her ex-husband, Eddie Roman.

I was sent to Clara's hospital room because I have a reputation for working with difficult patients. I told her I work for Dr. So and So, who is chief attending on the AIDS service, and how is the service in this joint, anyway? She didn't know whether to laugh or cry and while she was thinking it over, I picked up the clipboard attached to the bed and see the note: Restrict Liquids. This is the fate of the incontinent patient.

"Are you thirsty?"

"Yeah. Nobody lets me have any god damn water. Can you get me some?"

"Sure." She was already soaking wet from head to toe anyway because she has an intractable fever. She was a very small woman, not more than 80 pounds, with brown hair and very delicate, even features. Before she was sick, she was probably quite pretty.

I've shared many a drink in a bar where tongues were loosened and confidences were exchanged as the amber liquid flowed freely. This was the first time I open the floodgates with a glass of water.

"My daughters, they were 5 and 6 years old when I took them to the emergency because they both had some kind of pus coming out of their pee pees. The sonobitch nurses called the cops. The bastard detective acted like I did it or something. They wanted to take the kids away right there, but they were screaming for their mommy and I wouldn't leave the emergency room without them. It was a big fucking mess." She drank two more glasses of water; the night shift nurses would soon be plotting my death. "They came for Eddie the next day. I didn't say anything to that scumbag. I made the girls sleep with me that night, I told him they were sick.

"They told me I had to get tested for AIDS. The shit hit the fan. It was a good thing they took Eddie to jail because I would be there forever for breaking his balls open with an axe."

Clara and the older daughter tested HIV positive. There was only AZT then and nothing really for the kids. "I had to go to court. The fucking a-hole of a detective still treated me like shit. And you know how long Eddie got? A year in jail." I got another glass of water for Clara.

I begged the attending physicians to have her placed on the AIDS ward. Clara could drink herself silly there and no one would complain about changing the sheets.

I visited Clara every chance I had, since her new bed is next to my office. She seldom spoke about her ex-husband, preferring subjects like movies, television soap operas, and the private lives of movie stars. I cram for our chats when I am stuck in line at the supermarket where all those glossies are handy.

Yesterday, Clara sent for me. "Eddie is with an Ednitza somebody from his program. She's going to court to get her daughter back on Thursday."

"How old is her daughter?"

"Seven, maybe eight."

"Shit."

Clara lay back on her pillow with a peaceful look on her face. I fixed things up for her before; she had no reason to think I couldn't fix this, too.

I want to do something, but I'm sure what I could do. Legally, I could do nothing. Ednitza and Eddie are not patients enrolled in the clinic where I am entitled to access information about their health status, never mind their relationship or his prison record. There are strict laws about confidentiality in a hospital. In fact, legally, I could do nothing with the knowledge that Eddie Roman is HIV positive and had infected his ex-wife and her daughter.

Later, when I return to the AIDS ward after clinic, I watch a tall, thin dark-haired man holding a giant, shrink-wrapped pink bear approach the nurses' station. I hear him ask for Clara's room. I signal the head nurse behind his back. She invites him to wait in the visitor's lounge.

"I think he's Clara's ex-husband, don't ask me why," I inform the nurse.

"I think you're right. What should we do?"

"Let me check with Clara."

When I return to the nurses' station, we agree to call security. Clara had gotten a phone call from him. He wanted to see her; his life was turning around; he was so sorry for all the pain he had caused her. "Tell him to go to hell and fuck the devil while he's there," she spit at me.

The whole staff watches from the nurses' station while two guards accompany Eddie Roman and his pink teddy bear to the elevators. He makes no fuss; he offers no resistance; he requires no explanation.

I lay awake all night. What if I tell Louise DeSouza everything I know about Eddie Roman, ex-husband, ex-heroin addict, HIV positive child molester, and ask her if she could still go ahead with Ednitza's reunion with her daughter while he is living in their home?

Legally, I am required to say nothing. I don't have a license to lose, but the physicians I work for do. I would be breaking all kinds of confidentiality restrictions if I tell what I know, and this breach would rein down on doctors I work for and respect for their expertise and dedication. If I didn't tell Louise, could I live with myself knowing that a seven-year-old girl is at home with a man who not only had sex with other little girls, but infected them with a terminal illness?

If I am supposed to feel virtuous following the letter of the law, how come I feel terrible? I haven't told the doctors or anyone else about this, which is unusual in a hospital where you tell your colleagues everything. Being out of the loop is no defense in a confidentiality breach. Should I call Louise in the morning and tell her everything I know, or just hope that everything works out like the final scene in a weekly TV sitcom?

The real question is this: can I live with myself keeping what I know confidential when a seven-year-old girl is in danger?

In my cubicle this morning, I pick up the phone twice without dialing. Then I pick up the phone and dial, but hang up twice before Louise answers. This is hard, but no harder than taking blood from a newborn or a drug injector with collapsed veins or telling a young pregnant woman who has had only one partner and never used drugs in her life that she is HIV-infected and the baby she is happily carrying may also be infected.

I dial Louise's number and don't hang up the phone when she answers on the first ring. I mumble, "Ednitza's daughter…Eddie Roman was…"

Louise is way ahead of me. "I'm fully aware of the situation with Ednitza's boyfriend," she says crisply.

"Thanks," I say and hang up promptly. We know how to play this game and we want to keep the score perfect.

Traveling

> *How long I failed to heed ... the sound*
> *of the earth beneath my feet.*
>
> —Bill Brown

Past the garden heaped with leaves—
maple, oak for a sweet-sour soil—
beneath the apple tree, sere and gray
her withered fruit clinging through the cold

across deer tracks and close-cropped grass
dry zinnia seeds standing for titmouse
chickadee and junco, out to compost pile
with pear peelings, spinach leaves, egg shells

trekking back as light fades and red pillars
rise above the setting sun, into the house
where a quick scratching noise tells me
I've surprised the mouse who no doubt

thought me gone for the evening, where soup
simmers on a stove eye, cornbread brown
from the oven, my footsteps wearing
a forty-year groove from door to stove

from table to sink, a journey whose miles
could stretch coast to coast,
could span the Appalachian Trail,
a trip I had not thought to map.

Cleaning Up After Supper

The scrub brush bristles
and crushes the cussing leftovers. The power
of soap and bubbles celebrates

our trick of swallowing what makes
our bodies tick, of leaving behind what's last
and least—look how it swirls

in a whirl of sticky gray slime
that means "it's time to drain the sink and let
garbage be garbage."

The table that's taught us not
to eat off the floor and its old-timey wood
celebrate my up and down

strokes, and the sensuous
crawl of my seasoned cloth tickles each grain
and groove forced to remove

what we've spilled, the food
the tongue can no longer give meaning to.
And freed from the taste buds'

rough terrain, the hot oven of the
mouth, the blots and spots of spitted barbecue
and slaw—the knives, forks and spoons

get rinsed to a sweet pride, and return
to their glossy once-upon-a-time fairytale
of pure cut, scoop and tine. And you and I?

We celebrate by holding on tight
to this cleansing ritual that rules over the ruthless
force of our human appetite.

The Stigma of the Laundry Line

When I decided to hang our family's laundry outside to dry instead of using the clothes dryer, my husband David was his usual supportive self. "That's great," he replied when I made the announcement. He grinned at me, eyes twinkling, as though the laundry line was my gift to him.

Our next trip to town, we stopped at the local Dollar Store and purchased a 100-foot line and a bag of clothespins. Together we strung the line between high cedar posts on the hill behind our house, and with the slightest smile I hauled the first basket of damp clothes outside. David watched while I pinned pants by their hems and button-down shirts by their tails.

My motives for hanging laundry were to save us money and help preserve the planet. But as I stood there in the sunshine with my basket and clothespins, I realized how good it felt to be outdoors getting some exercise and using my body in a productive way.

For David, a lover of nostalgia, flea markets and junkyards, the laundry line held a different sort of appeal — a direct line to his past growing up in Louisville's Beechmont neighborhood in the late 1960s. As I clipped clothes to the line, he told me it reminded him of the days when neighbors talked across fences while hanging or gathering their clothes. He remembered his mother in a pink-and-green-flowered dress, and, curiously, Mr. Bratcher's underwear, plain and practical, drying on the line the next yard over.

Neither David or I can remember exactly when those T-shaped clothesline poles began to disappear from backyards. Somewhere along the line we were tricked into believing a machine could do a better job. In researching the topic on the Internet, I discovered that there are communities and neighborhoods across the country where citizens are banned from using clotheslines — places such as Lake Braddock in Burke, Virginia, Westminster Homes in Harrisburg, North Carolina, and Estates at Arrowhead in San Antonio, Texas. According to the Project Laundry List site, many residents are fighting for their "Right to Dry."

This atrocity is the result of restrictions imposed by city codes, homeowners associations and landlords. In 2004, a homebuilder in Fort Lauderdale, Florida, fought a resident all the way to City Hall over the issue. Poppy Madden's clothesline was ultimately protected by a Florida law that encourages the use of solar power. The homebuilder who lodged the complaint, Robert Strauss, told *USA Today*: "I objected to walking out of the new home I was building and seeing her underwear. And now she's flying it like a flag."

Strauss, who built two $3 million houses in Madden's formerly middle-class neighborhood, rejected the idea that hanging laundry outside is a form of nostalgia. "We're not living in the '50s," he said. "We're not driving Edsels. We have air conditioning in our homes now and clothes dryers."

No feelings of shame or disgust linger in my husband's memory of Mr. Bratcher's underwear hanging in a backyard on South 1st Street. The laundry line was the norm in the 1960s. Only 45 percent of U.S. households owned clothes dryers in 1970, according to the Bureau of Labor Statistics. Common sense outweighed embarrassment. There was no stigma in drying laundry on the line.

I hadn't even considered that possibility when we put up the clothesline. Our home is surrounded by oaks, pines and heavy thickets. Later that spring, after planting the garden, we moved the line out front, down the hill. It's visible from the road when clothes hang there, strung between trees.

As I carry my basket of laundry down the hill, I think of the clothesline as a way of inviting conversation from my scattered neighbors. With the slightest smile, I clip David's underwear to the line and wait for a breeze.

Housekeeping Tips

I leave the bed unmade,
the dishes dirty, stacked staggeringly high.
My open book, food-stained and left out on the table,
may catch Death's eye,
distract him from his dreadful chore.

Maybe the mildew, maybe the dust
will be too much.
Maybe he'll wheeze, and grope for the door.

The skate on the stair
is there
for a reason—
and the lone piece of lint
on my dark blue sleeve.

Keepers

Two centuries of old-growth hardwood are clear cut, brush and scrub dozed over the mountainside. Coal seam exposed and extracted. Money banked. Slurry stored behind dammed earthen walls, a patient poison leaching into groundwater, quietly troubling the offspring of the very ones who mined it until, finally, the fissure hemorrhages sending a toxic flow into valley, stream, church, school, store. Grown women and men cleave to their children as their last breath is sucked from their bodies. A fish lies flat on wounded soil, a single glassy eye turned skyward, unable to meet the gaze of vultures circling, circling around the ozone's jagged tear. Temperatures rising. Ice caps melting. A planet giving up the ghost.

Doral could not have nightmared such a thing, yet his own daughter brought this knowledge home from school with her. Brainwashed, evidently, by her new science teacher, Mr. Stanley, a treehugging atheist do-gooder who left the laboratories of Dow Chemical to prey on the minds of unsuspecting high school seniors. Or so it seemed to Doral, who was still trying to process how this man could take his entire class to the state capital to march in opposition to mountain top removal.

"How you aim to get to Frankfort?" Doral asked. "You ain't got no car, and no idea how to get there besides."

Missy chewed the corner of her lip and counted back from ten to one, not quite surprised by her father's simplicity, but somehow embarrassed by it just the same. "We'll take the bus, Daddy, just like any other field trip. All you've got to do is sign the paper saying I can go."

Missy had been talking these notions ever since school started back in August. Coal is bad. Electric cars are good. Green this and that. Save the whales. She was a girl on a mission. Had them recycling aluminum cans. Still, Doral had no intention of signing any paper. Nor did he anticipate any other response from the men he worked alongside in Slate Branch Mine #4. He just hoped there was some way he could talk good sense back into his daughter.

"That coal is ours, Missy. God give it for our use, just like he give us everything else. To subdue it. Have dominion over it. Lord, don't they teach you all nothing at church no more?"

"Mr. Stanley said Adam and Eve were the first stewards of the environment. Said God made them to be keepers of the garden. He read it from Genesis. Read it straight out of the Bible."

"I don't pay my tax dollar so some school teacher can read you the Bible," Doral said.

"Mr. Stanley used to be a lay minister," said Missy.

"A what?" Doral asked.

"That means he was a member of the clergy, but he wasn't ordained."

"You're talking gibberish. Is he a preacher or ain't he?"

"Well, he wasn't a preacher like Brother Roy, if that's what you mean. But he used to be a lay minister. Back when he worked for Dow Chemical."

"Well," said Doral. "Sounds like Mr. Stanley used to be a little bit of everything."

"Hey, you two!" Sheila called from the kitchen. "I've got green beans and tomatoes and a casserole. And there will be no debate. Take a thirty minute recess, then you all can pick up where you left off after supper. Now go wash yourselves."

Sheila piled plates high with vegetables fresh picked from the garden, corn bread baked in cast iron, pickled beets canned the previous summer. A pitcher of ice tea formed beads of condensation against the September heat. Heads bowed as Sheila whispered grace over the meal. The box fan sliced through a patch of sunlight and the family ate in silence. Missy finally spoke.

"I wish you could see an aerial photograph of an MTR site, Daddy. Mr. Stanley pulled up pictures on the internet and showed the whole class using a projector."

Doral had never seen any aerial photographs. He'd never even seen the internet.

"Missy," Sheila said.

"He showed pictures from Tennessee and West Virginia, as well as Kentucky. Daddy, the images were so powerful. It looked like the surface of the moon. There's even a website that shows how the whole power grid is connected to MTR. It's nationwide, Daddy. All you have to do is type in a zip code. We could go to the public library and I could show you on their computer."

"Missy, please," Sheila said.

"It's okay," said Doral. "I reckon I could go to the library."

Missy smiled, relieved to hear some trace of affirmation in her father's words. "Mr. Stanley said mountaintop removal is the rape of Appalachia," she said.

"Have mercy, mind your tongue." Doral said, his fork paused halfway between plate and mouth. "We're setting at the dinner table."

Missy and her mother sat alone, the storm door creaking as Doral stepped onto the front porch. Together they rose, mother and daughter moving bowls to ice box, plates to sink, scraps for the compost scraped into an old butter tub. Sheila washed and Missy dried.

"You're a smart girl, Missy," Sheila said.

Missy opened her mouth to speak, but her mother continued.

"Your Daddy's a smart man, too. You think he's not, but he just never had a chance. You've got to give him some time."

Missy said, "I just want him to listen, Mama."

"He listens," Sheila said.

Missy walked to her bedroom and unpacked her book bag. There was her literature textbook and her graphing calculator and her lab journal. And the permission slip.

"I think I know what I want to do now, Daddy. After high school." Missy had followed her father outside. Smoke vapored his face as he sat on the porch swing and rocked, stacks of mountains rising blue-grey across the road.

Doral squinted through the last sliver of evening sun, took a long draw off his menthol. "I thought you was going to the vo-tech."

"I'm going to Berea. I'm going to study chemistry." Missy offered this as a decision made, hoping her father would abide her words' resolve.

"Ain't no college money. You know that." Doral mashed the cigarette against the sole of his shoe, let the butt fall in a coffee can.

"All the students have jobs at Berea College." Missy sat down beside her father. She contemplated taking his hand, then thought better of it. "They don't even have to pay tuition. And Mr. Stanley thinks he can help me get a scholarship."

"May not be any college." Doral stood and cracked his backbone, stepped out into the front yard. "Obviously, this man is filling your head with thoughts."

Later, while she worked on homework in her room, Doral tapped on his daughter's door. "They's two sides, you know."

"What do you mean?" Missy asked.

"Two sides to an argument," Doral said. "Coal ain't near the devil your Mr. Stanley makes it out to be."

"Could be there's more than two sides," said Missy. "You mine underground. MTR is something else entirely."

"Well, I know it has its benefits," Doral said. "Mountaintop removal is safer. Cheaper. That's documented fact. And flat land's a premium in these parts. Why, they built a prison on reclaimed land over in West Virginia. Mountaintop removal creates prime real estate. Stimulates the economy. It's good for hospitals and shopping malls. Golf courses."

"Have you ever played golf, Daddy?"

"That ain't the point, Missy, and you know it!" Doral stepped toward his daughter and Missy rose to meet him in the middle of the room. "That mine is my job! Coal keeps food on our table. It's how I put them clothes on your back. You can't go messing with that. You can't go against a man's livelihood."

"I reckon there's lots of ways to earn a living. I know plenty of folks around here raise dope. Cook meth." Missy made her eyes into slits. Balled up her fists and jutted out her bony chin. "You want me to grow up to be a truck stop whore?"

"Is that a threat?" Doral spat the words, not knowing he'd raised his hand against her until he felt it fall back to his side, his neck blushing with anger and shame. He had never once struck that child, nor had he heard that tone of disrespect in her voice. Once more he reached for Missy, palms upturned, hoping she could see the sorry in his eyes.

Missy stood motionless, her body sprouted from twin saplings rooted in the hardwood floor, her eyes never leaving his. She shook her head. "Roger said you'd not hear it."

"Who's Roger?" Doral asked.

"Mr. Stanley. His name is Roger," she said, finally looking away. "The profit of a thing don't make it right, Daddy. That's all I'm saying."

Doral did not speak as he watched his daughter walk away. He picked up the permission form lying on the corner of her desk, then he shut the lights and left her room.

Missy came near again as her father watched the late news. She sat on the sofa opposite his chair and waited. Neither moved until commercial.

"You here to give an apology or to get one?" Doral asked. The lamp light made shadows across Missy's face, and he could see she'd been crying.

"I'm sorry, Daddy. Did you mean what you said?" Missy asked.

"I guess some parts I meant and some I didn't. Which part you speaking of?"

"About college," she said. "If it's the money, I can make my own way. I know I can."

Doral said, "We'll see."

"I just wish you'd listen to me, Daddy." Missy sunk back into the upholstery, closed her eyes. "I just wish you would open up your mind."

"Yeah, well," Doral said, turning his attention to the television set. "Wishing ain't getting."

Sheila set her book on the night stand when Doral came to bed. Flipped the lamp switch and reached for him in the dark.

"How long you all aim to fight?" she said.

"I didn't know we was fighting."

"Lord, honey, you were fixing to kill one another." Sheila pressed into him, felt the tense in his body. "How can you not see that?"

Doral stared up at the ceiling's black. "I don't know that it's as bad as you make out."

"Well, it is for Missy," Sheila said. "Maybe for you, too. She just wants you to listen."

"I listen," said Doral.

And then he slept a fitful slumber, transported back to the days of his childhood. Clear streams, squirrel and rabbit, grapevine swings. Bare feet running through pasture fields. Vegetable garden, smokehouse, chicken, hog. Frame house surrounded by high hills and mountains. A homeplace nestled among hemlock and laurel, razed by company dozers as his family looked on. The sound of progress ringing in their ears.

Dangerous Safety Tips

Steel toe boots are useless. If anything truly heavy were to fall on my feet, like a skid of roofing shingles, the metal half moon would just pivot backwards, severing my toes. We should have full metal plate, like plate mail, from toe to tongue. Until then, these sneakers will do. With my utility knife, I cut loose a bunk of treated 4x4 posts. Their wet arsenic edges thump off my shoelaces, down the round toe. My feet become extra hands, push plywood back into stacks, shove-kick heavy forklift forks apart for floppy drywall.

I can drive a forklift in my sleep. Saturday morning, my head starts to tilt down while the motor hums beneath my seat. I dream of lumber trucks lining up like ducks in a county fair game, I'm here to prove my three dimensional skill. The squeaking wheels and the forklift's boom whirs under my control. A neurotic manager disturbs my nap, so I stagger off onto a futon in the furniture department. Later jokes follow about forklifts as a major cause of drowsiness, but then again who hasn't sat on power and yawned?

Calfskin gloves make everything annoying. They keep me from feeling splinters and cinderblock corners. One afternoon, I slice a palm from thumb to pinky on a metal stud with paper cut precision, creating my own crimson glove above a sticky pool. Beautiful work.

Safety goggles block my eyes. I squeeze shut my left eye to look down the spinning saw blade, just above the board's pencil mark. Saw dust doesn't worry me and staples are so rare to cut through, their hot shrapnel flies off anyway.

There is too much gauze to shove into a first aid kit. I skip seatbelts and avoid back bracing it all. What is safe? Why do we try so hard to avoid the real and dangerous? I live for scars and bruises, each one a progression of evidence.

Sawdust

My father's hands are bleeding.
If I ask what tore the skin,
he won't remember: wood tears,
block crushes. Pain's a given.
He can ignore it or numb it, loosen
its yoke with weed or whiskey,
but tomorrow he'll begin again,
hands already bleeding.

In the darkness of the body,
cancer eats a man's bones.
Centered in his spine, it radiates,
spreading, a hurt that deepens
for years before breaking:
a day off for the doctor, no pay,
no insurance. Two months
and he's dead at fifty, my father's friend.
A day off for the funeral is a given.

My father's broad hands are bleeding
sawdust. At his feet it builds thin
pyramids like salt measured in
a woman's hand. Pain is constant,
whirring like a saw blade's spin,
like the blade that struck a knot's ring
and drove its hundred teeth through
flesh and tendons before bone held.

I am asking for someone to explain.
What of the hurt that's been growing,
grinding a man's bones like sheetrock?
I am asking: what tears the skin?
Tell me. My father's hands are bleeding.

Sure to Be a Fire (Paradise Revisited)

If you stop at the Citgo just off the interstate
You can pick up a pack of those Kentucky's Best
Give me the finest of burley tobacco
And you can take back the rest

Go left at the bottom, just past the Pentecost
Singin' that old-time refrain
You can follow the billows of smoke from the chimney
A hundred years back at the end of the lane

(Singin') *Where there's smoke, there's sure to be a fire...*

I was raised with tobacco in old Trimble County
It was down by the Little Kentucky we'd play
The work it was hard then, but we weren't scared of working
And we knew who we were at the end of the day

And life's contradictions and old-time religions
Were just lessons I learned as a child
Where they'd shame you for smoking
In the sermons on Sunday
In a church that was raised
On tobacco's own tithe

(Singin') *Where there's smoke, there's sure to be fire...*

Well my grandfather lived through the Hoover Depression
Said he hoped he'd live to see change
But come Reagan's new morning, 1984
He knew he'd seen the last of his days

They said times were changin' and I tried to change with them
I took their advice, and I near lost my land
And I've seen my share now of snake oil and hucksters
No mud on their boots, just blood on their hands...

There's sure to be a fire...

So go left at the bottom, just past the Pentecost
Singin' that old-time refrain:
(Singin') *Won't you take me to old Trimble County*
By the Little Kentucky where paradise lay?

Oh won't you take me to old Trimble County
By the Little Kentucky where paradise lay...

A Minor Prophet

Sometimes I took my lunch break right there in the cab
of my dozer with winter breathing hard, seeping
in the cracks around the door. I ate my baloney
sandwich and looked out over the valley: gray
mountain
after gray mountain
like piles of old weathered bones and all them
little houses
with coal smoke pumping out of their chimneys.
I envied the people huddled close to their stoves
while I was up here working on this old dam.
When the workday was over I trudged
across the frozen ground satisfied
I had done a good day's work and had a paycheck
on the way. And I drove to my own little house
just down Buffalo and sat by the stove alone.
Every single person I ever cared about
dead and gone, not a soul in this world to cap
their hand over the top of my head. The evening
before the dam broke we started hearing talk
that it was leaking. The company had done turned
me away by then (we can't have no big grown man
a-cryin
in the cab of his dozer now Amos) and me stumbling
through the world like a ghost. My neighborman,
Mathias, he hollered across the yard and said
They sayin the dam's pourin a leak couldn't you
fellers build it no better than that buddy? and laughed
but I didn't think it was nary bit funny.
Next morning when I heard the water's roar I stayed
right there in my bed and let the torrent wash
me away. I stretched out my arms and said Lord God
what have we done?

Highway 38: Jericol Revisited

In the spring of 1977 I was one of a dozen or so women who played folk music and came together for a performance at the International Women's Year Conference at the University of Kentucky. Out of that mixture of women the Reel World String Band emerged. At that time Reel World was one of only a handful of women's string bands in the nation and the only band actually from an Appalachian state. We were also one of the few bands whose music was focused on social justice issues.

After connecting with Guy and Candie Carawan and the Highlander Center, we were firmly planted as cultural workers whose lives would be dedicated to planting the seeds of human rights through our art. By 1978 we had enlisted in the ranks of those supporting the miners in the Jericol and Stearns strikes in Eastern Kentucky. So when the call came out to join the picket line in Jericol, I knew nothing would stop me.

I was filled with a profound sense of purpose as I began that day in 1978. It would be my first time on a picket line, not counting the times of picking my dad up when he had "union duty." I was aware of the real danger that faced us. Kentucky picket lines were notoriously bloody.

The four of us, Karen, Sharon, Pam and myself, made the journey from Lexington to Jericol in our big blue Dodge van. We'd named her Beulah Van after the old gospel song, "Dwelling in Beulah Land." In our early years we spent days at a time tucked away in her comfortably furnished blue womb.

We'd decided to go by Lois Short's in Evarts to play a little music before we headed on over to the meeting planned at Highsplint that evening. Lois was a banjo player, ballad singer, buck dancer and a wonderful storyteller. She was also among the many musicians who, at their husband's bidding, put their banjos, guitars, and fiddles in the closet, most never knowing music's sweet release again. But the power of music ran strong in Lois. Soon after her husband died, she reclaimed her instruments, her tunes and her ballads; she flatfooted and square danced from Tennessee to Ohio, once dancing with her leg in a cast from a broken ankle. Most of all Lois regained her spirit.

Playing with Lois that afternoon helped us gather resolve for the work to be done in the next 24 hours. We sang union songs, old and new, and Lois shared songs sung by generations before her, giving us precious family heirlooms with each tune she played and each tale she told. Like many of our activist musician elders Lois passed too quickly through our lives. She shared more than music and stories with us that treasured afternoon. She passed on to us an understanding of values and justice rooted in the heart of the mountains and the fortitude and persistence to pursue them.

The day was moving on towards evening and folks were gathering for the potluck meal and meeting to plan the coming morning's action. Dusk was settling heavy with fog and foreboding. Coal dust and snow mingled in the mist and piled up on the sides of the road that wrapped around cliffs like a black snake. Coal towns are often built along roads that run between rock and waterways with homes crawling up the mountainsides.

We gathered at the Highsplint home of one of the local UMWA leaders. We were meeting with Mary Lou, a schoolteacher and nurse who wrote several powerful songs about working peoples' struggles in Eastern Kentucky. Mary Lou had joined us for our first Highlander experience and we had all been deeply inspired to do what we could for social justice. We were also being joined by Linda and Liz from over in Southwest Virginia. They ran Grace House of the Mountains, an Episcopal retreat center that was always on the frontline of the social justice movement.

The dismal cold seemed to seep inside the small clapboard home despite the blazing fire in the large double barrel wood stove. The house filled to overflowing with angry, desperate miners, their wives and those of us who had chosen to stand with them. The conversations slid rapidly from light-hearted camaraderie to deadly serious discussions. Word was out that snipers would be waiting in the woods above the picket line site and that the state troopers would be more than willing to get rough. Some of the miners were pulling out ball bats and clubs, and some were speaking of more lethal weapons.

By the time the actual meeting began it was clear that though many of us had expected and preferred to participate in non-violent civil disobedience, there were those among us who were way past peaceful. Added to this mix was a group of folks from the North Carolina Communist Workers Party who were actually hoping for and encouraging violent resistance.

I found myself in a conversation with a small group of miners and the man who appeared to be the leader of the North Carolina group. He seemed to be the kind of small man who felt he had to make up for his small stature with machismo and bravado, though at first I was drawn to him because he looked like an old hippie. The more he talked and tried to tell the miners how to run the strike, the more frightening he became.

He asked the miners how they planned to respond to being arrested. "If you go peacefully the coal company wins. We have to resist however we can. They won't hesitate to use physical force against us and we must be prepared to use it against them."

My front teeth went numb as I tried to grasp the situation we were in. I was a sixties hippie flower child, a pacifist, I was standing up for a cause I knew was right, but I was suddenly casting my fate with radical crazies who were hoping someone would be killed. It didn't matter much to them who died or got hurt as long as it resulted in headlines. I was terrified, bewildered and disappointed. People, including my dearest of friends, might die the next day.

During that time in my life I was in a deadly battle with depression. Fantasies of death and injury had become a familiar and oddly comfortable retreat. I could quite courageously be a willing martyr, but I was completely blindsided by the possibility of losing any of the friends who had gathered there. A kind of terror screamed through my soul that I had never known before, nor have I experienced it since.

I was shivering from cold and fear and sat on the floor as close to the stove as I could get while the plans were explained to us. We were going to block Highway 38 that led to the Jericol Mine with burning tires and our bodies. We'd meet in Evarts, leaving most of our vehicles and ride together. We'd arrive at the site just before dawn. If there was trouble the miners would leave. A federal injunction would get them arrested and cost the union heavy fines if they were caught too close to the entrance of the mine. The words to Mary Lou's song, *Hey You Scabs,* describe the mindset of all the women present that day.

Hey you scabs in your armored trucks
Are you having a comfortable ride?
If you think you can slip through us women out here
You better wake up and have another look outside
Cause we're women out here on the picket line
And we don't intend to go away
Until you scabs dry up and Sigmund agrees
That the Union is here to stay

The goal of this action was to prevent scabs (replacement workers) from getting to the mine. It was expected that they would arrive in an armored bus, a school bus that had been converted to a strike-busting behemoth. Transporting scabs in the cover of a school bus was a source of great rage and fear for the safety of all the county's children. Strikes most always turn neighbor against neighbor and split families asunder. Deciding to stand with the union or crossing the picket line can look very different if your children are hungry. A few weeks after the blockade, a scab miner was shot and killed while riding the bus to the mine.

The meeting ended and the six of us walked over the hill to the home where we were sleeping that night. We stayed up late trying to assess the situation. The North Carolina crew was notorious for orchestrating violent incidents, including the infamous Greensboro massacre, so this was serious. We ultimately decided to go through with our plans to stand on the line, but also do what we could to keep the North Carolinians from taking control.

We were all sleeping in one room, some on couches, some on beds and some of us on the floor. Sleep was no match for worry and I wrestled the rest of the night with the notion that this was really a selfish, dangerous web I'd wrapped my friends in.

I had admired Sarah Ogan Gunning from the moment I saw her calm a riot on the Mall at the 1972 Smithsonian Folklife Festival by singing, unaccompanied, her song, "I Hate the Capitalist System." Less than six years later I met her at a Highlander Gathering. Sarah had been blacklisted and exiled from Kentucky for being a union organizer and a communist sympathizer during the "Bloody Harlan" strikes of the 1930s. As she slowly rocked in the circle of rocking chairs at Highlander, with a mischievous grin on her face and a deep anger in her eyes she said, "I don't know much about communism, but I know the capitalist system starved my two darling babies to death." Sarah had braved the picket lines with bullets flying while she sang of the injustices in the coalfields. So, was this my turn? I suddenly realized the full measure of Sarah's courage and sacrifice.

We were up and headed to the mine way before dawn, and the short drive to the site was agonizing. I was bartering with my unrecognized higher power. If one of us was fated to be hurt or killed it had to be me. I couldn't have it otherwise, though I knew that in truth I had no control over the events that would unfold.

The tires across the highway were already burning when we arrived. The smell of the burning tires reminded me of my father. He almost always smelled like cooked rubber, especially when he worked near the giant vats where Goodyear melted and blended rubber for the monster earthmoving tires often used on strip-mining equipment. Dad was a Union Steward for a while, and I thought about how proud he would be to see me following in his footsteps.

Soot fell like ominous black snowflakes dusting our winter jackets and hats. A river ran behind us and the mountain loomed above us, hidden behind rhododendron thickets and skeleton trees. Whose eyes were watching from up there, the ones whose hands are on the trigger . . . would they really shoot us?

I was shivering from the cold, shoulders raised to my ears to calm the quiver. My feet were turning from burning cold to numb and heavy. Sharon was, as usual taking photos of the event, which I worried, would make her a likely target for the snipers.

We were standing in a row behind the tires singing and chanting while we waited for the bus to come. Suddenly a jeep appeared, slowed for a moment, and then headed toward us gaining speed as it drew closer. We all scattered to the side of the road; it didn't seem strategically savvy to die at that moment. When we looked back, Mary Lou was still standing there, and it seemed as though she was not going to listen to our pleading screams to get out of the way. But at the last moment she was standing safely beside us.

The jeep continued to pick up speed as it neared the wall of flames we had created. I was braced for the jeep to explode as it collided with the tires. The moment tires connected with flame, the man standing next to me pulled a pistol from his coat pocket and emptied it into the vehicle as it flew on by us, windows exploding into a million glittery pieces. The jeep passed by and successfully made its way to the mine.

As all this was happening, a woman hollered, "Oh, Lord, they're shootin at us." All the reporters ducked to the ground. The newspaper reports suggested that shots were fired from both sides. I'm pretty sure the woman who yelled knew exactly what she was doing.

As planned, the miners disappeared, but they took all the vehicles with them. There we were, miner's wives, families and friends, a handful of radical communists and a gaggle of lesbians waiting for the "law" to arrive and do whatever they wanted to us. When the state troopers did arrive we refused to respond to any of their questions.

When asked for my name I started singing, "Oh, you can't scare me, I'm sticking to the union," my knees and voice trembling until the rest of the picket line joined in. We sang every verse we knew until the officer moved on.

Then the North Carolina agitators chanted, "Hey pig, you'd better start shakin', Today's pig's tomorrow's bacon." At the very first hint of a pause from the troublemakers I interrupted with "We Shall Not Be Moved" which is forceful, but less directly threatening. Finally, the troopers just left. So there was nothing else to do but walk the three miles back to town. Once we reached Highsplint and arranged for a ride back to Beulah Van, I let rigid resolve relax enough to realize I was frozen to the bone and shaken to the core.

I feared and hated violence and yet I had just taken part in it, however tangentially. I was worried that we'd all be charged with assault or murder if someone in the Jeep had been killed. It was my first real experience with desperation's demons driving gentle souls to violent deeds. The strike had gone on so long miners were struggling to shelter and feed their families. Poverty pushes even the most saintly to resort to previously unthinkable behavior.

Too disillusioned and depleted to talk much, the ride back to Lexington was a long quiet one. Beulah didn't have a radio, so only the drone of rubber on road accompanied my wrestling thoughts. Every now and again I would try to talk, but like a radiator about to blow, it seemed wisest to let only small amounts of steam seep out gradually.

The strike continued on into the spring and we were invited to play for a big UMWA rally in a school gym in Harlan County. When we arrived everyone was gathering to hear what the union representative had to say about the progress of the strike. We were all stunned when he announced that they were dropping the strike because it was "impossible to win and costing the union too much money." I didn't know unions could just decide not to support their members.

We joined the miners as everyone walked out. We spontaneously pulled out our instruments and played for the betrayed. We called square dances until they wore their rage down to a slow simmer. That was it. It was over and all the sacrifice and suffering they'd endured accomplished nothing. No wonder it's been so difficult to unionize Eastern Kentucky; the union has historically dished out its own share of injustice from time to time.

Through the years Reel World has played on several picket lines and protest marches and we've helped get people fired up at dozens of rallies, but none has ever left its mark on me like Jericol. I lost a bit of innocence there along with a romanticized version of social justice work in the coalfields. I got my first full dose of cynicism from watching both the Jericol Mining Company and the United Mine Workers exploit and betray the miners. It's somewhat like receiving a vaccination against a broken spirit.

It was for me, the beginning of a relationship with Appalachian people and culture that has truly sculpted the activist musician I've become. The sense of purpose that took me to Jericol was not diminished by the discouragement I met there; instead it grew and became my life's work. And like growing older with a dear friend, my bond with Appalachia has grown stronger for accepting it as being nearly as flawed as I am. Jericol demonstrated Appalachian's spirit and tenacity, and I am proud to have stood beside them on Highway 38.

Jay McCoy

paper quilts

Shoo Fly, Churn
Dash, Broken Dishes,
Monkey Wrench, Goose
Tracks, Job's Tears

Thanksgiving two years past,
Aunt Madge sat quietly at the end
of the dinner table folding dark brown
paper napkins printed with autumn
leaves, cornucopia, and child-like
pilgrims. She collected them
from gathered family members; her eyes
politely asked for more. She aligned
them in stacks of four, ever mindful
of the holiday wishes printed
on stark selvage to keep an even
cut, maintain square corners.

Drunkard's Trail, Dove
in the Window, Lover's
Quarrel, Old Maid's
Ramble, Contrary Wife

Sharpening creases between thumb
and forefinger, she found the bias
more forgiving in tissue than in familiar
linsey tops and muslin backings.
She smoothed seams with her crooked
pinky finger – reminiscent
of the grandmother who taught her
ancient Appalachian origami, and forever evident
in the hands of her sisters, daughter, nieces,
and grand-daughter to whom she passed on
her craft. Seamstress of more forgotten
than remembered Star pattern blocks –

Saw-toothed, Blazing, Cowboy,
Unfolding, Sojourner Truth, Susan B.
Anthony, Harvest, and Eastern –

she combined variations of *Feathered* and *Melungeon*
into that cherished counterpane made for my twelfth
birthday I still layer on cold winter nights
over Mother's crazy quilt of calico, plaid, paisley
patchwork, with yarn tacking and whip-stitched
edges.

Cherokee Sunburst, Eye
of God, Hearts and
Gizzards, Moon over
Mountains, Prayer Wheel

My mother reacts to demands for fabric and notions the next day, or another reason I don't have a job

Then there was the day I came home
from 8th grade sewing
class, required, despite already knowing
how to sew well enough to make my own
dress for a school concert two years earlier. (Imagine
sending every girl to her mother with pattern number and fabric
    specs, assuming
they'd return on the appropriate evening
with a floor-length, empire-waisted cotton gown

complete with ribbons.) So that although
I desperately wanted to learn woodworking that semester—
what the boys did—the shop teacher told me point-blank
that he wasn't having any females messing around dangerous
    machinery
in his class, so I would have to take Beginning Sewing. And that's
    why my mother
just exploded at "Items to Make a Purse," home at last from a
    long, late day at work.

Last Words

words and hugs
were not my daddy's tools
life was about work
hands were made to think

he communicated like his father
silently erecting monuments of
    pauses
even his gestures had commas

in his private workshop
behind a wall of resurrected TV sets
and engine parts
collected from the side of the road
he spent his spare time
polishing granddaddy's old saws
chisels and hammers
reconstructing assorted junk and found objects
into miniature antique furniture
and scale models of his dreams

just pidlin', he'd say
deflecting accusations
of creating something beautiful

no one ever called this man
an artist
no book spine whispers his name
yet every time i open my mouth
i can hear him sing

After the Move Back to Wichita
(Fall 1964)

Phoenix had been hell that summer
and for my father, hell on wheels.
How could he not fail: the new guy
from Kansas making cold calls
in the rusty, shit-green Pioneer Steel
station wagon, a.c. chugging out
more hot air. The sun was relentless
as the promise he'd made to us:
It's simple, so simple—there's a fortune
to be made out there! And then, day
after day, the blank order pads he'd lug
in from the car. The litany of nobody
buying, nobody buying . . .

Back in Wichita, the house we'd left
for a realtor to do his best, my father
knelt over a bucket in the driveway.
He lifted the green hose and watched
water trickle into powdered cement.
He stirred the silicate and aluminate
like a man trying to coax fire from cinders.

When he hobbled toward me,
pulled by the weight of the bucket,
I had already set the last stones
into the knee-high wall outlining
our garden plot. Our Best Boys
would luxuriate, green peppers
fatten in the sun . . .

Dad stretched out on his back
in the center of what we'd built.
He was tired of this, tired now
of everything. He folded his hands

over his chest. He barely breathed.
And I was happy to hear Mother clang

the cowbell for dinner, even though
we'd eat again in silence, the silence
saying that surely the man
who'd brought us this far and back
can find something as simple as a job.

Philological Downsizing

On a late summer weekday we convened poolside in a western suburb at the home of our esteemed benefactress, wearing modest cotton blends and economical Celanese Fortrels, nibbling on crudités, and sipping Café Macchiato and Ristretto to occupy our hands while the graying proprietor addressed us with his fly open. In a hostile takeover of time's business, he revised history while pleading poorhouse and unmitigated gall, while crying au courant exodus and hip dysphasia. Taking seriously our vocations as cultural arbiters, we succumbed to a litany of prevarications, a confectioner's assortment of hatreds, and the Darwinesque appreciation of the benefaction that we are not our ancestors. Most of all, we enjoyed the allegiance of ourselves, the companionship of clutch, herd, drove, with concomitant opportunities for ostracizing the odd fish, the ugly duckling, and the queer bird, and the luxuriant abhorrence of what is not we. So as not to be the one in the cocked hat, we listened in feigned accession while the proprietor concocted his syllogism proving downsizing as a bivalve mollusk isolates a foreign irritant with nacre. With an officious wave of her Hermes scarf, our hostess adjourned us to the indoor bowling lanes of her manse on the lake, where we pondered our resolve in the feverish manner of a raccoon washing his face and mask. Our putamens engorged, our premotor cortexes inflamed, we wondered if the desire to alleviate the pain we felt due to something outside the body was fueled by our Cartesian revulsion at that which might harm us, our nose hairs twitching at the whiff of a decadent pheromone. The crack and echo of pins falling around us, glare off the carnauba wax, sugary strains of a popular melody in our ears, we turned inward to the hope that every impulse has its opposite, every synonym its antonym, every marine his queen. Despite outward appearances, we ache for something to love, we search for something good. We reach for the spine on the shelf, a glimmer of hope that we are the ones first to find truth, so eager to spill our weighty praise and leave the group. What we want most of all is a cynosure, a map of our solar plexus, our nervous system writ large.

Piled Unemployment

Those welding goggles by the door
don't ride to work much anymore,
the white fence slats fall like soldiers
the drainage ditch kid looks around
for his absent father so much someone
may hand him an old trench periscope,
the businesses retool their rhetoric
getting greener, globalized, or gone,
the chop shop is face-masking grey
muscle cars for post-robbery resale—
everybody's intestines are dripping
from this tough bite neighborhood.

Unbeloved Community: An Imaginary Address to the People of Madisonville, Ohio, at the Conclusion of Their Bicentennial Year

I was standing between the Fiction and Poetry sections at Half Price Books last year near Christmas when a slender black man approached me and began to speak. I recognized the face and the voice, and when he told me who he was I immediately placed him, though we hadn't talked to one another for 28 years. Michael Wright graduated in 1980 from the high school I have taught in for going on forty years. We exchanged pleasantries and at last I asked him, "Where are you living these days, Mike?"

"Same place," he said, "on Whetsel, near Chandler."

That "same place"—where he lived when he was a student at Purcell High School—shook me. I didn't show it and the conversation moved on, but that "same place —chilling. It meant I have dwelled in the same village as he has for more than a quarter of a century. It is nine blocks from his house to mine, some of them very short ones of only five or six houses. And yet we had not run into one another until then—and our meeting was not in Madisonville, but in a suburban strip mall a mile away.

Madisonville is a neighborhood—formerly its own village, founded in 1809—of around 13,000 people, which makes it about one-third the size my hometown of Steubenville, Ohio was when I grew up there. I have lived here now many years longer than I lived in Steubenville; Madisonville is a place I should know even better than that first piece of the world I was given to study. I have walked, I believe, every block of Madisonville's streets, as well as its creekside trails and woods, its alleys, railroad right-of-ways, its cut-throughs and dead-ends, even its cemetery paths. To literally circumambulate the place takes less than a morning.

And yet, I had not seen Mike Wright for 28 years. I have shopped in Madisonville's groceries and Dollar Stores; I have patronized its post office and library; I have occasionally been a member of one of its parishes and of its Community Council. I have built two modest but conspicuous community gardens in its environs. I have raised two boys on its playing fields and streets. I continue to conduct a deliberate and long-lasting marriage here. I have thrown large parties to which dozens of residents have come, have been a destination for the Gardens and Historic Homes tours several times, and have held living room chats to which dozens of others have come. I have lived a public, front yard, street-level life here. And yet, I have not seen Mike Wright for 28 years.

Wendell Berry writes of what he calls "the beloved community." It is one based on "common experience and common effort on a common ground to which one willingly belongs." The complications, distortions, failures, and barriers that have kept Mike Wright and I from coming face to face in twenty-eight years of living in Madisonville, that have kept us from realizing common experience and devoting common effort and recognizing the common ground in our community, are what my most earnest occupations here have failed to repair. From my perspective, Madisonville, I am sorry to say, is broken badly: it is the opposite of a "beloved community." And further, as a resident here, though connected physically to it for thirty years now, I too am nevertheless broken, far from whole.

One very early morning, around two or so, soon after we moved here, I leaped from bed to answer a phone call. The voice on the other end said, "They's a bomb in your house. They's a bomb in your house. Be repaired!" I was so shocked that I fell into a kind of self-defensive chuckle. We had begun major restoration work and the place was already a mess. "O Lordy, I hope I will be repaired," I said agreeably into the phone. "I most certainly do," and hung up.

This was my first direct evidence that all was not well in our newly chosen neighborhood. Only a few weeks after that I was walking across the street from my house, when a black woman, a total stranger to me and, I presume, I to her, stopped in front of me, blocking the sidewalk, and said with a sneer, "We don't need your kind around here." She didn't seem at all open to conversation, tromping off without so much as a kindly how-de-do that might have diluted her bitterness, so I still am not sure "what kind" she might have thought I was, though the white kind seemed to be most obvious. There followed over the next months several minor rip-offs—a lawn mower, hand tools, a wicker chair from our front porch, given to us a housewarming present, and taken back, I guess, as a house-cooling warning like the other petty thefts.

I didn't let it bother me much; I couldn't. My wife and I had made a commitment, and not a blind one, and we knew there might be some friction in what was known by all the faculty and students in my school as a tough neighborhood. But I was from Steubenville, by God, where Tough was invented. Didn't Scrap Iron Kuzikowski still live in Steubenville? Didn't he almost eat an entire Cadillac back in high school on a dare? Didn't Bull Pulaski, one of the original Seven Mules who blocked for the Four Horsemen of the Apocalypse at Notre Dame, teach my naked and shivering sorry little self to swim at the Knights of Columbus Community Center right there in the downtown of the Ville? Didn't some of the meanest sumbitches ever to fight in the middle of the street, any street, at any time of day or night, still own Steubenville? Mad-Ville, as it was called by dopey inner-city crack-heads and beltless, self-hobbled gangstas on the street, couldn't be tougher, wouldn't be tougher. I was determined to last it out.

Christmas morning, a few days after running into Mike Wright, I awoke and made coffee and leashed the dog for his morning walk. I crossed over to the lot where I have struggled to keep the trash and junked cars and litter off about an acre of railroad-owned land, and where I have planted a dozen hybrid poplars, an ash tree, several shrubs, and built a raised bed for flowers in the summer from the solid flat blocks discarded by my neighbor when he renovated his house and removed a broken wall from his front yard. Here is what I saw in that place I have cared for: exactly in the middle of the section closest to our house, where the grass in the summer is lush and green after years of mowing and care, a great ragged circle of torn-up ground, the result of someone "doing doughnuts" with their car on the rain-softened turf, had been gouged into the earth. Under the tire ruts, the dirt was compacted; at the edges of each it was clumped up three or four inches, creating a twenty-foot wide circle of broken ground that would be impossible to mow easily, and would probably remain bare and spoiled, wrecking the calm expanse of green for two or three years.

I could still see the two ruts from an earlier drive-over that happened around the beginning of October, in which someone had run their car over the logs and old railroad ties I had set as a barrier at the edge of the parking area used by the music students of my neighbor, Lynne Miller. The tracks led right through the row of lilacs, forsythias, and Rose of Sharons I had planted a year before, crushing two of them, and tearing the branches off a third. It was the same effect one sees at the edge of woods that has been made by the reckless riders of all terrain vehicles (aka woods-wreckers, kid-killers) for fun. To me, such acts are not fun, but the equivalent of face-slashings, or those favorite old-time attacks with vitriol, acid splashed in the face of an unsuspecting victim, or of chain-saw wild attacks, done with as little heed as accompanies a greasy toss-out of fast food trash from a passing car window by some fat-addled cell-phoner—or with the same maliciousness as attends a rapist's work.

If what Wendell Berry writes—that we cannot treat one another any better or differently than we treat the land—if that is true, and I am afraid it is, then what chance for hope and blessed community here in Madisonville?

Right before school began in mid-August, I was talking with Kevin Sansone, my neighbor and fellow gardener on the block. We looked down to the corner the lot is on, where the City had, in an unprecedented and almost immediate answer to my request, installed a trash can just a day before. A white man, around forty, bearded and wearing work clothes, had stopped his pickup, jumped out, and was dragging long sheets of damaged drywall out of the bed, and then snapping them into pieces small enough to jam into the trash can.

Kevin and I looked at one another, and then walked down to speak to him. I said, "Sir, that construction debris is not allowed in trash pick-up. If the City workers see it in there, they'll not empty the can."

"That's just the problem," the man said, looking steadily at me and Kevin. "How the hell am I supposed to get rid of it if the City won't pick it up?"

"But the people who empty that can are the City. You can't put construction debris out for City pick-up."

The man was tall, fit, with a salt-and pepper beard. His truck was a new, over-sized, expensive model, with a ladder rack over the bed and a chromed tool-box against the cab. He looked familiar to me, but I couldn't place him.

"By the way," he said, still snapping the drywall into pieces. "How come you guys aren't at work?"

"What do you mean?" I said, looking at him sharply. It was August, right before school was to start again for me; Kevin was on lunch break from his job as owner of a landscaping business. It was clear that this guy's strategy was to play offense as his defense against our suggesting he was doing something wrong.

"I mean are you guys like the rest of the mooches and retards around here, sucking up welfare and sitting all day on your asses?"

Kevin is a lot more patient than I am with such stuff: I turned away angrily. Kevin spoke with the man for a minute or two, and all the time the man stared him straight in the eye and kept snapping the drywall and stuffing it into the can.

"Sir," I said, when I returned to the conversation, cooled off a bit. "I've been trying to keep this corner, and this whole lot, clean for almost thirty years. What's going to happen is that the City is going to see that construction debris in the can, refuse to empty it, let it overflow, and it'll be me who has to pick all your trash up. So I'd personally appreciate it if you wouldn't put that in there."

He suddenly stiffened. "What shit," he said. "What shit. Don't you know where you are? I've lived in this hole for twenty years, and I can tell you nobody around here cleans up their trash. You know what you should do?

"What?" I said.

"Give it up!" he cried."Give it up!"

Kevin and I stood astonished. The man stuffed the last piece of drywall into the overflowing can, clapped his hands together, got back into his truck, and drove away.

Let us imagine that I try to tell the "story" of this lot and its litterers and despoilers in a way that would be local and effective. By local I mean it would be heard or read by my neighbors—by the family next door to the Millers, an extended one with a bunch of cute kids, several dogs, and a cockatoo or conure that we can hear squawking all summer when the windows are open. By the Millers. By the man in the pickup. By the post person, and the furnance repairman, and the owner of the Palm Court Market, just a few blocks away. When I suggest it might be effective, I mean it would become a spur to new thinking and new acting. We'd all have a clearer notion of the bad that's been done to the place, and what our responsibility to the human population of Madisonville would be, and to the economic structure of the neighborhood, even to the aesthetic concerns over litter and ramshackle properties that come with an investment of care and concern by the citizens of any beloved place.

But I'm trying to imagine even approaching the guy I've dubbed Buffalo Bill—he has a long blond ponytail that reminds me of the 19th century Indian fighter and circus star. The new Buffalo Bill has bought a wreck of a house across the railroad tracks—just across: if the engineer spits when he passes, it hits Buffalo's back door. The first thing he did when he bought the place was to dump a load of used wooden pallets in a pile next to the tracks. They lay there in an increasingly weedy jumble for a month or two, and then one day—voila—there they were, nailed together, teeteringly standing on edge, no posts to support them, enclosing an unmown pie-wedge of litter and trash that I suppose he planned to be a back yard. He had told me when I first saw him there in the heat of the summer that he was going to do two things: "I'm going to get the railroad to stop blowing the crossing here and waking up my kids, and I'm going to make them put a fence up, for protection." When I told him I didn't think it would work, that the railroad was the most absent of absentee landlords, with their headquarters now in Jacksonville, Florida, he scoffed, "Man, I'm a Marine. I'll get her done."

The story of this lot, which is complicated, and interdisciplinary, and chronic—and which requires an investment of spirit and body into its upkeep— will not be heard by Buffalo Bill. He's into "making it," like the hottest hot-shot Americans, gung-ho for pulling himself up by his bootstraps, and oblivious to the fact that "making it" here often means "wrecking" something to do it. And now, as I write this later, I can confirm that he never moved in, never finished the repairs, never cleaned up the pallets, never picked up the rain-sodden disintegrating drywall he dumped in what was to be his backyard, never put down the slightest roots, nor said hello to anyone I know around here. And the railroad still blows the crossing, day and night.

In all fairness, I never learned much of Buffalo Bill's story, so I have little right to look down upon him and his frantic, helter-skelter remuddling time here. But the fact that he did not connect with the neighborhood, and it with him, is an ongoing phenomena; it is part of the rootlessness and distrust and fear and hurry and waste and displacement of American culture that Madisonville has certainly not escaped. Nor, as I have said before, have I. I do not live myself in poverty, but the culture of poverty lives around me; it is an environmental ill that is, in subtle and insistent ways, contagious.

I might have a little more luck telling the story of the lot to the family with the kids down the street, but I don't see them outdoors together much. When I do, they're in a hurry to go somewhere. The younger girl rides her bike for hours up and down the block, but never makes eye contact with me, or stops to chat when she sees me out front, or carrying water over to my chickens. What would she make of any story about the lot I'd try to tell her?

Nor will the story of the lot be heard by the folks all up and down the railroad on both sides for a thousand yards. I've walked the tracks all the way to Oakley, the next village in, and I've seen ruin and ugliness, what looked like an abandoned hobo village—if hobos have girlfriends (I'll spare you the details), a dead beagle, several galleries of graffiti and gang threats spray-painted on the inside of old bridges, and then stopped and turned back behind the steaming, stinking back of a paper mill. In all those thousand yards, there's only one garden by the right-of-way— a feature I saw many of during my riparian boyhood back in Steubenville, haunting the well-cultivated patches of watermelons, squash, and beans along the no-man's land between the Pennsylvania Railroad right-of-way and the Ohio River. Gardens, I have come to believe, especially ones tended by neighborhood folks as partners in a common enterprise, on more-or-less common or public ground, are one way to establish the beloved community. But even gardens cannot guarantee it.

So what's the story that might transform Madisonville? It clearly hasn't yet been imagined and told, though I know there are anecdotes of hopeful collaborations, of well-intentioned planning, of real barrier-crossing and reaching out. There are stories of the decade in which marvels were discovered in the ground here, once the largest and most important archaeological site in North America. I know there must have been interesting and stylish writings and orations delivered, back in the late 1800s, by members of the Madisonville Literary and Philosophical Society. But they are only disconnected stories, spare sketches, far from the sustained and sustaining chapters that a place with Madisonville's history and potential deserves. The story of our place remains a fragmentary one, with gaps where there ought to be bridges, ignorance where there ought to be common knowledge, resentments where there ought to be forgiveness and common cause, blank pages where there ought to be whole histories. It strikes me that if this story doesn't exist yet, someone may have to make it up. I, or you, may have to write it, or sing it, or dance it, or draw it. Maybe by imagining a Madisonville that works, that thrives as a beloved community, something creative and executive will enter the morphogenetic field, and actually make it so.

I propose that in two years I return with what I have written and gathered of that story. In the meantime, imagine what chapters, what anecdotes you might like to add, and come tell them to me, or let me know where you are, and I'll come to you, God willing and the creek don't rise. You know where I live by now, if you have paid attention to this, and tried to visualize the actual locales I've described, if you have really entered, physically, into our community. If you haven't, well then, just walk around on foot until you find me—it'll do you and the neighborhood all kinds of good. Maybe you'll even run into Mike Wright. And if you do, friend, neighbor—tell him what we're up to.

East Avenue Gulf

Richie kissed the starchy pavement,
when the ozone cracked a comma in the sky
and the mole on his neck took root, sending him
to soil he loved so well. Like a lit fuse he gardened
with a fury around the Gulf station he ran like a pit stop.

Now, nothing stirs in the darkened building.
Gas pumps seem beheaded. Graying aluminum hangs
a dirty bib around a garden that is no more.
The only movement, a note flapping on the door
thanking stranded patrons he rescued on the highway.

I gauged my safety by the vigor of his hair, watched
it wane from roan to dun, imagined serrated blocks
of chaos when they'd take the building down.
No more bougainvillea on the trellis, forked tongue
of iris, or bees sucking larkspur. His obituary
hangs on my refrigerator, as if evoking luck
when on the road alone. I touch it in passing.

Clutch

At the transmission shop, I talk with an old man
who tells me about his bad hip, the pipe that blew off
a semi and knocked all of his teeth out, his boy
running a crotch rocket into a van, getting steel rods
screwed into his legs, and riding again. None of this
amazes me as much as him telling me how he
microwaves his cigarettes for ten seconds, to make them
burn better, and how his wife microwaves them
for too long so that the nicotine drips down on the plate.
I'm just there to get a quote on a clutch. But it's cold
and snowy out, a slow day, so he keeps me
every time I motion to leave with another story.
Listen here, bub, he says. In the background I hear
a vicious motorcycle revving. In the background I hear
my own voice in my head, looking out the window
while he talks, thinking, I wonder if he thinks
I'm a chump, I wonder if the sun will come again,
I wonder what we'll have tonight for dinner.
The place is called GoForth Transmission,
which I thought was at least a stab at being clever,
like calling a beauty parlor Curl Up & Dye,
but it turned out that was his last name. He started
this place up after years on the road as a trucker,
and I think how life is strange like that, you begin
as Goforth, and drive and drive, and when you are
finished driving you help others do the same.
It's like this other Cuban fellow I saw in the news
named Jesus who believes he is the second coming.
All these perfect names. I get a little depressed about it
sometimes, too, because I'm not really sure
what a Matthews is supposed to be, I'm not really sure
what I'm supposed to be doing here. His boy
comes back around with my truck. We talk,
and while talking, to avoid looking at each other,
we look at one vehicle in the lot, and then another.

He says, We're not above anybody, take that old Ford
out there, I've had to replace nearly every part
in that thing, We've all got car problems.
And I think about how right he is, how we all
come and pray to the same god of muffler leaks
and blown head gaskets, flat tires and leaking oil,
the best of all perhaps: slipping transmissions,
these frequencies sent out that don't exactly make it
there, but get there in parts and pieces, strewn across
an oily shop floor, while in the background
someone is beginning another story.

Society Report

Young adults from a group home
for the developmentally delayed
and in trouble

come each Friday to an elementary
school in the most violent part
of the city

and fill backpacks for fifty children
whose weekend food security
is at risk:

peanut butter, tuna, boxed mac-
n-cheese, soup, crackers, cereal,
maybe chili.

"It's a perfect fit," their supervisor
says. "Filling the packs they practice
sequential skills

and they count lockers to know
which ones get the backpacks.
It's a win-win

situation."

I Hate My Mouth

I hate my mouth
When it speaks properly
I hate the white edges
Of the words themselves
Like razor blades
They cut from both sides
Forming, and leaving
My usual words slide sweet
Like molasses along the depth
Of a hot biscuit
I miss them
Sometimes they slip
Like forgotten memories
Into the creek pool where I learned to swim
My daddy saying, "Kick yee legs. That's hit!"
The half sunken snag where I learned to dive
A greasy mess of poke salet sweltering in black iron
Upon the stove
My mind slides two tracks
I concentrate hard to keep one at a time
To enunciate or smooth the edges
Depending on the company

Fighting Poverty

My father drives mountain back roads, across creek beds, alongside coal trucks, and in the dark through grey little towns that tilt toward the train tracks. The towns have funny names like Lick Skillet and Mousie, Hell for Certain and Whoopflarea. They are filled with mayors, county executives and coal operators who don't really want my Daddy there. He drives the mountains sometimes with sacks full of clothes and "learning" toys, but mostly with a head full of big ideas backed by federal money. We live in Frankfort, but he drives all over the mountains to go to work.

"Will you be gone all week?" I ask him.

If he is gone, Mama will be in one of her moods—smoking furiously, lecturing about religion incessantly, or sending me into the basement to iron blouses, pants and shirts. She had to quit her job because of me, because I am the child born in an odd year, which meant that when they closed the Negro schools and integrated us, there was not enough room for everyone to go to the same school together. My brothers go to school from 7 a.m. until 1 p.m.; I go to school in the same building from 1 p.m. until 7 p.m. My mother left her nice job working for the governor's office to stay home and "mother" me. She watches me like a hawk all day.

If I can't see my father or my brothers, I'd rather be ironing.

"Why do you have to be gone again?" I ask my father.

"Because," he says, "in one of those coal camps, up some hollow, or by some creek, there might be a child who is cold and hungry."

"Or lonesome," I say.

"That's right."

Daddy talks the mountain mothers into sending their children to one of his Head Start schools. He helps the community build playgrounds and brings round the public health nurses to give the babies their shots. He makes a point of getting things done that some people can't or won't do for themselves. That's why the mayors don't like him. He makes them look bad.

"You don't need an education to work in the mines," the mayor in Floyd County says.

"I don't want my baby to go to school," one Mama says. "She'll just get too smart and leave away from home. I don't want my boys going off to Detroit or Dayton and getting into trouble."

At a White House conference in 1964 Daddy received an award

and shook hands with President Johnson who congratulated my father for being "a frontline lieutenant in the War on Poverty." My Daddy wants the children of coal miners to read, to flush their toilets, to drink milk from a bottle, and to live in houses with bedspreads and curtains. He hires young men and women to drive across creeks and up dirt roads to take the children to school, to give them their shots, to fix their teeth, and, yes, to show them a world beyond the mines.

"While you're chasing the pot of gold for people you don't even know," Mama complains, "what is it at the end of the day that we get out of it?"

My father's search for a better life for others has left my mother bitter. While I'm trying to write a social studies paper describing John Trumbull's portraits of the Creek Indians, Mama is arguing with herself and my absent father behind my back. "I thought when I got married," Mama says, "that'd I'd finally have a real family with a husband who comes home and puts his feet under the supper table every night. I didn't know I would be a single parent raising three children."

One spring Daddy went to Washington to meet the nation's congressmen and shake hands with President Johnson. My brothers, Mama, and I went along with him in his green Impala. While he was in meetings we toured the Capitol Building, the White House, the Lincoln Monument, the Smithsonian Institute, and the National Art Museum. My father thought we should see something educational and interesting. From behind the thick, smoky stench of the yellow curtains on the fifth floor of the Francis Scott Key Hotel, my brothers and I peered out the rain-streaked window and down into the crowded street. We were hoping to see John, Paul, George, and Ringo step out of a cab. We complained to Mama that we didn't have tickets to see their concert. We knew The Beatles were in town because the hotel lobby was filled with memorabilia.

"I know your father is in town, too," Mama replied, puffing her cigarette and staring at the television, "but I don't get to see him."

Back home Daddy is still wooing legislators by driving with them through the mountains. They talk to miners, politicians, and moonshiners. Daddy puts his faith in his silver tongue and in the moonshine and the martini shakers, vodka, and vermouth inside the photographer's case that he has hidden in his car trunk. He used a Dymo Labelmaker to identify its contents. It reads "Poverty Kit."

Clear moonshine shimmers inside the water glasses in motel rooms along blue highways. My father's liquor funds his war on poverty. Late Friday nights, he comes home carrying his garment bag up the sidewalk and into the house. Then he drives up to the Windmill Liquors on the corner "to pick up a little something" in a paper bag. If I am lucky enough to go with him, I get beer nuts in a red-striped tin foil bag. Late at night alone on the sofa in the living room, Daddy watches Johnny Carson, laughs, and eats sardines on saltine crackers. His drink sweats inside its metal tumbler in the coaster on the coffee table.

The nights he does not come home I lie in bed, listening to one-sided phone conversations with Mama. "Tomorrow," she says, repeating him in a tired angry voice. "Tomorrow? Let me tell you where you can go right now."

Some nights when he comes home late, I listen to the sound of Mama breaking dishes. I think as hard as I can, shouting with my mind, "Don't do it, Mama! He'll just leave again!" But she has an angry cloud-roiling inside her so she doesn't hear me. Many weeks all I see of my Daddy is his back as he carries double-packed suitcases down the sidewalk, loads them into the trunk of his car, and drives away.

My father has worn out five cars going up and down mountain roads. He wrecked two of them. It's entirely possible he'd been drinking. I heard how the coal truck in Beattyville tore off the front end of his Pontiac; an inch closer and it would have torn off his legs. At night Mama makes us fold our hands and pray. We pray that Daddy will come home to stay. My little brother prays that Daddy won't lose his job and leave us homeless with no food to eat. He's heard about the mountain children living in cement block houses by the creeks with only a thin little stream of smoke coming out of their chimneys to make them warm.

"We've got a house," Mama says. "And food to eat."

"We've got Charles Chips in a can on the front porch," my youngest brother adds. "And a good mother."

"And a good Daddy," I say.

Mama bites her lip. She's trying not to say it, but she says what we're thinking. "If he was so good why isn't he home with his wife and children instead of out running the countryside?"

While lying in bed kicking at covers because I can't sleep I listen to the Mama side of the conversation. Daddy really does call her every night. "I would think if you loved me that much, you'd want to be at home with me." There's a long silence. "You're children miss you. I think they've almost forgotten what you look like."

When Daddy comes home, he brings me a cedar coin box that is stamped in gold across the top. It reads: "Natural Bridge State Park, Slade, Kentucky." I put it on my bookshelf along with the other cedar boxes in my collection. They are all stuffed with money. Quarters go in the Pine Mountain State Park box, nickels and dimes in the Cumberland Falls, copper pennies in the Springfield, Kentucky box, Boyhood Home of Abraham Lincoln.

"Put a dollar in the box," I tell Daddy.

"What's that for?" he asks.

"That's to buy us a new car for whenever you wear out or wreck this one."

"I can see your mother's been giving you her lectures again."

"That okay," I say. "She says you and me don't pay her any attention, anyway."

In the summer I ride along with Daddy to his meetings in Hazard, Jackson, Prestonsburg, or Manchester. Sometimes he takes bags filled with clothes, or checks, or music LPs and art supplies to the child care centers. I like to repeat the names of the towns through which we pass: Blackey, Greasy Creek, Buckhorn, and Hindman. The flabby-armed cooks at the centers squeal and jiggle when they see Daddy coming up the sidewalk. They lay aside special plates of cornbread and butter just for him. He rolls up his sleeves to eat.

It's summer and I'm with my father, so I don't mind waiting. I'm learning to do it well. In Isom I sit in a tire swing, spinning in circles, and I wait. In Vicco two little girls and I make crayon rubbings of burr oak leaves. In Wheelwright, a strange, narrow, soot-covered town, I sleep in the front seat of Daddy's Pontiac with the windows rolled down. The sun sets early in the mountains as I wait for him to finish his tediously long community center meeting.

I don't get to stay overnight, but one night I got to hear Daddy tell his office workers and some state legislators about his adventures. After he's written the checks and the centers close, he might accept a supper invitation at one of his staff workers' houses. Once after a meal, he sat in a wooden porch swing with a 90-year-old woman—his employee's great grandmother. They listened to her sons, Cyrus and Bill, play the fiddle and banjo, while Bill's wife and daughter clogged on the porch.

"Mr. Davis," the old woman asked him, "Do ye pick?"

No, he said, he didn't pick. "I never was too musically inclined."

She rocked a minute, thinking. Then she said, "Do ye dance?"

"Oh, I don't dance anymore," Daddy said. "My knees have given out on me."

She rocked a little more, thinking. "Well, do ye sing?"

Daddy laughed. "Oh well, I can't carry a tune."

The old woman grunted and looked up at my father with pity.

"Well," she finally mumbled. "Ye don't do much, do ye."

When Daddy tells that story he laughs and rattles the metal shakers in which he has mixed a very dry martini for one of the legislators. Their office aides laugh with him. He and Mama are entertaining Daddy's board members in the living room. It's Christmas. There's a fire in the grate and mistletoe hung over all the doorways in the house. Bing Crosby is crooning about being home for Christmas and Daddy is humming along. We've decorated the house with bright little sofa throws to hide the worn places in the couch. Mama's wearing a beautiful green brocade sheath that she made from discount draperies from her brother's home furnishing shop. She looks like a million bucks, but she's got her red lips pursed and keeps tapping her wedding ring in irritation against the metal tumbler of vodka in her hand. It sounds like someone beating a metal pipe with a wrench.

Daddy gives her a look. She gives him one back.

"No, I don't do much," he says, repeating the punch line of his little joke. "I don't do much at all." He gives the tumbler one last shake and pours the concoction into his state representative's glass. In the golden firelight Mama's eyes snap with their own kind of smoldering fire while the ice chips in the legislator's glass glitter like money.

Lightning Over Walgreens

I wait at the counter,
    watch a lone shopping cart's
chrome flash. For weeks nothing's

    changed. But now August's fist
closes and the city
    takes it hard on the chin.

All of us sucker-punched,
    down for the count. Outside,
the clerk lights another

    smoke, coughs, yells at the drunk
pissing into bushes
    behind the blue dumpster.

I leave my dollar for
    the paper. The front page:
a dark tree, a noose, and

    still no one cares waitress
pay is only two bucks
    an hour. We all do what

we can. Traffic piles up.
    Rain falls. The drivers stare,
wait for the light to change.

Work

A force applied through a distance.
—Sir Isaac Newton

Yesterday, in physics class
I learned about work. I had
often wondered what work is,
why it took so much of it.
The professor, matter-of-factly
said, *energy is the capacity to do*
work. What kind of bullshit is that?
I thought. Defining one abstraction
with another? Like love
being absence of hate. I am spent
trying to make sense of it,
working my ass off to understand
this stuff before the final exam.
I stared at equations the same way
I glared at you last night;
the force of my eyes strong
enough to have pushed you
across the living room.
It just doesn't work anymore
and you can't force me to stay
or be displaced. Instead,
I'll work my way to the door,
quietly slide out. No friction,
no work.

How the Heartland Works

When the state threatened
to take a mouth-shaped bite
out of his field on Highway 73,
old Farmer Beiser rushed
into court irate. "Farmers don't
like curves," he told the judge.
"Farmers like straight lines."
He rolled up plaid flannel sleeves,
pulled a pencil from his jeans
and drew the road
a new design.

When life outside the margins
threatens to take a bite
out of our writing class,
the professor we call Andy
diverts the curve.
He rolls up plaid flannel sleeves,
pulls a pencil from his jeans,
and leads us straight
through black lines of text.
Semester's end finds stories
and students too
designed anew.

Ecstasy

after Roethke

I have known the exquisite pleasure of hand tools,
Strewn about the floor, ecstasy of level and plumbline,
Mirth of mitre saw and measurements,
Elation in sawdust-covered work spaces,
Congenial bathroom, basement, back porch,
Unmitigated rapture of hammer and nail,
Ritual of roller, brush, paint,
Delightful repetition of staple gun and screen.
And I have seen leaves from the branches of trees,
Finer than flower petals, alive, more golden than sunlight,
Drift, almost silent, through long hammock afternoons,
Draping as adornments onto rocks and ephemeral ferns,
Dressing the soft grass, the rich moist fertile earth.

Blood Blister

The fleshy pad of my left thumb
caught in the work and distraction
of nail and hammer.

The nail, a galvanized
six-penny, has delicate crosshatching
on the head. The hammer belonged
to my father, sweat-stained hickory handle,
claw-back, a carpenter's hammer,
but I am not a carpenter.

Hard pinch breaks no skin,
a shape note of labor.

Knapping The Arrowhead

If you're afraid of splinters and cut fingers,
you will fail. Count any blood as sacrifice

for a good hunt. Only obsidian, glassy night-stone,
cuts fine and quick. You must strike hard

with a moose horn billet, but soft enough
to catch the flake. Rake down edges, chip away

what you must. If your strike splits the shard
clean through it's an overshot, reconsider your way.

Pure obsidian's got no grain. If you come to a hinge fracture
deal with it. Only you can say whether you'll settle

for ragged edges of *good enough*, or aim further.
Dress down sides for straightness. A full overshot here

will take the other edge, though a near one helps
streamline the thing. The closer you get to sharp

the smaller the antler tip, less force.
In the end translucent edges hold light.

GREGA McDONOUGH

Artifacts

I worked for a time at the Kentucky Museum on Western Kentucky University's campus. Being an anthropology major, I was relegated to the basement where I was given the task of cataloging a large collection of artifacts donated to the museum by an amateur arrowhead collector.

In those days, cataloging a collection meant sitting for long hours in dim light picking up a single flint chip, pottery shard, projectile point or squirrel bone, assigning it a number several digits long, marking the number with pen and ink—black ink on light objects, white ink on dark ones. I then recorded the item and its number on a note card that stood in a stack on the edge of the work table.

Girls majoring in textiles or interior design worked upstairs in the museum, rearranging the Victorian doll collection or polishing Duncan Hines' massive and ornate furniture. They stood in well-dressed huddles in the cool, long hallway, where they gossiped and giggled as they waited for the occasional museum-goer to pass through the heavy wooden doors looking for a tour.

I huddled in my jeans and sweat shirt between towering rows of metal cabinets and only got up to pull out another drawer of artifacts to begin the cataloging process all over again.

My work began early in the fall semester, and the afternoons were bright and full of promise as I descended the dark stairwell to my basement work station. The slanting light of early evening was full of promise still when I emerged three hours later, the cataloging done for the day.

One afternoon I capped the ink jar, cleaned my pen nibs, and climbed the stairs toward quitting time to find the museum lit by dim chandeliers and fusty little table lamps. The golden afternoons had slipped into a winter coat of darkness, slipped so suddenly that for a moment I was disoriented, confused. My walk home was moody, then stoic, as I gave over to that first coming of darkness, the one we have no cure for, the one we must simply wait out.

My anthropology career did not end in that basement, but it did not progress much beyond it, either. I became proficient in identifying bone fragments, human and forest creature, and in time I came to accept the importance of preserving the rusted bottled caps and bits of broken china that rode in the same shovel with the perfect Late Woodland projectile points.

In the first semesters of my archaeology coursework I assumed only the best specimens were kept, swaddled in cotton batting, catalogued, studied, and finally illuminated in glass cases for an admiring public. I assumed the broken pottery and vole bones were just so much backfill, an aggravation, the stuff that we tossed around carelessly to cover our tracks.

It turns out this material was almost as important as the artifact itself. The charcoal and bones from the midden serve as place markers and pointers to what might have occurred there, centuries before, buried under four feet of striped dirt. This bead predates the bit of pottery it is buried along side. It cannot be from this era. It must have been brought here from somewhere else, used as currency, perhaps, or possessing some other, deeper significance. It is the trash that tells us the bigger truth.

Of course, no green archaeology student is allowed to touch a whisk broom or garden trowel, much less a shovel right off the bat. First comes the field survey class, which is a class that is pretty much exactly as it sounds. Students spend every Saturday of the semester out in a farmer's field, stumbling over clods of newly disked dirt, walking in grids, surveying the ground.

We looked for anything of interest—flint, pottery, bone. And everything looked interesting. Convinced I was going to find a fully articulated skeleton my first trip out, I all but crawled on my hands and knees coaxing a skull to present itself. My eye was keen and within the hour I had a handful of teeth.

When we thought we had something, we pranced around our professor like puppies, all but panting and wagging our tails. Everyone gathered around as I presented my find. I was exhilarated but worked to arrange my face into a mask of nonchalance. The tooth fragments clacked like dice in the palm of his hand. He swiped at the dirt with his thumb, stood still for a pregnant beat. He gazed out toward the tree line in a study of contemplation.

"What you have here is pea gravel," he said.

He tossed the teeth over his shoulder and my classmates laughed.

Embarrassed, I returned to my little section of soybean field and continued to look for skeletons. But I trained my eye. I studied the lay of the land, looking for what I couldn't see as much as for what I could. I spit on a good many stones and rocks, rubbing at the dirt for a better look. I harnessed my enthusiasm until my experience and study caught up with my desire.

I developed discernment.

It was a good lesson for archeology. It was a good lesson for life.

There are no artifacts in my work now. I trade in ideas and talk, things not easily labeled with bottles of ink. I produce agendas and reports, academic plans and memoranda of agreements—documents we treat like artifacts, but they aren't, really. They are too easily changed, too often altered, to be anything more than a fancy to-do list written on good paper instead of on the back of an envelope.

We are comforted perhaps, by the neat rows of notebooks and file folders that march across our credenzas. Soon, these, too, will be extinct, because we are going paperless. The files we store electronically give us no comfort at all. They don't even exist, not until we print them out.

There are times when, working as I do, I feel disoriented and dismayed. It feels a bit like ascending the stairs of the Kentucky Museum, and wondering how did it get so dark, so suddenly, so soon? For a second—no longer—I don't know where I am.

It is then I go in search of artifacts. I long for them, those relics from the past, mine or someone else's, that connect me to right now, today. I rummage around in the basement, uncovering old tools, a jar of buttons, dried up paint cans, or my grandmother's tea pot. I dig in the garden, carefully sorting the pebbles from the shells, from the shards of red foundation brick. I place them in neat little piles on the deck before I discard them.

I look at old photos, or listen to old music, leaf through old books.

I take my time with them. Turn them over. Swipe at the dirt. I think about them, wonder. I can breathe, then, knowing they fit—for a time—small, and heavy, right in the palm of my hand.

the severity of my anxiety disorder

i am a gargoyle amongst gadflies
as fingers slip around my throat
and make speaking a felony,
the scream of some great soul machine
turning gears through rust at the sight
of yet another refusal to make phone calls,
one more chance to miss a hand
and slap my nose, i am at war,
an enlarged heart and a mouthless mind,
each armed with a shotgun
directed at my tongue, that innocent child

A Clown Without Pity

Listen up—when a liberty
horse stomps my foot
because I flicked a
                    cigarette
in the wrong direction,
                              my screams
are not for your
amusement. Even the show
has room for real hurt—
it's a pissed-off half-ton brute
and on his back rides
a showgirl who can't
save me. Sure, I know

my place—a fool's just
a funhouse mirror: your
grotesque twin, slaughtered
ten thousand ways to bust
your guts, to make you feel lucky,
like you could never,
                         ever be me:
sad sack, butt of the joke,
unbeautiful klutz, an effigy—

I only die once, but for such
  a long-ass time!

So when your kid whines
at the end of the show, don't
tug my sleeve. I got no more
balloon giraffes tonight.
Don't clown me to make
your girlfriend think
you're a bigger man. I am
a grown man in makeup

for you:
my feet too big, my car
too small, and all the heroes fly
through the air—yet here
I am with a pie in my face,
a fat foot, and Quasimodo's
limp/drag. We fools know:
no matter how many times
you fail, you all get up
and give it another go, though
the seltzer bottle's always
rigged,
the whoopee cushion always
lurks. We are tiny things,

downed like shots, and even
pratfalls bruise—so don't
laugh so hard, asshole: who
else could I be but you?

Thank you. That helps.

I've been down, as the singer said, but not like this before — so beat, toasted and done with it that talking to the department's administrative assistant today feels like taking opiates, time's gone all wobbly and weird.

I asked a question. That's all. And I knew she didn't quite get all of it because the answer was a cracked mosaic; it was a smashed baseball, its cover tattered and frayed, fluttering over a fence...going, going and gone, baby. But that was all right. I was willing to go along with her for awhile. I was even willing to say, "Thank you. That helps."

Why? Because so many days are like this now and maybe that's what she wanted to hear. And because saying "Thanks, that helps," out loud has kicked me hard, knocked me on the noggin, as my father used to say.

I'm seeing it and I'm appreciating it, my dear administrative assistant, the end of the game. I'm not dying exactly, but here it is—my career flashing through a glass, darkly...there's the beginning, when I thought holding forth in literature classes of my own design and choosing would be about genius—my genius. I'd be inspired and disciplined. I'd train myself to be some kind of super-specialist. I'd read until my eyes bled. Almost osmotically, I'd know everything there might be to know about this guy or that.

And for a while that worked. First it was Wallace Stevens. Maybe you read that paper. For a time it was WILLIAM FAULKNER. Especially *Absalom! Absalom!*, which took an entire drive to the tip of Cape Cod from Providence, Rhode Island for me to lay out its labyrinthine essentials to my beautiful ex-wife. I wonder if she ever read it. Oh that was a time. Nowadays, the characters just run away from me. I don't know a Sutpen from a Snopes. Wait, wait, give me a minute. Nopes.

Then it was Flannery O'Connor because she talked about how small she felt compared to Faulkner, like she was a flattened penny on some southern rail line after the steam powered train which was Faulkner came rolling through. I really liked that or the something-like-that she may or may not have said. Maybe I dreamed it.

Next it was Ethan Canin. I understand that as we speak, Hollywood is shooting the very story I chose to adapt for some fly-by-night screenwriting course I took for a raise. Lastly it was Spalding Gray because I thought I might also be Spalding Gray. Do you see a pattern? Of course, you don't. I see now that I never had a system. That's why when I say thanks, dear, and go along with this dizzy clerk of the works, this-soon-to-be retired papier mache lady of the lake, you have to believe I'm right behind her.

The truth is we're not on our game, neither of us. Whatever might have worked for us back when we thought we were getting anywhere has gone to sleep and now paces through a dream.

Today we are actors, nomadic players in an old road show that rolls into the same sleepy western town autumn after autumn. I'm the one downing the tonic and laudanum and sweating long and hard before the curtain goes up.

In the ramshackle hotel where the troupe stays, we run lines over breakfast. She's much younger and quite beautiful. She tells me I should relax. I've played the part a thousand times. Another actor puts *Ta-Ra-Ra Boom-De-Ay,* which is the number that opens the show, on the Victrola. I ask her for a dance.

Oh she's a gorgeous dancer, other-worldly light on her feet. I wrap my arm around her tiny waist and sweep her across the wide wooden planks of the dining room floor. The tables lean out of our way, the other guests disappear, the walls of the hotel open to a dusty street. We kick up great, twisting clouds of the stuff. Tumbleweeds spin around us, never touching us. We turn like a cyclone, out into the endless prairie beyond.

Photo in the Orchard, 1908

We look like bronze in this tintype.
I was stuck atop a barrel, in my one
red dress, the tribe's youngest produce, sour
as crabapple & ready to cry. All day,

men in green hats mumbled to me in passing
then climbed back into branches. Their cheeks
full, cider & sweat dripped from their chins.
Wagons heavy as lumber heaved away

& came back light. Though it remained hot
& close beneath the trees, Mother, with other
hauling women, stayed buttoned tight, soaked,
as top leaves fanned themselves again in breeze.

Juices seeping through baskets before them,
giant dobbins had little enough of water.
I imagined them leaning in harness
all day and dreaming of snow.

So, the tall ladders bounced until evening,
young leaves waving in light & our faces
burnished like fruit of the sun.

Clearing (a sketch)

If his hands ever stop smelling
of leaves,
I'll never find my way.
This dark smell of burning
arrives after trees
change odors—
just as they shed leaves.
I recall his hands knotting
my tie, how smoke
settled in the silk,
some Church Sunday
in front of a mirror.
Now I have a year to watch
this man
live without his eldest,
measuring his work
bare-handed,
clutching at leaves.
The trees begin to threadbare,
women and men
put on their coats,
all of them finding their way.
From my brother's old
bedroom window
I watch him working,
counting the hours
it will take to clear leaves.

Jewish Poet Swim

I don't dive into dark water,
not even at Sweet Briar Lake

where the girls pay—what? 60 thou
to float. The novelist

leaps in, the painters swan-dive,
but me, the Jewish poet with one leg

in Montgomery and one
in Brooklyn, I'll sit on the dock for a week

before I get the nerve to slide in.
Splinters are small price

for the gradual descent into the unknown
place my mother

and Daddy warned against,
and despite poem after poem,

the place where the two of them
lie now.

Piece Work

I lean over and kiss my father on the cheek, being careful of the wires sprouting out of the Telemetry box in his pajama pocket. If his heart starts to fail, the box will alert a monitoring station in another part of the hospital and attendants will come to his rescue.

"I told the doctor I don't want none of that pounding up and down on my chest if something happens," my father says. "I'm too old for that." He lets the bedrail down and sets his feet on the floor. "I feel like a dog hobbled to this thing." He slings the IV tubing and gives the IV stand a jerk. "I wish I was already dead. I do." Then he asks me not to tell my mother what he said.

I promise I won't and help untangle the tubing and roll the IV stand into the bathroom. This is the first time I've heard him say he wishes his life was over. Two years ago, when he was diagnosed with refractory anemia, he went to his garage every night and knelt on the concrete floor, praying aloud for Jesus to give him his life back. But the anemia continued sapping him of his strength. For six months now he has been taking medication for a bronchial infection. This stay in the hospital is the first time he has had Telemetry monitoring his heart.

My mother complains about the doctors. A couple of days ago, she said to me while my father was in the bathroom, "Them doctors are just not trying hard enough. I get so aggravated at that little foreign doctor. I can't understand a word he says."

Later, I ask the respiratory specialist if there isn't something he can give my father to clear up the bronchial infection. He looks at me as if I need a hug and suggests that I talk with my father's oncologist. "Dr. Lamb very nice," he says. "He explain everything. Your father have almost no platelets. He taking blood almost every day."

This is what refractory anemia is – the body not making enough blood to keep it alive. This is why my father's skin is taking on the lifeless look of a house that is being abandoned. I noticed two months ago that the skin at the top of his head looked dead. The muscles in his arms have shrunk to the bone. These are the arms that worked with his brothers and sisters, digging hillside fields with mattocks and hoes during the Depression to plant corn and beans to feed their family. These arms broke a steer to plow the hillsides. These arms hefted logs onto the back of a truck to help feed my sisters and little brother and me. When timber work wouldn't feed us, these arms went to work in a garment factory. They cut material into pieces for shirts and trousers and pulled heavy dollies loaded with thick stacks of these pieces to my mother and the other women to stitch together on their sewing machines.

Even three years ago at age seventy, these arms could wield a power saw and cut down firewood for the winter. Now these arms need my help to drag the IV stand out of the bathroom and over to the recliner beside the window when he says he wants to sit for awhile.

We look out at the cars lined up in rows on the black asphalt in front of the hospital. Wind swirls a gust of snow by the window and scatters the ragged clouds overhead. I watch their shadows move across the drab February grass in the parking lot medians.

"Your mother was crying when she called this morning," my father says. "I just told it to her like it is. I'm not going to get any better."

"Well," I say. "Well. . .," not knowing what else to say.

We are both quiet for a few minutes then he shakes his head, still looking out the window. "Look at how that grass is greening up. Oh, if I could just have the strength to plow that rich ground in the cove this spring. Just to feel that black soil again. One more year – that's all I would ask." He holds his head in his hands and weeps, tears dripping down the IV tubing attached to the top of his hand. "That's good ground."

I put my arms around him. "I know. I know," It's all I know to say. We sit there and cry together.

I remember the time he had five heart bypasses and the two times he had plaque cleaned out of the arteries in his neck. These procedures bought him ten retirement years to go to the cove and raise potatoes and corn. That many years to come back to the workshop behind his house in town and build birdhouses until past dark with my mother yelling from the back door, "Get in here to supper or I'm throwing it out in the yard."

My father says he wants to lie down and lifts himself out of the chair and sits on the hospital bed. I help remove his house shoes and hold the IV tubing while he tries to get comfortable. He flinches as his dry, calloused heels touch the sheet. I grab the hospital lotion and pour it along the purplish tops of his feet, easing it down over the cracked heels and up his legs below the knee. When I lift the leg that gave up a vein for the heart bypasses, it feels heavy, not quite alive, as if it had to give up more than a vein to save the heart.

"My life was rough," he says. "I worked like a brute. But it was a pleasure."

∾

Days when my mother sees my father lying in the fetal position, she pulls at his legs trying to straighten him back out. "Honey, you look so uncomfortable," she says. Then she stands back from his bed, waving her arms up and down like a cheerleader. "Honey, you've got to fight this. Hear me. You've got to think positive."

She skitters into his room every day at noon carrying a bag of Tupperware containers filled with biscuits, gravy, and whatever else she thinks he might eat. As soon as he hears her voice, he pulls himself up, bracing so he can get out of the hospital bed. She hurries to him and they grab one another and lock arms in a fierce embrace: he, shaky and looking a little tattered with the IV tubing rattling and splaying out from him, and she, neat but tiny and bent in her beige coat, her red hair fading yet still lively.

When they let go, my mother turns the hospital room into a country kitchen with the slightly scorched aroma of bacon gravy vying with the smell of antiseptic. She hovers over my father, watching every bite he eats. He forces as much of the biscuits and gravy and strawberry jam down as he can, saying they are the best he has ever eaten. But every morning before she arrives, he tells me that he has such a nasty taste in his mouth the thought of food almost gags him.

I remember how fast he could eat a bowl of soup beans and a plate of fried potatoes. How he used to slurp his coffee and bang his fork against his plate, my mother fussing all the while, "I want you to stop digging in your plate like you're hoeing corn." Glowering, he would stop chewing long enough to fire back, "If it don't beat the devil right out of torment that a man can't eat the way he wants to." He taught my brother and sisters and me how to hold our lips to our glasses and blow bubbles in our milk. He taught us to mix peanut butter with syrup and put it on our biscuits. He introduced us to the delight of eating fried bologna with syrup on it for breakfast.

Now, the turn of my father's fork is slow, its touch against the plastic container barely discernible except for its dig at my heart. Sometimes, I leave while he is still trying to eat and sometimes I stay until it is time for his bath. My mother insists on bathing him. "He doesn't want them little ole nurses messing with him," she says to me. Each day, she brings him clean pajamas and even brings washcloths from home. She shaves him, slicks his thin, gray hair down, and shines the dead look off the top of his head with baby oil.

Today, when I return after the bath, my father is sitting up in bed smiling. My mother has polished him up, giving him a cleaned-up baby look in spite of the age spots on his head and the bruises on his hands and arms from the IVs.

"He's feeling better," she says, straightening his pajama collar and rearranging the IV tubing.

"I'm going to plant five-hundred pounds of potatoes come spring," he says, not taking his eyes from her face. At this moment, he looks as if he could.

When time comes for me to gather up my purse and jacket and leave for the day, I listen once again to the instructions that my mother will repeat later in the evening over the phone: "Now in the morning, if your daddy needs Kleenex to spit in, go to the canteen and get him some. He hates these little things the hospital provides. And if you can get him to eat anything between meals, go to the cafeteria and get it."

The last day of my father's life, he spent the morning in his own home. His temperature was 102.6 degrees. My mother despaired of getting him to eat anything solid and persuaded him to drink Ensure. I took him back to the hospital and the doctor ordered more blood.

The IV tubing swung back and forth as his hand reached for the rail on the hospital bed. I assumed he was reaching for my mother. Perhaps he was. But later, she told me that when she was alone with him, he kept saying the name of a co-worker at the garment factory where he worked. He thought he was back in the cutting room. The steel rail was the cutting knife and he was trying to cut a stack of material into pieces for the women to sew.

Night Shift

Starlight Shift

The true children of the night
sport wounds as well as fangs,
and the parents of the night care

for them, as for us all: clean,
transport, patch, restrain, comfort
what's leftover, restless, and can't
wait until dawn. They are free

to dress casually, wear circles
under their eyes, their sacraments
are coffee, arc-sodium, and all night
radio. They make their own time

zone, shadows never move for them,
only switch on or off. They monitor
screens, walk perimeters, swash mops
over the soiled paths of daylight.

They roam a deserted world,
solitary pilots on oceans of dark,
steering by the stars and greeting
each other with a flick of headlights.

You see them at daybreak, blinking
and slow as they fill empty tanks,
stretch the night from their shoulders.

You judge them as hungover, and
they are: from the amphetamine of
responsibility, the strangest, longest,
wildest party of all.

Temple Square

You were like a ghost I watched fade away
With a wide-arm swing sheltering a tiny flame
As the song played out
You laughed at my doubt
Then disappeared in the darkness

Tonight I hold a pen that bleeds all through my hands
The old Moroni faces east, a pioneer makes her plans
The price of all these visions
Dearer than a newborn's cries
As the sun beats down on this pushcart prize
Pushcart prize
And faint goodbyes

Leaves on the branch sink in the rain
The sound of thunderbolts breaking over my head
Water pours down windowpanes
The wind's blowing up for rain
Mama said angels were crying

I cut my foot at the pool, you held me like a father
Suspended in your arms, terrified of the water
Hobbling away
To hide was the crutch
Ashamed of skin that could feel so much
Feel so much
And fear your touch

I approached with shaking hands
Then danced like a girl in your Netherlands
Defying the gods
Decisions all my own
Robbing cathedrals of their cornerstones

Amidst applause, we walked cobblestone streets
Showing special kindnesses to every person we met
And feasting for three
The common man, you and me
I opened my eyes and I could see
I could see possibility

Ancient drumbeats marking time
Breathing through the hammer thrust upon my spine
I heard the women's screams in concert with mine
As pain turned to morning

Hunkered down in black and turquoise
You drove 1000 miles to kiss my boy
Ah the medicine of love
It heals the sin-sick soul
But desire and longing has made me whole
Whole
Made me whole

Sun, moon, stars, the choir sings
Statues of mothers clinging to their offspring
A testament to life
The strength to cross the pass
And never more be an outcast

We're all out to find our temple square
Rising out of the desert, a palace we put there
But it's always East of Eden
We're forever a bit shy
With our hand on the plough
And face towards the sky

Towards the sky like Moroni
My Moroni, goodbye

Where I'll Be If I'm Not There

His mama named him with purpose, hoping it'd be a guide, but life is complicated and you can forget who you are, so Straight had given the last three years of his life to the State of Missouri.

Out now—he had difficulty with the word free—he worked at a job arranged by the parole officer; at a bakery, making bagels fresh every morning and pastries beside. The owner, Mr. Gilbert, was a Jew but they got on okay.

He worked four days a week, each starting at one in the morning. Measuring, mixing. Flour and water, yeast and malt syrup. Pounding. Forming. Proofing. Trays to racks. Bagel-shaped dough to boiling water. Everything into the ovens. And then the cleaning, that last hour. Washing, rinsing, sanitizing. Wiping the stainless until he was reminded that he was to polish the finish, not take it off. His day done, the work complete, nine hours after he'd started.

Back home, a quick shower. Close the blinds, eyes, mind. Fall to sleep. Restless sleep, but it passed the day. When Straight woke for a second time, it was early evening. Too late to bother anyone and he was glad for that. Some people he knew, but maybe it was best to stay away.

He'd sit at the card table in front of the kitchen window and drink coffee. Listen to time ticking off behind him. He might be coaxed to the window by the swatches of laughter and child's play. He'd stand there, watching and wondering ('cause he couldn't help but think of her), sipping the coffee even after it was cold.

He'd never been around enough. Even if her mama had kept pictures, had shown them to her, he wasn't the same. Least he didn't think himself to be. Or maybe that was what he should hope. Three months out and he hadn't spent time with anyone who knew him from before, so he couldn't be sure.

He wouldn't allow himself much thought on it. Just stand at the window, let minutes pass until it was time to go out again and he was in a world mostly asleep; him not a bother to it and the world not giving one thought to him.

∾

He sweated: lifting 50-pound bags of flour, the heavy bulk of dough, the heat of the oven. Straight bought an oscillating fan from the Salvation Army thrift shop. It didn't move the air around him much (he couldn't put it too close to the dough) but he liked the company of it moving crookedly through space, going only so far before changing its mind and heading back in the opposite direction.

∾

His fingers trembled as he worked the key into the lock on the door. Better than two weeks now and his having access to the place continued to unnerve him.

"You think I want to keep getting up in the middle of the night?" Mr. Gilbert had asked.

Straight thought yes, finding comfort in someone else allowing him entrance and locking up behind.

∾

"He comes by more often than the Health Department man," Straight commented after the Rabbi had left.

Mr. Gilbert laughed and explained the frequent visits as he counted out a week's pay.

Straight didn't have a bank account so he cashed his paychecks at the bakery.

"Big plans for tonight?" Mr. Gilbert asked.

Straight shrugged.

"You never bring any family around."

Straight shrugged again. "You sure you don't want me to come in tomorrow."

"I appreciate your hard work, but this is a job; it shouldn't become your life."

∾

Straight only glanced at his blurred reflection as he ran the towel over the face of the oven, the prep table, the refrigerator, polishing them to brightness. Done, he tossed the rag aside, lifted the skirt of the apron he wore and ran it over his face. Letting it fall, he looked out into the front of the store, not looking for anyone in general or particular and there she was.

Perhaps she felt his stare because she looked up from the display case and over at him. She did nothing but nod before making a purchase and leaving.

How she knew where to find him, he didn't know. That she even knew that he was out surprised him.

Straight raced out the back door, down the alley, around the corner.

Her or not, he would've been content to just watch. He called "Minerva!" and he waited for the woman to keep walking as if he'd been confused and wrong but he'd never forget the way those hips moved beneath snug skirts.

She stopped, turned, waited.

Stepping toward her, Straight searched the space between them for something he could grab hold of, use to explain and then he was there before her and he hadn't constructed anything. He looked away.

"You look good, Straight," she told him. "No worse for the wear."

He made himself meet those eyes warm, soft and brown as the coffee he stared into most days. He thought he saw some forgiveness and patience but — ?

"Ain't nothing changed," she assured him. "The phone number neither." She turned and, to his delight, strutted away.

Straight didn't sleep. Couldn't. At home, on the bed, he lay on top of the covers, hands under his head, staring at the ceiling.

He'd thought that the world had not been waiting for his return. But her words – *Ain't nothing changed*. Maybe it was true. Maybe he hadn't lost anything at all. Just hid it away some and now it was time for him to bring it out again.

He rose and went to the phone. The number he still knew, would always know.

"I want to see you," he said simply when she answered.

"It's 'bout time."

"Tonight," he said without thinking on what else he'd planned.

"Let's meet at Eddie's."

He was disappointed. He'd wanted her to himself—he wanted the feel of her beneath his fingertips, her sigh dancing in his ear, the delicious sweetness of her lips—but he agreed.

"Say about eight?"

That thing poking at him, he realized, was reminding him that he had somewhere else to be at seven.

"That's not good for you?" Minerva asked.

“I was heading over to see Rose,” he told her, hoping his explanation would calm the frustration he thought he heard in her voice. “I been sending her Mama some money but I think it’s time I show my face.”

“I understand, Straight. You need to set things right.”

“Kosher,” he said.

“What?”

“Nothing. I don’t know how long I’ll be.”

“You’ve been gone awhile, it may take awhile.”

“Woman,” he said, with slight laughter. He shook his head, listened to her breathe. “I’mo try not to keep you waiting. I’ve done that too much, too long.”

“Lord knows that’s the truth, but we can do this another time.”

“I need to see you and her both; I just got ahead of myself. I ain’t got no right, but I’mo ask you to stay put. I’ll get to Eddie’s soon as I can. I’m just letting you know where I’ll be if I’m not there.”

He hadn’t slept the night but as he readied to go to the bakery, he didn’t feel worn. He had seen his daughter and Minerva and afterwards his whole body buzzed, felt alive, with some kind of possibility.

When he reached the bakery, entered and turned on the light, he saw a note attached to the oven. It was something Mr. Gilbert did, knowing that turning the appliance on would be the first thing Straight did.

“I won’t be in until eight. Please open the shop and I will compensate you for doing so. The office is unlocked and the cash drawer is on the desk.”

Straight felt his breath changing, the pace of his heart. Mr. Gilbert had added instructions for running the register. The paper trembled in Straight’s hand. This was bigger than the key to the door.

It was Minerva’s voice, what she’d told him last night when he’d confessed he sometimes felt hopeless about getting her back, his child, that calmed him.

“It ain’t gonna be easy,” she’d said, “But that ain’t no reason not to try.”

Straight took a breath. He gave that familiar face of fear a nod then he pushed himself forward. There was only so much time and he had work to do.

Third Shift

One pair of shoes, that's all this job is getting,
these ugly black twins, tight and twisted
from the anger in which they were laced,
hunched close to the shining floors,
splattered as the mop flings bleach, blood,
and grease-water like diamonds back onto their
tongues and soles. All remnants of the
anonymous bar fight now gone, they move
with heavy toll, each crawling tumor, tar
complexion and clinging to the tile as if with
interminable love, each sticking cephalopod creak,
moving onward into the night, waiting to expire, for
these seams to burst, their sticky black shells
spilling the soft whiteness within, like crab-meat,
this matching pair, impatient for tonight to be put
finally to rest, to be buried beside it, but first
the time to dig the trench, for tomorrow's
dreams swirl distantly like oil within water.

dream

In the dream world there is not much
color much light there
is only The Foreman screaming
that when you get up

only the old man with wizened face scraggle
beard old teeth in your face hot
breath says when you
Wake up wake up with sticky mouth

wooden headed feet
slide like rattle bear trap on the hard floor to the mine
on your way out the vision blaring from the corner
till you cross the thresh to dark to dark

the men huddle shadowless by the bound door
await you in the dark with axes
and shovels and barrels of hoarded slate
till the corner the old man staring cloudy eyes

at the dead boy the boy dying till he stops
till he stops dying the way you were
the way the night held your hand
took you home safe

but in the dark there is no color
in the dream world
the Foreman and the old man tell each other dirty secrets in the
        whisper corner
and what they wish is prophecy

a held on secret that drives the moon
can you see the time ghosting in their mouths
the shadowed hall caught in their deep throats
the men take no heed only clatter and gamble

crying Daniel Daniel
the little boy preaches from the pit
from the den of horrid lions
in the corner the old man and The Foreman fill each other's throats
with bile

while the unshadowed men harbor axes and picks against the wall
forty lashes bloody shouldered against the wall
till finally the bottom of boots a half leg gone above the knee
Daniel Daniel crying it's already night it's already night

no clamp jawed lions
the Foreman hauling out the pale ledger pen in hand
in the dream world there isn't much color
in the dream world the Foreman and the old man cackle and suckle
the dry bones

and when you clamber past the men to cradle heads,
to lull soft throats to sleep
then is when the Foreman and the old man slip in behind
what they ask

what they ask O Daniel crying out in the dark
what they ask is if you are ready to be next
are you ready to be slipped off in the night
still sleeping in your scaly shoes

are you ready to wait the years until your
throat will open again

Dreaming Granddaddy

A child, I dreamed you as those black and whites
in Grandma's family album, your miner's lamp
like a third eye perched at the brim of your hat,
your skin black with coal dust you still bring up
with solid coughs. I dreamed you tall
before the mines bent you to the curve
of twenty-five years' pickaxe and shovel weight
and the black rock you hefted onto carts and belts.

Lately, I've dreamed you
as part of the mountains – all six feet of you
stuffed into a coal seam, the way you said
you shoved cartridges of powder
into an auger-drilled hole, packed it good
and tight with the tamper and lit the fuse.
Sleep hinges on that moment of soundlessness.

I wait for the shift of slate,
the slipping face of coal walls
that signal the shaft dwellers to come,
shovels in hand, and lift the broken pieces
onto carts to be dragged toward the light
of surface and grass.

Telling

On TV, a man in a hard hat
talks about a mine explosion.
It is night there, and cold—
his breath comes in ellipses, telling
the anguish of waiting.

He says there are no signs
of life, no sounds, no answers
to signals tapped onto a pipe
the crew lowered into the shaft.
As he talks, his words walk
dark corridors, carrying small lanterns.

Once, I looked out the window
to see my father in the yard
on palms and knees, talking
to my son, crouched like a man
with a great weight on his back.
Later, when I asked, my boy said
Papa was telling him how men
used to crawl through mine shafts
dragging sacks of coal behind them.

The man on TV stops talking, squints
into the brilliant light of the camera.
I go to the phone, dial
my father. I wait for the ring.
Through the line, static taps out
the word *home . . . home.*

Synchronous

For the nine previous evenings he had counted lightning bugs, but tonight, Sam relaxed at a barbecue.

The hosts' arthritic black lab waddled across the tile to sniff Sam's pant leg, his toenails *click*, *click*, *click*ing like sleet on a barn roof. Eldon was the dog's name. Or was it Quincy? No, Quincy was the incontinent basset hound who stayed out on the carport.

Sam lowered his face to the barrel-shaped dog. Streaks of gray were brushed across Eldon's face.

"Hello, puppy dog. Are you a good boy? Yes! You're a good boy! You nasty son of a bitch."

Eldon wagged his tail, then wandered around the room like a nervous hog, searching for a spot out of the way of all the human footsteps to flop down and gnaw at his various and private itches.

"Oh, Sam!" Elisa called out from a huddle of women in the sun room. "Someone dropped off a litter of darling kittens at the shelter. Could I interest you in a sweet little kitten?"

"Shit no."

Elisa grinned and shook her head. "Well, if you know anybody."

Whenever the doorbell rang, Sam would straighten himself on the couch to see over the heads of the mingled crowd, to see who might waft in from the carport with the white barbecue smoke.

"Sam is an entomologist from the University of Missouri. He's in town this summer to study the synchronous fireflies." Elisa explained this to a new couple with different last names, attorneys with an environmental advocacy group. "He's researching how development impacts them. Sam, tell them about your research."

He forced his eyes – which had just pulled shut against his will – to open wide, and he lifted his gaze to the polished, middle-aged pair at his host's side.

"Count lightning bugs in the clearings. Count lightning bugs in the campground. Count lightning bugs in the timber. The end."

Sam slipped his finger into his shirt pocket and touched the check from his parents that he'd kept in a Gideon Bible for over a week. Tomorrow, he'd go cash it. Another swallow of Early Times burned his throat.

He needed to piss but knew he'd lose his seat and have to stand propped up against the doorframe if he excused himself now. Ben shuffled past him, disappeared down the hallway and then returned with his banjo in hand, and two or three of the guests applauded. In his Brooklyn accent, Ben introduced his first composition, "Snowdrops," which he followed with "Falls of Richmond," both deftly delivered with index and middle fingers splayed in the clawhammer style.

After the music had waned, Sam excused himself and made his way out to his pickup, where he opened the door, pulled out his penis and drained his pressured bladder. It was a clear, cool evening, and a layer of fog had begun to rise off the grass and now hovered about knee-high. Pyralis fireflies—*Photinus pyralis*—flickered in all directions, as random as could be.

A mile or so before he got back to the motor lodge, he switched off his headlights and pulled into a wide spot in the road directly across from the little convenience store operated by the family from India. The store was closed at this hour, but in the trailer next to the store, he watched the bluish flicker of light in the window. He sat parked there for ten, fifteen minutes, then stepped out of his truck to piss again, steadying himself with his hand on the door handle. Then he drove away.

On Saturday morning, he drove to the laundromat and to the bank to cash the check from his parents. He bought coffee and saltines, cereal and milk at the IGA. He watched westerns all afternoon while he worked on his data analysis.

Over in Elkmont that night, he settled into a familiar spot at the edge of an old field where, within a half hour, a group of tourists stumbled from the woods into the clearing. They trailed behind Janis, a summer naturalist with the Park Service.

"Hi, Sam," she whispered as the group filed past.

Some of the tourists gawked at him; others offered nods and smiles as they shuffled by him in his camp chair, aluminum clipboard in his lap, an insect net and a thermos lying at his feet.

"An entomologist," Janis told her group. "Studying the fireflies."

As they walked to a spot on the field's edge just a few dozen feet from Sam, he listened to Janis's introduction: how the patterns of light attracted mates, how there also exists a species of synchronous fireflies—*Pteroptyx malaccae*—in Thailand and Indonesia. The fate of our species, *Photinus carolinus*, explained Janis, remained relatively more secure than for these fireflies' Asian relatives, because the preservation of the Great Smokies ensured a sizable habitat.

Soon the tourists stood open-mouthed as the first faint blinks began at one side of the field, setting the rhythm, and in a matter of seconds the entire population throbbed luminescent with their brethren, *dark, light, dark, light*, all as one, nothing like the independent fireflies they'd seen before.

Janis said the Smokies' synchronous fireflies weren't even discovered until 1991.

Janis had once told Sam over beers on her porch that it wasn't unusual for the tourists to weep when they saw the synchronized flickerings, chalking this up as nothing short of a spiritual experience. At least a few on this night were probably seeing fireflies (of any species) for the first time.

"It's an entomological orgy," Sam had replied. "Light equals lust."

They had speculated that evening that, in any given clearing, one hundred thousand fireflies wanted to fuck the moon.

The tourists stretched across their blankets or in their folding chairs or else shifted their weight from foot to foot and vied for the attention of Janis, and Sam calculated that some of the males hoped to woo her, unaware that she wasn't into guys.

"Yes," Sam mumbled. "Glowing asses would sure take out a lot of the guesswork."

He sat in his chair and watched the show long after he'd collected his data. It was just before eleven when most of the tourists climbed aboard the last shuttle back to Gatlinburg or else retired to their campers, and then he walked back to the campground and had a beer with Janis at a picnic table, over the stench of a citronella candle and to the sound of crickets and muffled giggles.

"How are the folks?" he asked.

"Good. Enjoying retirement."

"When do you leave?" she asked.

"Classes start Wednesday after next. I'm leaving right after Ben and Elisa's get-together on Friday."

Janis slid the citronella to the far end of the table and fanned it with her hand. "I'll be there, for sure," she said and smiled. "I'll share one more beer with you before you head back into the real world."

"Oh yeah, the real world."

"Yep. The one they always warned us about."

Sam slipped the tip of his pinkie finger into the mouth of the empty beer bottle.

"You know what," he told Janis. "I've thought more than once about just walking away from my job and my tenure and all. I could move back to Grundy County, get a job teaching high school biology and just stay close to where I grew up."

"There's good and bad about staying home. Do you think you could handle it?"

Sam didn't have an answer.

They left the campground at the same time, and he followed behind her white Park Service Bronco all along the curvy road to where she turned into the driveway of her place. Sam continued another five miles to the motor lodge.

He managed to write up a few sloppy pages on his study that week and drove back over to Elkmont one more time on Thursday.

On Friday, he was packed and loaded up and checked out by noon and wandered through town – to the pizza place, to the gift shops – for several hours and then got to Ben and Elisa's about six. Ben was on the carport with his banjo, and two middle-aged women who may have been twins played guitar and fiddle.

Quincy and Eldon greeted the guests one by one, licking hands until they received kind words and pats on the head.

"Sam? Tell Deloris about your research." Elisa poked her head out the sliding door. A handsome half-Asian lady stood behind her, clutching a glass of homemade wild blackberry wine.

"Deloris?" said Sam. "I watch lightning bugs fuck."

Even when the skillful playing ceased, the music played on: the crickets, the sizzle of beef over charcoal, laughter and conversations in a range of accents. The people and voices were diverse – the lawyers from Boston, the Pakistani cardiologist and his Thai wife, the Spanish instructor from the high school, three different exchange students, the family from India who owned the convenience store, plus a handful who had grown up right here in and around Cosby. Ben and Elisa themselves were originally from Brooklyn and Vancouver.

Janis showed up close to dark. The two of them sat and listened to the music and watched the guests for a long time. He turned his attention again and again to Avnee, the college-aged daughter of the couple who owned the store. She rubbed Eldon the dog's forehead and spoke softly to the environmental lawyers. He regarded the shiny black hair pulled into a braid, the silver earring dangling and the cappuccino-colored cartilage stretched tightly on her ear. And he noticed how, when he closed his eyes, the music was old, but the voices were newcomers, and he liked the pattern of sound he heard: old-time music, followed by the chatter of men and women foreign to these mountains but content with one another's kindness at the moment, followed by another tune born in the soil of this place.

"I've decided to stay with the university for now," he told Janis. "Maybe in a year I'll look at other options. We'll see. But for now, I'm staying put."

When it was time to depart, Sam walked from person to person. He told them what a pleasure it had been to get to know them – even the smallest bit – this summer. He shook hands with Ben and Dr. and Mrs. Malik. Elisa embraced him in a motherly hug.

"Come visit us," she said.

Janis promised to email often, giving him an update on the remainder of her seasonal responsibilities and the next adventure on her horizon.

Sam drove slowly away from the house, and he stopped again at the wide spot across from the convenience store. Although the entire family was still at Ben and Elisa's, the television inside the trailer played unsupervised, and the blue light flickered through the sheers on the window.

Sam eased his way down the embankment beside the road, kicking his ankles through wads of knotweed that tried to grow around him and pull him under. He reached the creek and, relying on the glow from the store's fuel sign for illumination, he stepped from one rock to another, passed through a dense stand of sycamores and more knotweed to an overgrown field, bushhogged maybe once every summer.

He studied the mist that hovered on the weedy field. The lightning bugs here weren't the synchronous ones, the ones that the tourists traveled from their cities to see. These were just plain old *Photinus pyralis* and maybe a scattering of other species. Thousands and thousands of them sent out their cries for love, one by one, each tiny glow piercing a blue halo in the fog.

A picture came to Sam's mind, although he couldn't say if it was a real or imagined event: his father, in a dark hayfield, held a quart jar full of fireflies to his face and grinned at them.

Somewhere not far from here, tourists were packing suitcases and stuffing RVs full of paper plates, charcoal and folding chairs. They were jotting thank you notes to the ranger and the campground host and Janis the summer naturalist. They were gathering around the campfire for one final evening in this wilderness, and as they lay down in their campers and tents, the excited conversations they had begun earlier in the night would continue, and they'd toss and turn through a restless night as their thoughts collectively swayed back and forth between the homes they knew and the ones they imagined.

The Union Steward Switches Back to 3rd Shift

By midnight, he is already tired.
His hammer is a 50 lb weight,
loose lugnuts and bolts slip
through his fingers. He has to heave
his full weight against the tool cart
for its wheels to turn, the metal edge
leaving a bruise on his belly,
just above his belt. Twenty years ago,
he is sure, the women didn't wear
pillow creases on their cheeks
like stretch marks, the men's faces
weren't shallow with shadows and dark stubble.
Even happy hour at 7 am is sour,
beer sticking like cotton to his tongue
and the back of his teeth, a hangover
that sets in only 20 minutes after that last drink.

Sabbatical

Miroslava had a fierce sense of commitment. She prided herself in the work ethic reflecting former generations of her Mom's family in Kiev. She worked 10 years at St. Mary's Psychiatric Hospital, eventually becoming Social Worker Supervisor for the adult short-stay unit. She was good at her job, but the pace and paperwork eventually got to her, nearly hurling her into a nervous breakdown. She missed the days of spending time with patients, running groups, and walking the night hallways with a flashlight and a keen eye. She drafted the letter on a Tuesday, and by the next Friday was given her schedule as Principal Mental Health Technician out on the unit, trading pay grade for sanity.

Brad was the kind of supervisor whose primary concern was having warm bodies in the halls. It was 6:42 that next Friday evening when she got the call. She thought it might be Kelly running late for vespers, and was surprised to hear Brad's voice on the other end.

"I need you to come in tonight," he told her. "Kendra called in and we have 3 level fives on the unit."

"I'm not scheduled tonight," she answered.

"I know, but I need you to come in," he said curtly.

"Brad, I've never worked on Friday nights or Saturdays."

"Everyone has to work weekends, Mira." Brad sounded irritated.

"I can come in Sunday, but not tonight," Miroslava insisted. "It's the Sabbath."

"Look, no one likes calls, and no one likes to work Friday and Saturday nights. You don't get preferential treatment." Brad's irritation was joined by suspicion. "I thought the Sabbath was Sunday anyway."

"Seventh Day Adventist," she clarified.

"Well I'm not going to argue. The rules are the rules, and if you are committed to this job, you have to follow them. Come in by 8:00 or you will be written up."

Miroslava's face heated up at the click of the phone. His words were just enough to send her back to the brink she had been trying to avoid by taking this position. She paced the floor, the word "committed" scrolling through her head over and over. *Was he serious in questioning her commitment?* The kitchen swirled around her as her pacing picked up speed. Within minutes, she found herself on the floor, head rested on the heating vent, staring at crumbs by the baseboard. She did not hear Kelly knock.

Miroslava came to on a plastic mattress, staring at dark shadows on a blue-white wall. She turned toward the creak of the door, just in time to catch the full blare of a flashlight in her eyes. The light slid down and out as the door creaked back to almost closed, and Miroslava realized where she was. She wanted to scream, to run, to bang on doors and make a break for it. Instead, she turned back toward the wall, closed her eyes, and smiled. All that seemed too much like work, and this was the Sabbath, after all.

Celestial Farmer

The last shall be first
and the first shall be last
That's what the scriptures say
but I ain't betting any money on it
I reckon when I get to heaven
John D. Rockefeller
will be sitting
on the left hand of Jesus
and John Paul Getty will be on the right
and I expect I'll be doing the same thing
in heaven that I'm doing here on earth
Be a celestial farmer
stumbling behind some ol' plug mule
Only difference will be
I'll turn clouds instead of earth
break up clods of stars instead of clay
and plant rain rather than pray for it
Farming's the onliest thing I know how to do
and I don't figure dying's going to make me any smarter
I'll work my tail off to get a good harvest
and after I go to market
they'll take half of it to pay
for Getty's new angel wings
or Rockefeller's harp collection
I don't expect anything to change
just because I'm dead

The game's been rigged
ever since Adam got turned out of the garden
We've been working ever since to get back in
but I know when we get there
there'll be a turnstile at the Pearly Gates
Cost you half a halo or three strings off your harp
to pass through
and ever' evening that Rockefeller

or that Mellon feller or that Getty feller
or some other rich feller will come collect
the proceeds that all us working fellers
had to pay just to get in

And once you're in there
if you want to go swimming in the River Jordan
there'll just be a little place roped off
where working folk can get their toes wet
and it'll be so crowded with angel farmers
and angel miners and angel truck drivers
that you won't be able to spit
Of course just a ways up the river
there'll be a whole mile of water
with nobody in it
but one little ol' president of Standard Oil
and guards set up on either side
to keep us common angels from getting in

No I ain't expecting it to get any easier
I ain't expecting it to change one blame bit
I'll die and be living in a shanty on Heaven's dirt road
while the rich folks are sitting pretty
in them many mansions on those streets paved with gold.

Elegy for a Hay Rake

To every thing its season, and to every tool
its final turn; to the Farmhand rake my father
bought hard-used in 1976, rust has eaten away
all your labels, all your sheen and simple function;
to what I hope is my last sight of you, unhitched
and standing in the field like a photograph
from the Great Depression;
farewell to the cut hay left
scattered on the ground to rot, nothing ate you
but the soil that birthed you; to the tractor tire
those long grappling points missed by inches
on every sharp turn, you survived without puncture;
to the long afternoon hours spent digging clumps
out of the balers' clenched teeth, good money
cannot buy you back;
so long to the lucky machine,
lucky I won't sell you as an antique, that no one will
paint you red, white, and blue and plant you in a garden,
or hang you on a restaurant wall; goodbye to the five
leaning wheels, their crooked tines turning, reaching up
like broken fingers to wave hello, hello, goodbye.

Clearing Out My Closet

Here's a shirt that was my Dad's. I know
the cigarette burns, the drips of roofing tar.
He wore it hard, I couldn't throw it out.

I didn't cry when Daddy died. Those angry
years I didn't cry for anything,
but here's this shirt that was my Dad's. I know

it makes an odd memento, wedged between
my out-of-fashion suits, an old work shirt
defiled by burns and drips of roofing tar,

but I can smell him when I look at it –
Camel smoke and sweat and Ancient Age.
He wore it hard, I cannot throw it out.

Ridge Runner's Commandment

Gather in the harvest,
put up for lean times.
Preserve them,
fat or lean, red or green,
for you may face
disaster.
Cap tightly.
Let simmer over an open fire,
flames of orange to baptize
ancient glass.
Let the smell fill your houses,
the lungs of your children,
so that they may know it well.
Store, safe from rot, in a dark place.
When darkness falls over you,
therein will be your portion of light.

Great Grandma's Crow Lament

Talk about bad signs—one time
a crow flew in the breezeway door
right into the kitchen. Quick,
I slammed down a skillet still
hot in my hand. That bird bled
out a rain puddle, black glass eyes
chilling me to the bone a hundred
nights after. I kneeled down to Jesus,
cleaned that shadow the minute
it took to my threshold. No matter—
by season's end your Papaw was dead
and me alone with things falling down
around my head, save two babies still
sleeping in the cradle. Years I tried
to keep us tied together—told how
that man could sing, could hew us a table
out of stone-hard ash, how he downed
a wildcat in one shot up there on the ridge
in the fallen dark. Hear me good, girl:
set your mind to lose what you done got
in this world, cause nothing steals back time
or keeps a man in place once he's called—
not even a sharp-eyed woman quickened
by cast iron, hell bent on barring the door.

Painting the Fence

Scrabble of squirrels in red oak—
acorns ding your fresh coat
fast as you apply it.
The brush dips, sweeps.
You are not a quitter.
I can't say the same. One day
I will unlatch the gate and go.

At night you lace up steel-toed boots,
pack a pail for your midnight shift—
slice of meatloaf, saltines.
When you return,
smelling of iron and cold,
I tiptoe out the door to day jobs
I can barely sit still for.

Young husband, no one
has instructed you
as I must be instructed
in all household things.
Your large hands take up tools—
the lock on the door,
the shingles that won't blow down.

Stool too low for your legs,
your grasshopper knees poke up.
Scorch of July,
your long back bronzes,
rhythm of your hand constant
as I am not.

Redeeming Jewell

Jewell Willis met Dickie Joe McDowell during the worst summer of her life. She had been a high school dropout for less than a week and even though she couldn't bring herself to admit it, she was already regretting her decision. After working only one shift as a carhop at the Tastee Freeze, she hated everything about the dingy little drive-in. As she walked home that first night, smelling of grease, the muscles in her calves throbbing, she practiced telling Old Man Stubblefield she was quitting. She folded her arms across her stomach and felt the sticky traces of ice cream grab at the front of her shirt. She had made dozens of dives that night headfirst into the big silver freezer. Her toes barely touched the floor as she stretched down to reach the row of brown cardboard tubs of ice cream nestled deep at the bottom. Every duty associated with her job hacked away at what little dignity she carried with her when she walked out of Dwight D. Eisenhower High School for the last time. Every time she pushed her weight against the swinging door at the drive-in, she imagined a large butcher knife sticking out from between her shoulder blades, pushed in deep by whatever force it was in the universe that had set her down in the arms of a mother like hers.

Jewell had long believed her mother had one reason for being - to make sure her daughter was every bit as miserable as she herself was. She was convinced she was nothing more to her mother than a sad reminder of things she sought to escape. And now it pained Jewell to think it looked like she was destined to climb right into the same miry pit her mother struggled against.

It was a sad truth the Tastee Freeze was the only place in town that would hire sixteen-year-old dropouts. She was disgusted to have to admit that she was finally free of the agony of high school, only to find herself carrying metal trays of burgers and fries to the same despicable girls she had quit school to avoid. On Friday and Saturday nights she saw them all as they sat in shiny cars, lined up like soldiers, arranged in neat rows and ready to attack. All those sprayed and fluffed smug-faced girls from school, pressed up against over-Vitalised boys, smirking as they watched her walk hundreds of miles up and down the sloped blacktop of the drive-in's parking lot. She cringed when they acknowledged her, called her by name, pretending to be sociable. She hated it even more when they acted like they didn't know her. She spent much of her shift just wishing she could slap somebody.

The Saturday night that changed her life was an especially miserable one. Marla Ingle was giving her a hard time, posturing for her latest boyfriend as she entertained the couple slouched in the back seat. Marla was a despicable human being on every level, and Jewell had hated her on sight. She felt ill every time Marla's cackling laughter rose above the tinny voice of Elvis Presley declaring he was "All Shook Up" over the loudspeaker at the drive-in. She was with a different boy every time she showed up at the Tastee Freeze. Everyone knew there was most certainly another reason for her immense popularity with boys besides her rich daddy.

It was a muggy night and a fine mist was just beginning to turn loose from the low-lying clouds. It clung to the skin and coated the windshields of the cars like wax. Jewell could feel it settle in her hair, and her t-shirt stuck to her back. She had been assigned the section of the parking lot known as the hill. It was a favorite spot for the teenagers who came to the drive-in more to see and be seen than to eat. It was also the best place to watch those who were "making the circle"—driving at a crawl through the middle of the Tastee Freeze parking lot, screeching out on to Highway 25E, turning around at an abandoned truck stop two miles down the road and looping back through again. As Jewell passed by, Marla leaned across the driver, a boy with a mouth too full of very white, very crooked teeth. The couple in the back seat were giggling profusely. Marla stuck her hand out the window as Jewell passed.

"Girl," Marla said, her voice taking on the nasal quality she applied when she was feeling especially full of her own importance. "Excuse me, Girl." Jewell cringed. She knew good and well Marla knew her name. "This cup that you brought me? Well, see, it has sauce all over the side. See? It's icky and it's getting all over my hand. Would you take this back and make me a fresh sundae?"

Jewell glared first at Marla, then at the boy, reached out and snatched the cup from Marla. Without taking her eyes off Marla's face, she wiped the cup across the front of her apron. She reached it back through the window, barely missing the boy's face, and waited for Marla to take it from her.

"Well, for heaven's sake" Marla said. "I'm not going to eat something you wiped all over yourself like that. And besides. Look at it. It's all melted and nasty looking. Plus . . . you forgot my cherry," Marla said.

"Honey, I think your cherry was forgot about a long time ago," the boy said. Marla rolled her eyes and playfully smacked his arm as the couple in the backseat burst out laughing.

The rain was getting harder and Jewell's hair felt like wool as it crept down across her eyes. She threw the cup on the ground and pushed her hair back. She crammed her fist hard into her hip and breathed deep until she felt her chest settle. "I'll tell you what," she said. "Why don't you and your cherry just get the hell on out of here and go somewhere where somebody gives a crap whether you live or die? How about you just do that?"

Marla's eyes widened and she grabbed the steering wheel, pulling herself closer to the window. The boy leaned back against the seat and the couple in the back let out a collective gasp. "Why, you little bitch," Marla said. "Who do you think you are? Your ass is so fired. You just wait and see. You're nobody. Do you understand? Don't think I can't have it done either. Let's go, Nathan. Right now."

Jewell kept her feet planted on the blacktop as the car squealed out of the parking lot and pulled onto the road. She looked down at the mess, a puddle of diluted soft serve ice cream and chocolate syrup gathering around her shoes. She turned when she heard clapping behind her. A boy was peering out the passenger window of a blue Ford pickup truck. Jewell noticed the rain was running together into quivering fat pools on the hood of the truck. A cigarette dangled from the corner of the boy's mouth and he was grinning at her.

"Well, that show was sure worth the price of a cheeseburger," he said.

Jewell stared at him briefly, then burst out laughing. He was sunburned and his arms and neck were a stark contrast to the white undershirt he wore. His curly brown hair was tangled and twisted in corkscrews on his forehead. Jewell noticed his eyes were the exact same color as his hair. He leaned over and pushed opened the passenger side door. "Get in," he said. She untied the apron and let it fall to the ground. She stepped over it and climbed into the truck as coins from her apron pockets rolled down the slope, made dizzy circles on the blacktop, coming to rest in a rainbow-colored oil slick.

A bra that fits

Frosty Mullins is on
her second ten minute
coffee break of the night
and she is thankful
that Paco had a little
bit of bourbon
and that he slipped
a two fingered shot
into her cup
she slips her thumb
inside her uniform
and under the tattered silk
of the strap
that slides off
and then below
her shoulder
more often than
she cares to admit
someone told her
that in big cities
like Lexington or Knoxville
rich women can
go to special places
where they can get a bra
that actually does its fucking job
she snaps the strap into place
feels it bite against her skin
Frosty feels the sting
it's not a bad sting
just a sting
to remind her
that other women
in other places
have things
she's never going to
like a bra that fits

Job Hunt

Don't have a name
for what echoes inside me.
Today, I'm a man as hollow
as a bulb, an upturned jar
waiting for some kind of light.

I Hear America Weeping

I hear America weeping, the diverse cries I hear,
Those of unemployed teachers, each one weeping for loss of
    purpose,
The automobile worker weeping as he beholds a factory closing in
    Detroit,
The recent college graduate weeping because she can't make ready
    for work,
The baker weeping as he makes less and less loaves, and his
    apprentice weeping as she punches the time clock for fewer
    and fewer hours,
The realtor weeping as more inventory adds to an ample supply, the
    stock trader no longer secure in his trade,
The grandmother weeping because Katrina washed her life out to
    sea,
The wildlife weeping for their habitat destroyed by *Deepwater
    Horizon*,
The homebuilder weeping as the bank forecloses on her dream,
The father weeping beside an interstate, holding a sign announcing
    his willingness to work for food,
The soldier weeping from a seven-year war, thousands of her
    comrades dead, missing, wounded,
The president weeping because hope was not enough to stop
    America's tears,
The disheartened voices of my fellow citizens weeping, their cries
    lingering throughout our immense and stricken land,
Each weeping what was lost to him or her, but to those willing to
    hear,
The remote voice of our America-loving poet, her melody urging us
    to believe,
we will sing again.

The Papers

Babe sits at the table
in the bright, white kitchen light
and pours a drop of coffee in my milk.
She laughs like a coyote at Red Skelton's latest plight.
My head leans on her knees that feel like silk.

She hands me half a Brillo pad and
we begin to scrub
the stove, the sink, the table and its chrome.
When gray linoleum's shining and
there's nothing left to rub,
we fill our cups and talk about her home.

Chorus:
Oval portrait of her love: all that woolly, black hair raging,
glowering at us from above on the wall.
And the praying hands of Jesus in a golden, lighted frame
sees us all, he sees us all.

"Well, I was doing mill work when I was just your age."
She says this as a fact, without regret.
Then she pulls out some papers from a little cedar chest —
a ritual that I won't soon forget.

"My dad was from Montana, a Blackfoot Indian boy,
the meanest indins in the old wild West."
I touch the papers' edges like
they are the sacred scrolls.
Her story takes the turn I like the best.

Chorus

"My daddy and his daddy joined
the troupe of Buffalo Bill.
They traveled east and camped out at the zoo.

They played the part of Indians in the wild west traveling show.
That wasn't hard because that part was true.

When grandpa got in trouble in a bar in Portsmouth town,
they sold my daddy to a farm up there.
These papers tell how daddy would work 'til 21 for
readin', 'ritin', 'rithmatic and care."

Chorus

Babe folds up the papers with her hands so smooth and brown
and tucks them very gently in their place.
The ceremony ended, we drink our coffee down
and share a little silence in our space.

Chorus:

> Oval portrait of her love: all that woolly, black hair raging,
> glowering at us from above on the wall.
> And the praying hands of Jesus in a golden, lighted frame
> sees us all, he sees us all.

A Prison Guard's Confessions to His Daughter

Clinton Correctional Facility, Dannemora, New York, 1964

Tonight I have to work the wall
he noted with dread, much more
than saying. His elbows, roosting
birds on the blue, smooth surface
of kitchen table, propped rugged hands
that braced a face of fear. In roiling disgrace,
he explained the wall,

its narrow walk, the guard station at each bend,
the intermittent rails. He spoke through fingers thick
with worry. *If it weren't for the rails, I couldn't do it.* He wore
a shroud of starched blue shirt, creased grey slacks.
I thought the wooden stick at his waist might keep him safe
from inmate crowds, guards gone sour. *But no,* he said,
the billy club's useless...you see, it's high
and narrow, that concrete wall. There's nothing,
nothing to save you if you fall.

He swore that all the cons inside the blocks
could be cajoled into flocks of ovine
sleep. But steep shoulders of sheer wall
swelled like abject fright, jailing him night
after cloistered night. He clutched
the worthless billy club tight, as in his mind
he fell and fell and fell.

Need to Know, March 1954

"Make atomic energy your future," read the poster inside the administration building where new Fernald workers got their first glimpse of the company. An assembly line of initiation, where they issued you an ID badge, a new set of clothes every shift, safety goggles and gloves, a pair of steel-toed boots, a goofy white paper hat and wooden shower clogs—like these would protect you. Doc Quigley ran you through his medical hokey-pokey. But before all that, you had to beat the FBI and their Q clearance, where they stripped your past down to the bone, and you'd better have been flying right or they'd toss you back like day-old fish.

The government meant business, no matter how friendly they tried to look with National Lead's Dutch Boy fronting for them. The feds wanted you to track every iota of material unloaded and loaded into those railroad cars at Fernald. They had guys weighing and sampling the dirt the minute they popped open the lids of the drums brought all the way from the Belgian Congo, or so Jeter'd heard. They measured the mix in the gulp pot. They counted the derbies and numbered the bars, calculated the purity of every hunk hauled out of that place. With the almighty right hand they examined and labeled and tried to keep pace with the paperwork, but Jeter bet the government would just as soon not know the left hand was releasing, pumping and dumping the runoff. He got the sickest feeling whenever they ordered him to drain the sump and shoot that waste over to Sewage on third shift.

Jeter could bounce his fears off nobody but himself because Clyde Bingham's Security warned that if a guy wants a job, let him have it but if he starts nosing and asking around, get rid of him because your country's got to have some secrets.

He followed mud tracks up the steps into Les Flick's bar, then sidled up to the first break in bodies.

John Steitz was saying, "My Paula don't know none of it."

Though Ray Missioner usually didn't speak without weighing majority opinion, he nodded. "You better be keeping your mouth shut about your output on the line."

When old Cliff Emminger leaned forward, his long arms embracing his beer, all the guys in between him and Ray sat up and out of the way of Cliff's eyeballing. Ray hunched over his beer.

"Well, they're working on your head, you know, until you're thinking anybody could be a goddamned spy," Cliff said. "Sitting right here at Flick's, ready to compromise American secrets if they could catch one of us bellyaching about a shoddy line neighbor or a piss-poor supervisor." He gulped as the crowd, mostly Fernald second shift, waited.

"Shit." Cliff waved like he might be ordering Jeter the drink he longed for, if he could just catch Les's eye. "Supervisors off by the panel board taking a smoke, pipes are leaking, pipes are hissing, a goddamned sieve, HF escaping. And what do they ask for? Yellow tape. That won't fix nothing. Production, production. Production comes first.

"You tape off the area like they tell you to—more yellow tape, the same damn tape you're hoping will hold the leak—until Ray here can get down to you with some piece of pipe, not new, mind you, something they took in from elsewhere and cleaned up so's you can use it because meeting that bottom line means they ain't going to buy you new parts. Stuff's in the air you're breathing until they get around to fixing with a used pipe from God-knows-where."

John's quiet voice wove in. "They took me on at the very beginning, said *If you can scratch gravel for six months you can keep on here*. Took their chances on this farm boy from Paintlick. Even when I came back from Korea they found me my same place in Six. We're so busy I could work seven days double shift every night if I wanted." He paused and swallowed. "I think I got a good job, and hey, it's a risk if you walk down the damned street, so..."

"I see no excuse for not being happy," Ray said. He looked around, maybe wanting confirmation or maybe searching for the spy who'd turn him in to old Clyde Bingham for talking.

Even among friends, Jeter knew they shouldn't have been grousing but he couldn't help adding his two cents. "We're some of the highest paid chem operators in the state." He brought $65 a week to Lydia.

Les took notice and started pulling a draft for him at last.

John nodded. "One of the best paying plants in the Ohio Valley."

With the mug lifted to his mouth, Jeter caught Les's eye. What cool relief, the Pabst sliding down his throat after breathing and eating the air of the plant. Normally he'd been on third, but Jeter took whatever shift they asked.

"All's I'm saying is you better learn how to dance," Cliff said. "The shit I've had to slog through over in Five this week? It ate up the soles on three pairs of boots."

Ray said, "You can go out the same road you came in. It's not blocked."

Everybody drank. Maybe Ray was a spy.

John shook his head. "Shit. I just want to keep my job."

"Don't we all?" Now that was more the Ray they knew.

John sighed. "The kind of leaks Cliff's talking about, spies couldn't care less. They want quantity and richness of metals we're shipping off."

"Well, hell, don't none of us know specifications like that. Everything's on a need to know basis, as you well know."

A joke, because Cliff and Jeter and any of them sitting there knew enough about what went on in the other eight buildings and the Pilot Plant. For as much as Clyde Bingham and the managers and even the company rag, *The Atomizer*, pounded "loose lips sink ships," a man was smart enough to see the process from beginning to end, if he'd just open his eyes. Some preferred to sleepwalk through their jobs, but that was being blind by choice.

Cliff drew himself up tall on the stool, and he *was* already taller than the rest of them. He imitated the foreman, Mr. Benedet, who they all knew despised third shift, not because of the workers but just on general principles. Every supervisor had to take a turn at it, in two weeks bumping down from first to second and then third, six weeks gone by before the whole rotation started up again. It was part of the foremen's responsibility, and probably why he cleared such good pay.

"Now you boys don't need to concern yourselves with what's happening down the line in plants other than your own." Cliff aped Benedet's nervous blink. "You don't care what happens to the green salt after you put it through the process and make it orange. All you need to know is that orange salt is precious to the race we're running with the Russians. To beat them out, we've got to count on every damn single one of you."

Jeter couldn't help himself. "So patriotic it almost makes you weep."

Laughter shook their shoulders, relaxed them some.

Cliff grabbed back the spotlight. "Well, you better not be whispering company secrets to your sweeties, now."

Who did Cliff think he was, telling guys what they could and couldn't talk about in bed?

Jeter leaned past John and Ray, and they arched back on their stools so Cliff had full view of him. "Maybe *your* woman ain't interested in where you've been and what you've been doing all day."

That drew a good laugh. Everybody knew that Cliff's wife, Junietta, could tell a story on just about all of them, their wives and the families they came from, the folks they'd gone to school with or had dated, even if it happened in another county. If Junietta didn't know, it wasn't known.

"Maybe Junietta's on government payroll," said John. He seemed pleased to be able to crack this small joke.

"Could be, could be," Cliff said. "The woman's got secrets I still ain't learned of."

Les slapped a wet dish rag on the bar. "You're into a bunch of Dutchmen out here, and they ain't going to tell you nothing anyhow." That seemed to punctuate the whole damned conversation, though he was the only one of them who'd never stepped inside the plant's perimeter.

Jeter quickly downed his beer. Maybe some of the guys had no women interested in what they did at the plant. Maybe, like Lydia, they were just grateful to see husbands walk through the door, eager to rub soft arms along those that, inside different sleeves earlier in the day, might have shot up to shield from a spill. What did Lydia know green salt from orange salt from the pure white out of the Morton's box from the pantry? It wasn't that she didn't care. She'd say, "I made you some noodle dumplings." And Jeter would thank his lucky stars he'd married her. He'd stand and stumble as he caught the picnic bench in his hurry-up legs. "Well, let's eat," he'd say.

What was he doing plopping even a few dear nickels on Les Flick's bar when Lydia had delicious things warming and waiting on him?

Lydia was trying to talk him out of working Easter.

"Someone has to run the lines at Fernald."

Lydia stubbed out her cigarette on her dinner plate. "It's not as if you haven't built up the comp time," she said. "Whenever Fernald calls, you fly in to the place."

Jeter scraped the food and spent cigarettes from her plate in the pail before he sank it in the dishpan. What she said made sense, but he worried if he lost his easygoing reputation he'd end up losing his job, too. Rumors of layoffs were floating around, especially with the unions threatening strike.

"What about that place draws you so?"

"You know Fernald pays wages better than most."

Her sarcastic laugh trilled. "You rarely treat yourself to anything with the piles of money you earn."

The plate in his hand dripped soap on the new linoleum he'd put down in October as he turned to watch Lydia adjust the sides of her robe and re-cinch the belt. She hadn't bothered getting dressed again today, and her belly swelled so lovely between her bust line and her hips. Even though she was pregnant, Doc Magel had her following some special diet.

"You're not eating enough," he said.

"I'm not hungry, and don't change the subject."

Jeter rinsed the plate. "I don't make piles of money." Wages were nothing to him at the moment.

Lydia grabbed a fresh dishcloth from the drawer and squatted to blot up the water around Jeter's feet. As her robe loosened again, he took in the sight of her straight through from neck to bottom.

"I've had money," Lydia said to the floor. "It's not enough of what's needed."

Jeter stuck the plate in the drip rack.

She said, "I know you're thinking disaster and financial emergency and, Jeter, that's your mama talking. You're a Depression baby, if ever there was one."

Next to him she tossed the dishcloth in the sink's suds, where it hardly made a sound, just absorbed bubbles and hot water as it sank. He could smell cigarette smoke and setting lotion in Lydia's hair, she stood that close.

"Disaster is the furthest thing from my mind," he said, her robe's silky material clinging as his wet hands touched her shoulders, then at her waist, finally settling on the curves he knew like the inside of his own mouth.

His hands roamed back up to feel her ribs. The thin fabric might as well have disappeared. Her hip bones were still prominent, making him think of knives.

He said, "I'll put in for the day off."

As they kissed, she swished her head this way and that. Jeter felt she was idling, with only half her brain engaged, half her heart. This division of affection confused him, and he wasn't sure how to go about angling for her one hundred percent. Wasn't that one thing marriage was supposed to have guaranteed?

Under his fingertips, Lydia's nipples weren't puckering like Jeter expected. He twisted one to what he thought had to be near painful, and that he liked the idea of hurting her just then scalded him.

"Pay attention," he said.

"What are you talking about?" She squirmed so his hand fell away and settled on her ribs. The right side of her head lay against his chest, leaving her left ear open to the sounds of the room.

This exclusion tapped into his other fear, the one that fell like a curtain between him and all the world's elements the few times he'd seen a guy throw a valve open too soon in the green salt plant.

Lydia took her arms back, she took everything back. She worked the robe's halves to conceal evidence of the child she was carrying.

Jeter turned on the tap and said, "Bring me that last dish."

She did. Slipping past Jeter's outstretched hand, she frowned at it dripping again over the linoleum, and picked up the pail of vegetable peels and parings and bones.

"I'm dumping this back in the weeds."

Jeter watched Lydia step outside. "Feeding the raccoons?" he teased.

He watched her walk without a coat, wearing some silly shoes for this soggy season—feathery slippers with high heels he'd bought her in Vegas, how many years ago? Seemed like ten or more since they'd gone anywhere but their own neighborhood. Lydia had a thing about leaving home. She didn't want to.

Jeter rubbed his eyes and tears soothed the itching. He'd do whatever Fernald asked. He welcomed the hum and jolt and non-stop commotion of the place, of being part of a greater purpose, a project of national security.

In the cafeteria he caught enough of stories to know the different plants each had pros and cons.

Furnaces in Plant Five ran so high they didn't need to tap into the boiler plant. Workers tore the sleeves out of their coveralls, bare arms against company rules and the strict safety standards the union had been demanding. You could give a lineman all the heads-up in the world, but if he ain't going to heed the caution, who's to blame?

In Six and Nine the lathes and shavers and saws made an ungoldly racket, and the heat of running all those machines, even in winter, meant they kept the doors wide open to breathe. Once Jeter had seen sparks on the floor, and full flames in some places licking the puddles of shavings. Whatever metal they cut, and it was probably uranium, the grinding required to meet specifications left plenty of extra to catch fire. They said when a piece of uranium hit the floor it crackled just like gunshot, said the stuff was combustible, that it would ignite all on its own. They'd have to call the fire department, the *company* fire troop, nothing from outside. The plant had its own laundry, fire department, cafeteria with three hot meals a day, showers and locker rooms, medical department and hospital.

The process Jeter contributed to in Plant Four put off a chemical that had etched the windows so you couldn't see in or out. The green salt they processed into orange worked its weird magic, causing snow on the roof to turn green as grass. Old George Wunder, Plant Manager, head honcho from NLO, had this little addage he worked in to every speech and every issue of the plant newsletter: *Plan your work and work your plan.*

Jeter didn't connect danger with Fernald any more than with the other manufacturing or chemical plants up and down the Miami River. Sometimes he'd drive over the bridge in New Haven and look down at water running blue or green or red, depending on what dyes Champion Paper up in Hamilton had dumped over night. Fernald wasn't the only plant with run-off.

Lydia came in smelling of wood smoke.

"Playing with matches?" Jeter teased.

"Someone's got a fire," she said.

He grinned. "Oh yeah?"

"Outside," she said.

He kissed her.

She pressed her hips into his, and Jeter imagined her standing outside, gathering the cold and smoky smells into her robe and her hair specifically to drive him crazy. He wanted to dive in and root it out of her. *Work your plan*, he thought, but it wasn't as simple as switching a valve or cutting back the pressure. He'd developed expertise in reading the bank-long gauges and meters that kept a lid on elements too dangerous to talk about, but fumbled in this romantic moment. Cliff Emminger would claim, "Pathetic. But you'd still best not spill your guts, using it for method in cozy-ing up with your woman." Cliff talked sense all Fernald workers subscribed to, but just once Jeter wished he could tell Lydia what spooked him when he walked third shift and caught steam escaping where he stood on the mezzanine, a lonely observer, taking on knowledge he had to swallow like the Alka-Seltzer.

Keeping Our Silence

In the heart of a government agency,
commonly known for stoics and taciturn
strategists in shiny suits, lives a poet,
humming with words.

Far down the block-long hall, an actor,
a dancer, and a weaver, at work in their
separate cubes, secretly ponder their arts,
savor their heart's desire.

After hours, they follow the music, whatever
form it takes. One plays his saxophone
on street corners in Georgetown. Another hits
the boards at theaters in and out of the beltway.

One carries paint past the scanners,
spends nights in her government office
painting bright colors on walls restricted
to gray, beige, or putty. No one stops her.

Evenings, we sip champagne,
tip cobalt blue stemware. Lights
on runways far below rise and fall. We write
our poems, otherwise keep our silence.

The Night Librarian

Tonight, the heft of books
and aching lives weigh her down
like grim cathedral hymns.
Outside, the moon pulls tides,
loiters with lovers,
sharpens knives. Inside,
fluorescent lights hum above
stacks of sleeping tomes.
She's quiet queen in this
realm of men—the old drunk,
face lit blue by computer screen,
lonesome widower bowed
over the current *Time*,
pimpled teen sprawled
reading Dumas. Some nights
she wants to ask them,
where else could you be?
Doesn't something linger,
calling your name?
Some nights she wants to shove
through the glass door, dance
along the sidewalk under that moon,
leave and never look back.
But dust settles, she sighs,
piles books on the cart.
She's the keeper of words,
light beyond thin glass
against darkness that howls.

Flightless

As Cory settled her back against the trunk of an ancient oak, a rueful muse reminded her that this place was as close to home as she'd seen in a year. She allowed that voice to soften her finely-honed edges. Pulling a jack knife from her pocket, she picked up a nearby pine knot and began whittling.

Grandpa had left Cory his carving tools and the gift for paring something from nothing. When Cory's parents died in an accident, Grandpa had become her guardian and she his farm hand. From the age of six, she grew resilient and resourceful. She could drive a combine, bail hay, and shear sheep as well as any teenager in FFA. Unfortunately, she couldn't solve Grandpa's financial woes, and when he "bought the farm" she lost her family, her home, her livelihood. Fight or flight? She signed on to the first job to come her way.

The gloom of evening came down just as Cory finished her carving. Returning the jack knife to her pocket, she smoothed and polished the finished sculpture with her fingers, allowing her own sweat and body oils to bring up the wood's grain.

Cory looked over the clearing, watched the fireflies rise, and yearned to, like them, fly above this world.

Around the fringe of the field, understated watch fires flickered. Once in a while a wave of laughter would find its way to her, but otherwise cricket song hushed the sound of humanity. An owl called from a limb above. As though hunting with Grandpa, Cory sat very still. Soon, her head nodded and the carving slipped from her hand.

Brrooooooommmmmmmmmm! A menacing rumble restarted her senses. Her eyes flew open to see lights stabbing and strobing the sky above the eastern tree line. Cory shuddered. Grandpa had taught her that the worst storms blew in from the east.

Her fingers combed the ground for her carving, a simple dove honed from a resilient knot of pine. She cupped it wistfully, then left it to take her place under the shelter of the spreading oak.

Standing, she clipped the strap of her helmet under her chin, gripped her rifle, and heeded the orders of her commanding officer. Uncle Sam was a relentless taskmaster.

Under the oak, the dove retained its poise as Cory's unit engaged the approaching tempest.

Forty-Two Seasons at Sea

All we have become
are bodies corroded with brine,
leathered and sour-blooded,
fingers like knotted frays of rope
from holding lives taut
against the madness of our own company
glaring as sun crests its ferocity
and home becomes a place bleached and forgotten,
left behind like our names.
We are re-chistened bosun or mate and
even captain holds no weight of a man
in its crusts of salt
licked away so easily
by one sweep over the bow.

We've seen dreams scurvied over
by the wakefulness of the sea,
its hunger for bones,
watched for signs of imagined shorelines
in the eyes of the sleepless,
blustered through mention of wife or sun.
And we are tired of the albatross
that trails a ship for days,
finds it cannot follow to port,
that its wings are too wide
for gasps of inland winds,
that its only course
is of waves that rise and vanish
and no one remembers their passing.

Circle

my brothers
old past what they looked then
went to clean up the old house after
the river opened the front door
they came back home the long way
with what was left
after the flood
a three-legged table
a copper pot
the clock with just a minute hand
they were sapped
hollow

there is little I remember of it
but I do remember how
they said that at night
with the wind hard and the rain still steep
they would lay under the wagon to sleep
no pillows
only the others' feet
three brothers: head to foot, foot to head
a cold tired circle
hiding from the rain on the way back home
I'll never forget that

Silent Hope
(Clark's Childhood Memory, 1946)

When news came my father was returning from war, Mother left to meet him on the West Coast. Aunt Mary and J.D. drove me from the Mississippi Delta to the Tennessee River hills where my grandparents had me a warm feather bed, a dog-trot for my toys and a sooner hound named Bob.

That night, I stared out the dark window hoping by some miracle to see my mother's small frame, when a truck door slammed and a man's dark shape walked across the porch. A commercial fisherman from Perryville had rammed two large fish hooks in his one good hand, had driven with elbows up the bluff for GrandMilt to cut them out.

Extra lanterns were lit around the kitchen table, while GrandSally boiled thread. The fisherman slowly spread his cramped claw for us to see, one hook buried in the palm, the other in the index finger. My grandfather poured the only whiskey served in the house, a glass for the man and the rest into a washbowl. I watched as he forced the barbs through flesh and skin, clipped them off, then pulled the shafts back out. He lanced the punctures so they would bleed and held the man's hand in the bloody moonshine without a word. GrandSally sewed the wounds, bandaged them with strips of sheet and Milt drove him home. I fell asleep that night awestruck that I had witnessed what I had only heard about from books.

Soon my homesickness eased with days filled with feeding tomato peels to chickens and running the close fields with old Bob. Nights after supper, my dark window showed dreams of my mother's return, her tense smile melted into my father's arms, and I would remember the tight shoulders of that fisherman as he moved toward the silent hope of my grandparents, cradling his good hand in his left arm like a child.

My Father and Steel

I don't know much
about my father and steel.

I own his hardhat and belt buckle,
his social security card,

a Polaroid of his retirement party
in the maintenance shack

at Edgar Thomson where he worked
for forty-seven years.

He slices a sheet cake,
a crucible of white

heat iced onto it.
He and his smiling comrades,

millwrights, wear asbestos:
Pete Roman,

Joe Cockaruda,
Sam Garritano,

Bucky Williams,
Cigar Sam Wyland –

hacked like I-beams
into the tiny brown pad my father carried,

but never wrote in.
Just certain names.

Afterbirth

for my father

Your death was a short
hard labor, both our bodies
given up to it. You worked
to leave your flesh,
I to let you. Pains came
in waves to make you groan,
me weep, regular as the beeps
of the watch you still glanced at
on your wrist. Breathe,
just breathe, I'd say,
kneading your shoulder
and palm, an effleurage of calm.
It will pass.
At the end
I had you, still and lovely
in your peace, still warm
beneath my hands and lips.

awake

it's true, the last few days, 10 in fact, i've been in a state of constant sleep and
wake and eat and rejoice and cry and celebrate and new life and breath and
breathe and exaltation and exhalation and kisses and dirty diapers and genie
garbage pails and el malecon chicken with rice and beans and tostones with
salt and hot sauce and cluster feedings and sore breasts and love, love, love
and my heart wide and flailing and another, smaller set of lungs and a heart
too, and two fists and two feet, ankles and a chest and an open eyed little
baby girl who we call birdie sometimes and little bird because she is, and
smart and sophisticated and genius and batgirl of wings and whistles and
family and directions for swings and the alphabet and *new york magazine*,
bankrupt hospitals and c-section scars and recovery and abdomen opened
and Ibuprofin and nursing and naked house girl, me, and *parents magazine*
and reading, reading and poet-ing and writing and praying and paying
bills and baby bird asleep and my own wings of absolute and love, love and
harbor.
you are all and all. each day with a freshness. all.

The Last Woman in America to Wash Diapers

lugs the full pail down to the first floor,
heaves it in the washer, makes it spin its offal load.
How many diapers has she sloshed in the toilet,
how many neatly folded stacks has she raised skyward,
soft white squares of cotton, pieces of cloud,
how many double and triple folds has she pinned
on little bottoms? How many nights
of checking beds did she find those buns
raised in the air, loaves resting on a bakery shelf?
She knows the power of bleach, the benefits of rinsing.
On winter nights, when the snow comes down
in glittery drifts, she sees Ivory Flakes,
their slippery iridescence. When it comes
to dealing with the shit in her life,
nothing else is so simple, so white, so clean.

After Reading Sylvia Plath in Appalachia, 2005

I knew you weren't sick, Daddy, that there wasn't
a cold you *just couldn't shake off*. You didn't
need all that medicine, or all those batteries,
either. We didn't have fancy toys.
I knew that stuff you mixed underneath
the porch was dangerous.
Nothing good smells that bad.

Are you in hell, Daddy? Preacher
says no one knows what was in your
heart, says maybe you were making that stuff
to sell because you really needed money,
but Mommy says, *He was a selfish*
son of a bitch too lazy to work for a dollar.
She says you are going to rot in hell
for what you did. Hell must be hot,
and I don't want you to be hot.
You loved when summer ended
and the leaves started to change,
said there was hope in the smell
of dead leaves. I hate you

like you hated summer, the way
it made you sweat through
your t-shirts. But I don't want you
to burn. Did you burn
when the house blew up?
Did you even feel it?
Did you have time
to think of me and hope
I hadn't come home from school yet?
You were supposed to come
to my soccer game. I needed new shoes,
Daddy, but I could have waited—
I could have gone without.
I could have gone without.

No Fairytale

A better morning, for I'm not standing in four inches of basement water. Oh yesterday, when I could not go back to sleep at 2:30 a.m. and decided to fill the chlorinator system—water, water everywhere in the basement. So I checked the sump pump (a little one-armed pump that sits in a hole, measures water depth and pumps surface water out when it rains), unplugged it, fished it out of the sump hole, plugged it back in and SMOKE. Not a good sign. I grabbed the mop bucket and started to bail, but there was so much water in the sump hole and water is heavy. My arms are not what they used to be. I could not get ahead of it. Though I didn't want to, I woke my husband.

David waded straight into it with me. Cold-ass water, barefoot, 2:35 a.m. I tell you, it was a Kodak moment. He rolled his jammys up like knickers and took the green plastic bucket from my hands. Over and over, fast, fast he bailed and bailed and bailed and bailed. Seventy years old. Heart trouble. Bladder cancer. Entrapped sciatic nerve. Blood clots in both legs. Fingers mashed and cut off in a mill accident. Tired and needing his sleep. He rose to save our tiny house in the country, the bread we have baked and eaten together these forty years.

Under the trouble light, I kissed him and we laughed (for what else is there to do?), both my knees stiff, creaking, aching (so much I can no longer kneel). He did. He knelt on the cold cement, the watery floor and put his shoulder to the wheel of night work we had to do. And then, together we bailed bucket after bucket from the floor.

The water kept coming in.

There has been rain for two days, and water doesn't know what time it is. It follows the path of least resistance. At some point the floor is ready for newspapers. I gather them from the recycling pile. I carry soaked throw rugs to our back porch banisters. It's very dark. Quiet. Only the stars see me in my old flannel gown. Hair all asunder. No panties, bare, wet, cold feet on the porch. Grunge on my hands, forearms and under my nails. The hands of a nurse? Icky, but doing my work, helping as I can this man, this doctor who holds our old sump pump in his hands to check its parts. No heart beat. He is a magnificent fixer. Alas, the rusty bolts collapse and it falls, ruined pieces hit and hit the floor. It crumbles like a handful of leaves.

Kapoot, it's done for, David says to me, to himself, to the basement. The pump had served us well, but even a sump pump's heart has only so many beats, and when the end came, we were not present. It drowned. It drowned as it had lived. In darkness. In cold water. Alone. Crying out? I don't know. A machine must feel something when its time approaches. So many parts to a sump pump. (Who knew?)

I walk upstairs to call the only all night store—Wal-Mart—which I hate, but now it's the only store open. The girl who answers says, "What's a sump pump?" You know when you live in the country you need them in your basement to pump surface water out because there's no sewage system. "Oh," she says for a long time, "I'll talk to somebody in hardware." There's a wait, but she's trying to hunt for an answer. Answers are time-consuming especially when the question is not really yours and the vocabulary is foreign and it's 3:15 a.m. in the morning. "We don't have those, sorry," her young voice finally says. Okay, I tell her and hang up. I find another number. Lowes. I call and get a recording. *Thank you for calling Lowes. Your call is important to us. If you're calling about the store hours, we don't open again until 6 a.m.* My heart leaps up and does a shaky dance under my breastbone. In three more hours we can buy a new sump pump. We have to bail until then, but hey, we can do it.

Back I go to the cellar carrying my bit of good news. David is cleaning a part from the sump pump's hose. We find two big fans, plug them in to help with convection. For no apparent reason, I think about febrile children, how often I taught parents how to give tub baths as a way to hasten breaking fevers in sick kids. I used to work pediatrics, full time, midnights. It was thirty years ago. Can that be possible?

David turns to me. What about opening a couple of windows? To help with the process of drying. Yes, I say, good idea. It's only forty-five or fifty degrees outside, but it might help. David's hair is snow white. This is no fairytale. This home we've made together. This yellow house we have plumbed and hammered, shaped and roofed and painted is ours. But not for long. We're just passing through (as the cowboy says), and our horses needed water. We needed a bed and some grub. Soon, we'll be the stars and grass and every pink sunset.

Who will love this house for us? Who will rise in the night when it weakens and can not cry out? Who will kneel to scrub its floors and wrestle the God of water in its basement? Who will dress quickly and have the good sense to fix the hard parts as they wear down, wear out? Who will they be? This couple who is out there now struggling with letters and numbers and broken crayons. This freckled boy who has just learned how to tie his tennis shoes. This pony-tailed girl letting teacher trace her small hands on manila paper. Are they the ones? Are they the ones who'll stumble into each other on the shady sidewalk at college and start talking? Get married? See the FOR SALE sign in this front yard? Be handed a key that will open to my bright kitchen? The land of a thousand meatloaves and a million blessings.

Braid

Each side divided, three by three, the kneading
warms down to my toes, a ragdoll on the stool.
I have begged until she relents, comb parting
the middle to the ticklish nape, strange feel of egg
broken, seeping. *Your mama don't like this,*
but she keeps on, her girth like an oak behind me.
Plaiting, she calls it, crossed over and under,
rope stronger than many fallen loose. I am secretly
glad Mama won't like it, the waves going crazy
unspooled. I think nothing of how long my grandmother
stands, her corns and bunions, boxy shoes cut away
to ease their throb, nothing of her shoulders' ache
at the factory machine, its constant harangue
on the bus, at supper, in her toothless sleep. I think
she is spinning the straw of my hair to gold,
wheel oiled in the old retelling. Come morning,
her handiwork aglow, I know we will never be parted,
her uncomplaining days braided in every hair
of my head, her presence even now bound
sure as first memory.

Lockjaw

Flossie White grieved mightily
because she was barren.
Dennis Hicks, her brother,
educated and sworn to treat
the ills of mankind,
should have known
the oath he took didn't mean
to leave women out.
But he was deaf to women's hurts.
Besides, he didn't have
the patience of a gnat.
He told Flossie to stop carrying on
and find a child to love.
She sat in a dark cloud for many days.

That was before *his* daughter Matilda
passed away from lockjaw,
twenty-six years old,
wife of Elijah Ault, the sheriff,
mother of Lavinia, aged three.

He couldn't understand
how it happened.
Just a scratch from a stob
in the fencerow.
He told her to put iodine on it.
He'd treated worse hurts
hundreds of times.

When Matilda came down with fever,
headache, sore throat,
he thought it a summer complaint.
He didn't worry till Elijah
told of her stiff neck and limbs.
Her locked jaw set him into a panic.

He knew the gut-wrenching spasms,
the death coma would follow.
He could do nothing,
but help Elijah hold her on the bed,
whisper his love.

Now, he sweats whiskey,
his hands twitter,
feet clatter
like a limberjack
dancing on a paddle.

Plastic Surgery

Barbie's had some work
since the sixties;
these breasts perk,
hips curve like drumsticks.
The first to operate complained,
"Nipples look like pitted prunes."
Snip. Today no flab mars her silhouette.
Little girls still ooh and ah over Barbie's
blonde tresses, wedding dresses, glittery gowns.
But when play time is done,
Barbie and her sisters lie at rest,
arms outstretched, ready for the next playdate.

Next to them lies a smiling Ken, asexual
as the girls. An abandoned tangle of naked legs,
he and Barbie cannot make even their eyes meet.
Imagine how they might have looked,
loose boobs draping one over another,
Ken's head at rest on a soft belly.

Paradiso Lost

When you tell people you run film projectors for a living, there are typically three questions they will ask you about it. The first is if you watch all of the movies that you show. When I was a projectionist, my answer to that was always that I am like the baker who doesn't eat the bread she sells. When I get off from work, the last thing I want to do is stay longer and watch a movie. The second question is if you have ever spliced a frame of pornography into a kids' film, like Brad Pitt did in *Fight Club*. People don't seem to realize that home video has made actual film prints of pornographic movies almost non-existent. If I had a 35-millimeter print of a porno, I'd tell them, I definitely wouldn't be chopping it up into frames. I would be selling it on eBay. The last question is whether you have seen *Cinema Paradiso*.

For years, my answer to that was no. I knew the gist of the movie—an old man works as a film projectionist in a small Italian town and takes a young boy under his wing, whom he inspires to become a filmmaker. I avoided seeing it for so long because I had no desire to romanticize a profession that I considered to be a mindless day (well, usually night) job. Running projectors was what I was doing until someone decided to give me a real film industry job, not an end in itself.

I did finally see the movie, however, after I had soured enough on the film industry to give up wanting to be a part of it and started writing fiction instead. Much to my surprise, I came away from *Cinema Paradiso* thinking I should have watched it years before. Alfredo, the projectionist character, doesn't romanticize the job at all; he sees it for what it is: a dead end. He wouldn't have made me complacent; on the contrary, he would've kicked even the tiniest amount of complacency out of me, just as he does Toto, the boy who ensnares him in a trade-off to make him his projectionist protégé. Alfredo resists teaching him for as long as he can, pretending to dislike the boy to scare him off. Before Toto suckers him into their deal, the boy asks Alfredo why he won't teach him how to run the projector and Alfredo becomes adamant, saying:

> Because I don't want to, Toto! This is not a job for you. It's like being a slave. You're always alone. You see the same film over and over again, because you have nothing else to do. . . . You work on holidays, on Christmas, on Easter. Only on Good Friday are you free. But if they hadn't put Jesus Christ on a

cross… you'd work Good Fridays too!

Amen, I thought as I read those subtitles. I had spent many Christmases, Thanksgivings, and even Good Fridays in the booth watching families come in after big dinners and see movies about other families enjoying their holidays together. A couple of times when my parents visited me on a holiday I had to work, I sneaked them into the booth and we ate Chinese takeout or deli sandwiches on a grimy desk surrounded by the mechanical whir of several projectors. It's the being together that counts, I told myself, even as I envied each audience member who got up and left the theater after their movie was over.

Later in *Cinema Paradiso*, when Toto is grown, Alfredo insists that he leave the booth and their little town in Sicily to make his own way in the world. "I don't want to hear you talk anymore," Alfredo tells him, shooing him unmercifully out of a nest that is no longer serving any purpose except to hamper his growth. "I want to hear talk about you." He tells Toto that if he comes back to the little town, he won't even let him in his house. By this time Alfredo is not only a grizzled old pro, but blind from a nitrate film explosion that happened when Toto was still a boy. Through his physical blindness, Alfredo can see that this fresh-faced young man who took the old man's place in the booth after his accident is already becoming a carbon copy of himself. If Toto doesn't make a break now, he will never get out.

When I first started out as a projectionist in Blacksburg, Virginia, I worked at a downtown theater built in the 1920s that had fallen into disrepair. I began as a volunteer just when the community was getting behind it and making plans to renovate it. By the time I graduated college three years later, I had become a paid employee and the theater had received a major facelift. What was once a big dank room with broken seats and dirty wall tapestries was now a showplace where little kids sat in a balcony for the first time in their lives, where college kids (including myself) went on dates, and where people from all around the region saw artsy movies that were previously only available to them on video months after their theatrical runs.

The movie theater is the place where, like Toto in *Cinema Paradiso*, I learned what sacred felt like. Although I didn't cross myself when I entered the Lyric like he did at his theater (maybe I would have if I had been raised Catholic), I treated the place like a church, polishing everything from the popcorn popper to the films themselves if they arrived dirty or in disrepair. Working there made me feel like a bright, shining cell in a great, luminous body. Not only did I care deeply about the films and the place itself, but also about the people who came there, who were just as excited about it all as me. And *everyone* came to the Lyric, just like everyone came to the Paradiso. We were all caught up in this vibrant endeavor together, laughing and crying and talking endlessly about the movies we saw, while breathing life back into our shared downtown at the same time.

As my college days drew to a close, however, I knew that my time in that snug, hallowed nest would have to end as well. That day came a couple months after I graduated, when I left Blacksburg for New York City to begin an unpaid internship at a film production company. As I toiled away painting blood on severed limbs for *The Toxic Avenger IV* in a stuffy Brooklyn warehouse, telling myself I was turning my filmmaking dreams into a reality, the Lyric itself began to feel like a dream. Although I was finally not just watching films but helping make them, I missed the community of the Lyric and the feeling that I was a unique part of it. On the film set, I was no different from any other free pair of hands, but at the Lyric I was known and loved. There was no going back, though, because as Alfredo tells Toto in *Cinema Paradiso*, "When you're here every day you feel like you're at the center of the universe; it seems like nothing ever changes. Then you go away, one year, two . . . and when you come back, everything's different. The thread has broken."

No, I couldn't go back, but being a projectionist at the Lyric remains the most fun job I have ever had. While it didn't pay the most, it made me happy and also gave me the skills I needed to join the film projectionists' union in New York City. Several theater companies were opening multiplexes in Manhattan when I moved there, so for the first time in many years, the union was looking for new members. I needed something to pay the bills and since I already had three years' experience in the booth, I got the fast track and ended up working at Sony's Lincoln Square, and later AMC's Empire Theater in Times Square, both of which are still two of the top-grossing multiplexes in the country. Going from making eight dollars an hour in small-town Virginia to twenty-seven dollars an hour in New York City in a matter of months made me think I had hit some kind of big-time. At first.

While the machinery was pretty much the same, being a projectionist at a multiplex for a major theater chain was a completely different world from working at a single-screen non-profit. Since my crew members and I didn't split our days into shifts and Manhattan theaters open early and close late, my workdays were usually no less than thirteen hours on a weekday and seventeen on a weekend. A few times when we had special events, like a midnight opening of the last *Star Wars* movie or the world premier of *King*

Kong, I worked a full twenty-four. I spent most of my workdays alone and was contractually obligated not to leave the booth while on duty, which meant a lot of packed lunches, take-out dinners, and quick wash-ups in the employee bathroom.

Every hour or two, I would get up from one of the ratty chairs that had been cast off from the manager's office and thread a round of projectors, eventually getting my time down to two minutes or less per film. Speed was much more important at the multiplex than at the Lyric because I was now responsible for not just one projector, but twelve. If I lost track of time while reading or writing, as I often did, I would have to run to get a movie on screen on time.

Like the Lyric, multiplexes at that time were on a platter system, which means each film is not broken into reels, but rests as a whole on a timed platter and feeds from its middle into the projector, then back onto another spinning platter. Unlike the Lyric, however, multiplexes used this system to shoehorn as many screens as possible into one location. Since films can start on timers and one projectionist can potentially run a large number of machines, overhead is kept low while the number and variety of films is kept high.

Platters were the big new things a few decades ago and displaced many projectionists like Alfredo in *Cinema Paradiso*, who learned to run one film at a time, one reel at a time. Even though the Lyric used platters as well, it had only one screen and we didn't use a timer, so when I started a movie there it was a holy ritual, just like at a reel-to-reel theater. I would wait in the lobby until about a minute before time for the show and if people were still coming in, I'd wait a little longer, letting them get in and find seats. Then I would start my climb up the carpeted stairs, make my way past a row of teenagers or college kids who liked the seclusion of the balcony, up another set of steps and into the booth. I always got things ready early, so the projector fans would be droning when I got there and a ribbon of film would be hanging from the top roller of the platter to the top roller of the projector. I would look out the port window as my finger hovered over the start button and take in the people, the blank screen, the anticipation. Then, *click*. My finger would press down, the lamp would pop on, the gears would chatter, and the film would start to move. I'd wait for the shutter to clang open and take a look at the screen before leaving, making sure the image was in focus and properly framed before starting my slow descent through the now-darkened theater.

Starting a movie at the multiplex was a non-event because I was almost never standing at the machine when it happened. Films would start and end all day around the desk where I sat, but the sound would inspire nothing more in me than a casual awareness that things were running as they should. It was this kind of sense-deadening routine that soon made me realize that the job I had originally thought was a sign of great fortune was actually drudgery. Alfredo would have lambasted me for taking a safe route like this, which was never even really safe, just familiar.

Ever since my first day on the job in April of 2000, I knew digital projection was a looming threat to every projectionist in New York. Digital was the next big thing and once theaters began converting to it, the effects on the industry would be much more devastating than what had happened when platters were put into use. Projectionist job loss would be almost total because digital projectors are completely automated and require no film handling at all. One minimally-trained person can program an entire multiplex in the morning and barring any problems, the movies will start and run on their own for the rest of the day, in the same pristine condition as they did the first time. No scratches, no dirt, no misframes.

"Don't plan on having this job more than five years, maybe ten at the most," the booth chief at Lincoln Square told me when I first started there. I knew he meant this to scare me, but I was relieved to hear it. I didn't want to get comfortable in the job and knowing it had an expiration date wouldn't let me.

"That's fine with me," I told him. "I hope to be doing something else by then, anyway."

He looked hurt when I said this, and I worried that I had offended him. He had a mortgage and three kids, one with severe diabetes, and very much wanted to hold onto this job that paid well and provided health insurance, no matter how boring the work was or how long the hours. I had only myself to take care of and although I also appreciated the money and the insurance, I couldn't let myself be satisfied with those things. I wanted to make my own art, not just show other peoples'.

So I continued to work low and unpaid jobs in the film industry and dream about one day leaving this unstable security that felt like a trap. Eventually, however, those unrewarding jobs and the long, lonely booth hours killed any desire I had to see most movies, let alone make them. I began writing fiction instead, which was much more gratifying to me than planning films that never got made. When I was done writing, I had a finished product, not something that still needed to go through several more people and processes before it was complete. In the three years following the switch, I started working toward a Master's degree in creative writing, got a story published, and finally let myself see *Cinema Paradiso*.

Now that I wasn't interested in making movies anymore, though, I resented the long booth hours even more. Each year that passed brought more talk of the digital takeover and more bad morale amongst my crew-members. We would bicker between ourselves constantly about things like who didn't clean the desk the night before, or who started a show late. But the only real question in any of our minds was whether to hold out for unemployment or find something new before the bottom fell out.

I found something new. It was the summer of 2008 and my year-old Master's degree was gathering dust. Rather than wait for an uncertain severance package, I found a low-paying adjunct teaching job at a community college. That job is insecure, too, because whether or not I have a class to teach depends upon enrollment, but so far, that hasn't been a problem. With the economy sinking lower and lower, many people who are out of work are returning to school to start new careers or just bide time until perhaps their previous employer calls them back.

In the two years since I left the booth, almost all professional projectionists in New York City have joined this group of job seekers. This is because every major New York multiplex, including the two I worked at, has now completely converted to digital projection. This saddens me in a way I never thought it would. It's not that I want to go back – I am very thankful to be able to teach writing for a living – but I do have a hard time getting used to the idea that projectionists are no longer the bakers who don't eat their own bread. Now we are the blacksmiths who had to scramble to learn a new trade after the Model T was invented. Of course, there is no stopping progress no matter what the industry, but since we can't all be film directors like Toto, or make do on minimum wage, what is it exactly we're supposed to do?

Recently, while visiting my parents in Virginia, I returned to the Lyric Theater and found the experience just as Alfredo said it would be. Most of the people I knew were gone and even though the place looked the same, the atmosphere had changed. It was no longer a new, exciting venture, but an entrenched institution. People who were kids when I first started working there thirteen years ago have now grown up with the place and will probably bring their kids there one day. It hasn't converted to digital yet, but undoubtedly it eventually will to stay competitive with the nearby multiplex. I don't think it's likely to meet the same fate as the theater at the end of *Cinema Paradiso* – it's demolished due to declining audiences, which the owner says is a result of TV and home video – but the day the 35-millimeter projector is dragged out, a little piece of me will go with it.

Poem to Non-Poets

You probably think writing poetry
is an odd pursuit,
a little worse
than stamp-collecting,
but better than necrophilia.

I know: you make the world go.

What I do is build these little constructions,
places to sit, to contemplate,
to love the dappled world a little more.
You'll have to trust I'm not just wasting time,
goofing off. I admit it looks a lot like goofing off.

Notes on Contributors

Darnell Arnoult is writer-in-residence at Lincoln Memorial University where she teaches writing and literature classes and co-directs the annual Mountain Heritage Literary Festival. She is the award-winning author of the novel *Saving Grace* and the poetry collection *What Travels With Us*. She is much in demand as a writing workshop leader, teacher, and speaker.

Victoria Bailey has worked as an animal cage cleaner, a waitress, a longshoreman, a meter reader, and a parking enforcement officer. She is now the co-owner of a small land surveying company in western Kentucky. She considers writing poetry her real work and is a member of Green River Writers.

Janice Willis Barnett writes from her home in Unicoi, Tennessee. She is the author of *Unicoi and Limestone Cove* (Arcadia Publishing.) Her essays have appeared in numerous anthologies and journals. She is also a frequent contributor to West Virginia Public Broadcasting's "Inside Appalachia."

Jennifer Barton grew up in southwestern Virginia and currently teaches writing in Knoxville, Tennessee. She completed her MFA in Creative Writing at The New School in New York City in 2007. Her stories have appeared in *Pindeldyboz, Lost, Hawk and Handsaw, Kudzu, Motif v2: Come What May, Wilderness House Literary Review* and *Pine Mountain Sand & Gravel.* She recently completed her first novel.

Marilyn Bates, author of *It Could Drive You Crazy*, is a "Poet in Person" with the International Poetry Forum and a fellow of the National Writing Project at the University of Pittsburgh. Her work has appeared in *The MacGuffin, The Paterson Literary Review, One Trick Pony, Poet Lore* and *The Potomac Review* and anthologized in *Pass-Fail, My Auntie's Book, Voices in Italian America, Along These Rivers* and *What Rough Beast: Poems at the End of the Century*. Her one-act play, *Life Without Nipples*, was produced by the Pittsburgh New Works Theater Festival in 2007.

Joseph Bathanti's poetry collections are *Communion Partners, Anson County, The Feast of All Saints, This Metal* (National Book Award nominee), *Land of Amnesia* and *Restoring Sacred Art*. His novel, *East Liberty*, won the 2001 Carolina Novel Award. His latest novel, *Coventry*, won the 2006 Novello Literary Award. His book of stories, *The High Heart*, won the 2006 Spokane Prize. He is the recipient of Literature Fellowships from the North Carolina Arts Council in 1994 (poetry) and 2009 (fiction), the Sherwood Anderson Award, and many others. He teaches at Appalachian State University

David Baxter lives and writes in Bowling Green, Kentucky. He is an elementary school teacher and a producer of Barren River Breakdown, a weekly roots music radio broadcast airing on WKYU-FM. His stories have appeared in all three Motif anthologies.

Bill Brown just retired as a part-time lecturer at Vanderbilt University. He has authored five poetry collections, three chapbooks and a textbook. His three current collections are *The News Inside* (Iris Press, 2010), *Late Winter* (Iris Press, 2008) and *Tatters* (March Street Press, 2007). Recent work appears in *Prairie Schooner, North American Review, Tar River Poetry, English Journal, Southern Poetry Review, Connecticut Review, Atlanta Review, Asheville Poetry Review* and *Southern Humanities Review*. Brown wrote and co-produced the ITV series, "Student Centered Learning" for Nashville Public Television, and has been the recipient of many poetry fellowships.

Lauren J. Bryant was raised in Louisville, Kentucky, and settled in Indiana after experimenting with life on both coasts. She is co-editor of *Women with Wings: An Anthology* (Pen & Publish, 2009) and author of the chapbook *Now Comes the Petitioner* (Finishing Line Press, 2011).

Jeanne Bryner is a graduate of Trumbull Memorial's School of Nursing and Kent State University's Honors College. She has received writing fellowships from Bucknell University, the Ohio Arts Council and Vermont Studio Center. She has a new play, *Foxglove Canyon*, and her books in print are *Breathless, Blind Horse: Poems, Eclipse: Stories, Tenderly Lift Me: Nurses Honored, Celebrated and Remembered* and *No Matter How Many Windows*.

Bobbi Buchanan, MFA, teaches writing at Jefferson Community and Technical College. A Kentucky Foundation for Women grant recipient, she received the 2010 nonfiction prize from *Still: The Journal* for her essay "In the Woods," selected by acclaimed writer Janisse Ray. Her work has appeared in *Motif v2: Come What May, The New York Times, The Louisville Review, The Courier-Journal, Literary Mama* and other publications.

Julie Buffaloe-Yoder is a recipient of the Ohio Arts Council's Individual Award in Excellence for poetry. Her work has appeared or is forthcoming in several journals, including *Southern Women's Review, Calyx: A Journal of Art and Literature by Women, Trailer Park Quarterly, storySouth, Grain Magazine, Ouroboros Review* and *The Raleigh Review*. Her chapbook, *Price Reduced Again*, is available through Backpack Press.

Jeremy Byars' first poetry collection, *Eyes Open to the Flash*, was published in 2008. His poems and reviews have appeared in many journals, most recently or forthcoming in *Verse Wisconsin, Writer's Bloc, Pirene's Fountain, Welter* and *Stymie*.

Sherry Chandler lives on a small farm outside Paris, Kentucky, with her husband, the woodcarver T. R. Williams. Her poetry has appeared or is forthcoming in *Calyx: A Journal of Art and Literature by Women, Light, Kestrel* and *Verse Wisconsin*. Her poetry collection is *Weaving a New Eden* (Wind Publications, 2011).

Lucia Cherciu is Associate Professor of English at SUNY/ Dutchess in Poughkeepsie, New York . She published two books of poetry in Romanian, *The Abandonment of Language* (Editura Vinea, 2009), and *Grafted Laughter* (Editura Brumar, 2010). Her writing appears in *Riverine, WaterWrites, ESL Magazine, ISLE, Off the Coast, TETYC, Chronogram, Journal of the Short Story in English* and others.

James Cihlar is the author of the poetry book *Undoing* (Little Pear Press) and chapbook *Metaphysical Bailout* (Pudding House Press), and he has placed his writing with *American Poetry Review, Prairie Schooner, Mary, Rhino, Painted Bride Quarterly, Emprise Review, Verse Daily* and *Forklift, Ohio*. The recipient of a Minnesota State Arts Board Fellowship for Poetry and a Glenna Luschei Award from Prairie Schooner, James is a Visiting Instructor at the University of Minnesota in Minneapolis and Macalester College in St. Paul.

Suzanne Coker lives and works near Birmingham, Alabama. Her writing has been described as "fearless" and seeks the uncertain area between personal experience and philosophical inquiry. Her poems have appeared in *Birmingham Arts Journal, Motif v1: Writing by Ear* and the Big Table Poets collections *Poems from the Big Table* and *Einstein at the Odeon Café*.

Samantha Cole is a recent graduate of Berea College with a major in Appalachian Studies. She was a student editorial assistant at *Appalachian Heritage* magazine. Her work was most recently published in *Still: The Journal*. She hails from Beattyville, Kentucky.

G.C. (Gayle) Compton has worked as a coal miner, mail carrier, broadcast journalist, English teacher and service coordinator for a heavy equipment company. Nominated for the Pushcart Prize by *New Southerner* in 2010, he has been published in numerous literary journals and anthologies. His short story collection is *Black Lung Washing Machine* (Wind Publications, 2011). G.C. works, writes and fights mountaintop removal coal mining in Pike County, Kentucky.

Sean L. Corbin lives in the poetry section of Camden-Carroll Library in Morehead, Kentucky. He has served as co-editor of *Inscape* (Morehead State University) and has published work in *Inscape, Aurora, Still: The Journal* and *Vinyl Poetry*. With Christopher Prewitt, Corbin is co-founder of *Antilachia*, a writing collective interested in introducing new aesthetics to Appalachian literature.

Wayne Cresser is an Associate Professor of English at a small New England college. He is also co-founder and managing editor of the online journal, *Shaking Lit*. When he can manage, he blogs on things pop cultural at www.popkrazy.com. His fiction has been nominated for several awards and prizes and published in the previous two Motif anthologies and in numerous print and online journals including *Wandering Army* and *Long Story Short*.

Barbara Crooker's books are *Radiance*, winner of the 2005 Word Press First Book Award and finalist for the 2006 Paterson Poetry Prize; *Line Dance* (Word Press, 2008), winner of the 2009 Paterson Award for Excellence in Literature; and *More* (C&R Press, 2010). Her poems appear in a variety of literary journals and many anthologies, including *Good Poems for Hard Times* and the *Bedford Introduction to Literature*.

Ann Curran, author of *Placement Test*, is a contributing editor of *Pittsburgh* magazine. Her poetry has appeared recently in *Ireland of the Welcomes, Notre Dame Magazine, Off the Coast, Pittsburgh Post-Gazette,* and the anthologies *Along These Rivers, Thatchwork, and Motif v2: Come What May*. She edited *Carnegie Mellon Magazine* and taught English at Duquesne University.

Anthony D'Aries received the 2010 PEN/New England Discovery Award in Nonfiction. He is a graduate of the Stonecoast MFA program and served as Randolph College's 2011 Emerging Writer-in-Residence. His work appears or is forthcoming in *The Literary Review, Solstice: A Magazine of Diverse Voices* and *Tarnished: True Tales of Innocence Lost* (Pinchback Press). An excerpt from his recently completed memoir received honorable mention for Fourth Genre's Michael Steinberg Essay Prize. Anthony currently teaches creative writing and literacy in correctional facilities in Massachusetts.

Liz Dolan's first poetry manuscript, *A Secret of Long Life,* which is seeking a publisher, was nominated for the Robert McGrath Prize. She has been published in *On the Mason Dixon Line: An Anthology of Contemporary Delaware Writers.* A five-time Pushcart nominee, Liz won a fellowship from the Delaware Division of the Arts in 2009. Her second poetry collection, *They Abide,* was recently published by March Street Press. She is most proud of the offsite school she ran in the Bronx and of her nine grandchildren who live on the next block in Rehoboth. They pepper her life.

Hilda Downer works as an ACTT nurse in Avery County, North Carolina, and teaches in the English Department at Appalachian State University. Having written mostly poetry in the past, she is working on non-fiction at present culled from her experience in the nursing field of mental illness, disease, and child abuse in relation to her philosophies of raising her own children.

Donna Doyle is a native of Knoxville, Tennessee, where she resides along the southern base of Sharp's Ridge with her husband, David, and their cats, Ki and Abdulah. Most recently, her poetry has appeared in *The Journal of the American Medical Association* and in *The Southern Poetry Anthology Volume III: Contemporary Appalachia*. Donna is the author of a chapbook, *Heading Home*, published by Finishing Line Press.

Elizabeth Drewry is a Shakespeare enthusiast, a yoga practitioner, and a half-hearted cook except for her specialty, peach pies. She's a charter member of the National Blues Foundation, headquartered in her hometown of Memphis, Tennessee. Now retired, she was a newspaper executive for twenty-five years in New York and California. She lives in the beautiful foothills of the Blue Ridge Mountains, where she writes poetry and is working toward her first collection.

Caroline DuBois has been living in Nashville, Tennessee, with her singer-songwriter husband and two children since receiving her MFA in poetry. She teaches high school on the side. Her poetry has appeared in various journals, including *The Journal of the American Medical Association, Southern Poetry Review, Dry Creek Review* and *Fox Cry Review.*

Terry M. Dugan worked as a researcher at Bellevue Hospital Pediatric AIDS clinic. She has published academic articles about AIDS and lectured about human rights and AIDS in Africa at Oxford University. Her poetry and fiction about working at Bellevue have won numerous awards. She was invited to read her poetry at the United Nations.

Judith Duvall has been passionate about writing since producing her first poem, a masterpiece in crayon, at age four. Her poetry has appeared in the poetry anthology *Bleeding Hearts* (Tellico Books). Her poem, "In the Presence of Trees" won second place in the 2010 poetry competition for *Kudzu* literary journal, and her poem, "I Shall Not Think of War Today" garnered an honorable mention in The Portraits of the Past poetry competition sponsored by Old Gray Cemetery, Knoxville, Tennessee. Her fiction was included in three anthologies published by Greyhound Books.

Joyce Dyer is the John S. Kenyon Professor of English at Hiram College in Ohio. She is the author of three memoirs and the editor of *Bloodroot: Reflections on Place by Appalachian Women Writers.* Joyce has won numerous awards for her writing, including the 1999 Appalachian Book of the Year Award and the 2009 David B. Saunders Award in Creative Nonfiction. Her latest book, *Goosetown: Reconstructing an Akron Neighborhood*, was selected as a finalist for the 2011 Ohioana Book Award.

Normandi Ellis has authored three fiction collections, including *Sorrowful Mysteries and Other Stories*, winner of the Bumbershoot Award, and *Fresh Fleshed Sisters*. Her short story collection, *Going West*, is forthcoming from Wind Publications. A recipient of an Al Smith Fellowship from the Kentucky Arts Council and numerous grants from the Kentucky Foundation for Women, she and her husband operate PenHouse Retreat Center.

David Eye earned a midlife MFA from Syracuse University in 2008. His poems have appeared or are forthcoming in *The Louisville Review*, *Stone Canoe* (vols. 1, 2, & 5), *Waccamaw*, *roger*, *Fearless Poetry Anthology* (vol. 2) and *Consequence Magazine*, where he was a finalist for the 2009 Consequence Prize in Poetry. David teaches writing and poetry at Manhattan College in the Bronx.

Erin Fitzgerald is a writer of songs, short fiction, sketches, and lists on index cards. She lives in Louisville, Kentucky, with her brilliant children.

Jenrose Fitzgerald is a Kentucky-based singer/songwriter with a soulful voice and eclectic writing style. Inspired by songwriters from Loretta Lynn and Emmylou Harris to Michelle Shocked and Patty Griffin, Jenrose's songs cover a wide range of musical and lyrical styles. The common threads that run through all of her music are a passion for storytelling and an appreciation of the well-crafted song.

Elizabeth Glass has a Masters degree in Creative Writing from Miami University, Ohio. Her work has appeared in *Chattahoochee Review*, *Georgetown Review, West Wind Review, Blue Moon Review* and *Writer's Digest*. She is the recipient of a Kentucky Arts Council Grant and lives in Louisville, Kentucky.

Susan F. Glassmeyer is co-director of the Holistic Health Center of Cincinnati where she integrates The Feldenkrais Method®, Psychosynthesis, Sensory Awareness, and other healing modalities in her practice. Susan promotes experiential poetry classes and workshops through LittlePocketPoetry.Org. She has a chapbook of poems, *Body Matters,* from Pudding House and a second chapbook, *Cook's*

Lunch, forthcoming from Finishing Line Press.

Jesse Graves teaches writing and literature classes at East Tennessee State University, where he is an Assistant Professor of English. His first poetry collection is *Tennessee Landscape with Blighted Pine* (Texas Review Press, 2011). He recently served as guest editor for a special issue of *The Southern Quarterly* on "The Poetry and Prose of Robert Morgan" and is co-editor with William Wright of *The Southern Poetry Anthology, Volume III: Contemporary Appalachia.*

Connie Jordan Green lives on a farm in East Tennessee where she writes and gardens. She is the author of two novels for young people (*The War at Home* and *Emmy*), two poetry chapbooks (*Slow Children Playing* and *Regret Comes to Tea*), and a biweekly newspaper column. She and her husband have three grown children and seven grandchildren.

Michael Gregory has published widely in periodicals, anthologies and on-line. He is the author of several books and chapbooks including, most recently, *re: Play* (Pudding House, 2009). *Mr America Drives His Car: Poems 1978-2010* is scheduled for publication by Education in Reverse in 2011. For many years an internationally-recognized toxics activist, since 1971 he has lived off-grid near the Mexican border in southeast Arizona where he raises organic fruits and vegetables.

Ellen Hagan's poetry and essays have appeared in literary journals, magazines, and anthologies. She holds an MFA in Fiction from The New School University. Ellen is member of the Affrilachian Poets, Conjwomen, and co-founder of the girlstory collective. *Crowned,* her debut collection of poems, was published by Sawyer House Press in 2010.

Richard Hague is author of 13 volumes, including *Ripening, Possible Debris, Alive in Hard Country,* winner of the 2004 Appalachian Writers Association's Poetry Book of the Year, and *Milltown Natural: Essays And Stories from A Life,* nominated for a National Book Award. His nonfiction has been a finalist for the AWP Nonfiction Award and The Bechtel Prize, and has appeared in *Creative Nonfiction.*

Pauletta Hansel's poetry has been featured in journals including *ABZ, Southern Women's Review, Still: The Journal, The Mom Egg,* and *Appalachian Journal,* and anthologized in *Motif v2: Come What May* and *Boomtown: the Queens MFA Tenth Anniversary Celebratory Anthology.* Her poetry collections include *What I Did There* (Dos Madres Press, 2011) and *The Lives We Live in Houses* (Wind Publications, 2011). She is a current editor of *Pine Mountain Sand & Gravel,* the literary publication of Southern Appalachian Writers Cooperative. Pauletta received her MFA from Queens University of Charlotte. She lives in Cincinnati with her husband, Owen Cramer.

Barry Harris is editor of the *Tipton Poetry Journal* and lives in Zionsville, Indiana. His poetry has appeared in *Silk Road Review, Saint Ann's Review, Grey Sparrow Journal, Boston Literary Magazine, Night Train, Hiss Quarterly, The Centrifugal Eye, Snow Monkey, Writers' Bloc* and in anthologies *Twin Muses: Art and Poetry* and *From the Edge of the Prairie.*

Matthew Haughton is the author of the chapbook *Bee-coursing Box* (Accents Publishing). His poetry has appeared in many journals including *Appalachian Journal, Now & Then, Still: The Journal,* and *New Southerner.* Matthew lives in Lexington, Kentucky.

Irene D. Hays, a Washington State native, has lived and worked in Idaho, Hawaii, Colorado, California, and Washington as writer, teacher, and education director. She has two poetry chapbooks published: *The Measure of Loss* (Pudding House, 2007) and *Witness: Landscape to Inscape* (Foot Hills Publishing, 2008.) Her poems have also appeared in literary journals and other media.

Caroline Herring is a singer/songwriter based in Atlanta, Georgia. Herring has released five albums, including her most recent, *Golden Apples of the Sun,* on Signature Sounds Recordings. She has appeared on *Prairie Home Companion* and has been featured on NPR's *All Things Considered.* Herring tours nationally and in the UK and Europe. She recently participated in the Cecil Sharp Project, a musical collaborative based on the Appalachian journeys of English ballad collector Cecil Sharp and his assistant, Maud Karpeles.

Paul Hiers received his MFA in Writing from Spalding University. His short stories have been featured in several publications, including *The Louisville Review* and *Eclipse.*

Susan Hodara is a journalist, memoirist, editor and teacher. Her articles have appeared in *The New York Times, Harvard Magazine, Communication Arts*, and others. Her memoirs are published in a variety of anthologies and literary journals. She is the co-author with three other women of a memoir, *Still Here Thinking of You*, about mothers and daughters.

Thomas Alan Holmes lives with his family in Johnson City, Tennessee, where he writes and teaches as a member of the Literature and Language Department of East Tennessee State University. A contributor to *The Southern Poetry Anthology, Volume III: Contemporary Appalachia,* some of his work has appeared in *Appalachian Journal, South Atlantic Review, Now & Then,* and *Black Warrior Review.* With Gwen Hale and Mike Mutschelknaus, he has also edited *Diversity in the Composition Classroom.* He is currently involved in a project that focuses on the contribution of country music lyricists to the American literary canon.

Stephen M. Holt has three collections of poetry: *Late Mowing* (Jesse Stuart Foundation), *Elegy for September* (March Street Press), and *A Tone Poem of Stones* (Finishing Line Press). He teaches in the Russell, Kentucky Independent School System and at Ohio University Southern. His writing and teaching careers were featured in a 2007 segment of Kentucky Educational Television's series *Kentucky Life.*

Jennifer Horne is the author of a collection of poems, *Bottle Tree* (2010), the editor of *Working the Dirt: An Anthology of Southern Poets* (2003), and co-editor, with Wendy Reed, of *All Out of Faith: Southern Women on Spirituality* (2006). She received an Alabama State Council on the Arts Literature Fellowship in 2008. She currently teaches in the University of Alabama Honors College.

Ron Houchin has five books of poetry published: *Death and the River, Moveable Darkness,* and *Museum Crows* (1997, 2002, and 2009, respectively, by Salmon Publishing of Ireland), *Among Wordless Things* and *Birds in the Tops of Winter Trees* (2004 and 2008 by Wind Publications). His work has appeared recently or is forthcoming in *New Mexico Poetry Review, Now & Then, Pine Mountain Sand & Gravel, Congeries (Connotation Press: An On Line Artifact),* and *YourDaily Poem.com.*

Silas House is NEH Chair of Appalachian Studies at Berea College and is a nationally bestselling author of six books including *Clay's Quilt* (2001) and *Eli the Good* (2009), as well as two plays. His work has appeared in *The New York Times, Newsday, Oxford American* and many other publications. He is the winner of the New York Public Library's Storylines Award, the Appalachian Book of the Year, the Kentucky Novel of the Year, the Fellowship of Southern Writers' Award for Special Achievement and many other prizes. House is co-founder and fiction editor of *Still: The Journal.* He lives in Berea, Kentucky.

Elizabeth Howard lives in Crossville, Tennessee. Her work has appeared in *Comstock Review, Big Muddy, Appalachian Heritage, Cold Mountain Review, Mobius, Poem, Now & Then, Slant* and other journals.

Lee Howard (1953-2003) grew up in the mountains of Kentucky, West Virginia, and Virginia, and worked as a poet, sociologist, and vocational counselor. Her poetry collection, *The Last Unmined Vein*

(1980), inspired many Appalachian writers. Recently Howard's poetry and fiction were gathered and edited by George Ella Lyon in *Harvest of Fire: New & Collected Works by Lee Howard* (MotesBooks).

Dory L. Hudspeth of Alvaton, Kentucky, is an herbalist, freelance writer and poet. Her poems have appeared in *Rattle, Wavelength, Shenandoah, Sow's Ear Review, Slant, Runes, Atlanta Review* and other journals. Her first poetry collection is *Enduring Wonders* from WordTech Press and her chapbook is *I'll Fly Away* from Finishing Line Press.

Jessie Janeshek's first book of poems, *Invisible Mink*, is available from Iris Press. The co-editor of the literary anthology *Outscape: Writings on Fences and Frontiers* (KWG Press, 2008), Jessie holds a Ph.D. from the University of Tennessee-Knoxville and an MFA from Emerson College, Boston. She will spend the 2011-2012 school year as a Visiting Assistant Professor of English at Bethany College in West Virginia. Also a freelance editor, she promotes her belief in the power of creative writing as community outreach by co-directing a variety of workshops.

Mark Allen Jenkins completed an MFA at Bowling Green State University in 2004 and is currently a Ph.D. student at the University of Texas at Dallas. His poetry has appeared in *Memorious, the minnesota review, Muse & Stone, South Dakota Review* and elsewhere.

Libby Falk Jones teaches writing and literature at Berea College, where she is Chester D. Tripp Chair in Humanities and Professor of English. Her poetry chapbook, *Above the Eastern Treetops, Blue,* was published in 2010 by Finishing Line Press. Her poems have appeared in regional and national journals and anthologies, including *13th Moon, Connecticut Review, New Millennium Writings, PMS poemmemoirstory, Blue Fifth Review, New Growth: Recent Kentucky Writings* and *Low Explosions: Writings on the Body*.

Marilyn Kallet is the director of creative writing at the University of Tennessee, where she is also Lindsay Young Professor of English. She is the author of 15 books, including *Packing Light: New and Selected Poems*, and a new translation of Benjamin Péret's *The Big Game (Le grand jeu)*, both from Black Widow Press.

Erin Keane is the author of the poetry collections *Death-Defying Acts* and *The Gravity Soundtrack*. She lives in Louisville, Kentucky, where she writes about theater, books, arts, and culture and teaches in the National University MFA program.

Sandi Keaton-Wilson has been preserving Appalachian words and ways in poetry, prose and plays since the 1980s. Her work has appeared in numerous journals and anthologies throughout the region. She has traveled as a performance artist/reader and enjoys watching people fall in love with her southeastern Kentucky dialect.

Leatha Kendrick is the author of three volumes of poetry, most recently *Second Opinion* (2008). Her poems and essays appear widely in journals and anthologies including *What Comes Down to Us: Twenty-Five Contemporary Kentucky Poets* and *Listen Here: Women Writing in Appalachia*. She co-edited *Crossing Troublesome, Twenty-Five Years of the Appalachian Writers Workshop* and wrote *A Lasting Thing for the World—The Photography of Doris Ulmann,* a documentary film.

Kit Kennedy's *While Eating Oysters* is published by CLWN WR Press. With Susan Gangel, she co-authored *Inconvenience*, published by Littoral Press. Her work has appeared in *Glass, Karamu, Motif v2: Come What May, Otoliths, Runes* and *Up the Staircase*, among others.

Clyde Kessler lives in Radford, Virginia, and is a regional editor for *Virginia Birds*, a publication of the Virginia Society of Ornithology, and the editor of a quarterly bulletin for the Blue Ridge Discovery Center, a history and natural history education organization with projects in schools in the mountains of North Carolina and Virginia. His poems have been published in *Grab-a-Nickel* and *Still: The Journal.*

Alan King's poems have appeared in *Alehouse, Audience, Boxcar Poetry Review, Indiana Review, Mi-Poesias* and *RATTLE,* among others. A Cave Canem fellow and VONA Alum, he's been nominated for both a Best of the Net selection and Pushcart Prize. He writes and lives in the Washington, D.C., metropolitan area.

Cyn Kitchen teaches creative writing and literature at Knox College in Galesburg, Illinois. Her fiction and nonfiction have appeared in *Carve, The Louisville Review, Opium* and *Ars Medica.* "Answering the Call" is from her Marine mom memoir, *Disaster Preparedness.* Her first book, a collection of short stories entitled *Ten Tongues,* was published in 2010 by MotesBooks.

Tiana Knight received a BS in Africana Studies from Tennessee State University. She is currently working on her poetry at The Writer's Loft, Middle Tennessee State University's low-residency Certificate in Creative Writing program, with her mentor Bill Brown. She has published in *Sisterhood: Voices of Teenage Girls* and *The Southwestern Review.*

Christopher Knox is from Stanton, Kentucky. He hopes to pursue his MFA after graduating from Morehead State University in the spring of 2011. He lives in Berea with his wife Koula and their four furry children, who all speak fluent "Tooten Toos."

Cathy A. Kodra, a native New Yorker, now writes and edits in Knoxville, Tennessee. Her poems and prose have appeared in *Main Channel Voices, Birmingham Arts Journal, New Millennium Writings, Roanoke Review, Cavalier Literary Couture, Common Ground Review, The Medulla Review, Still Crazy, Slow Trains, Motif^{v1}: Writing by Ear, Now & Then* and others. Cathy is a contributing editor for *New Millennium Writings.*

Alison Kolodinsky is a poet and translator whose work has appeared in *Poetry, Alaska Quarterly Review, Cream City Review, Motif^{v1}: Writing by Ear* and *Motif^{v2}: Come What May.* Her poetry collection is *Since the End* (MotesBooks, 2010) and she co-authored *Into the Blue Reach: Selected Poems and Prose by Rainer Maria Rilke,* a bilingual edition translated with Ingrid Amalia Herbert of Germany. She lives in New Smyrna Beach, Florida.

Kate Larken is a rover, writer, editor and musician. All of America is her front and back yard. Her publications, performances and recordings are numerous. Among many other honors, she was most recently awarded the Sallie Bingham Prize from the Kentucky Foundation for Women (2010) and a research fellowship in the Appalachian Sound Archives at Berea College (2011). A literary edition of her award-winning play, "Teddy's Piece," was published in 2011. She is MotesBooks' founder.

Landra Lewis is a native of Hyden, Kentucky, deep in the Appalachian mountains. She grew up surrounded by coal mining and its impact on the region and the people. She has a BA in Political Science from the University of Kentucky and a certificate in mediation from Duke University. She resides in Berea, Kentucky, where she practices mediation and writes prose, poetry and folk songs.

Scott Lucero writes and teaches in southeastern Kentucky, where he lives with his wife and two children. Evening with Poets, the poetry reading he directs celebrates the publication of the magazine *Kudzu* and is one of the biggest readings in the state. His recent work appears in *Black Words on White Paper* and the online magazine *Toasted Cheese.*

Sylvia Lynch is Assistant Professor of Education at Lincoln Memorial University in Harrogate, Tennessee. She has published three books of non-fiction and her short fiction has appeared in *The Louisville Review, Nantahala Review, Kudzu,* and in several anthologies, including the previous *Motif* anthologies. She was the recipient of the 2008 Gurney Norman Prize for Fiction.

George Ella Lyon, originally from Harlan County, Kentucky, works as a freelance writer and teacher based in Lexington. Among her recent books are *Back: Poems* (Wind Publications) and *Harvest of Fire: New and Collected Works by Lee Howard* (MotesBooks), which she edited. A picture book, *"Which Side Are You On?" The Story of a Song* (Cinco Puntos Press), will appear in 2011 as will her poetry collection, *She Let Herself Go,* from the LSU Poetry Series.

Amy Walsh MacKrell teaches literature and creative writing at Simpson College in Iowa. She is a graduate of Oregon State University's writing program and received her Ph.D. in creative writing at the University of South Dakota.

Eileen Malone lives in the coastal fog at the edge of the San Francisco Bay Area. In her past life she taught for local community colleges, hosted and produced an interview television show for Channel 29 and founded the Soul-Making Literary Competition. Her book of poetry, *I Should Have Given Them Water,* was recently published by Ragged Sky Press.

John C. Mannone, nominated three times for the Pushcart, has poems in *The Pedestal, Glass, Lucid Rhythms, Prime Mincer, Paper Crow, Mobius, Apollo's Lyre, Pirene's Fountain, Motif*^{v2}*:Come What May* and others. He edits poetry for *Abyss & Apex* and *Silver Blade.* He teaches college physics in east Tennessee and is a NASA/JPL Solar System Ambassador.

Linda Parsons Marion is an editor at the University of Tennessee and author of the poetry collections, *Home Fires, Mother Land* and *Bound.* She served as poetry editor of *Now & Then* magazine for many years and has received literary fellowships from the Tennessee Arts Commission and the Associated Writing Programs Intro Award, among others. Poems have appeared in journals such as *The Georgia Review, Iowa Review, Shenandoah, Asheville Poetry Review, Prairie Schooner, Nimrod, Potomac Review, Poet Lore, Connecticut Review* and in anthologies, including *The Movable Nest, Listen Here: Women Writing in Appalachia, Her Words: Diverse Voices in Contemporary Appalachian Women's Poetry* and *The Southern Poetry Anthology, Volume III: Contemporary Appalachia.*

Belinda Ann Mason (1958-1991) was born in eastern Kentucky and worked as a journalist, fiction writer and playwright. Two of her plays were produced by Appalshop's Roadside Theatre. After contracting the HIV virus in 1987, she became an AIDS educator and activist. She co-founded the Kentuckiana People with AIDS Coalition, was elected president of the National Association of People with AIDS, and was appointed by George H.W. Bush to the National Commission on AIDS, the first person with the disease to occupy a seat on the commission. An excerpt from her novel appeared in *Motif*^{v1}*: Writing by Ear, An Anthology of Writings about Music.*

Sue Massek is a founding member of the Reel World String Band. Since 1977, they have created seven recording projects and played a variety of venues from community gatherings and picket lines in the heart of the Appalachian coalfields to the Lincoln Center in New York City. Sue's solo recording project is *Brave is the Heart of a Singing Bird* (Nekked-Rekkedz, 2010). She works with the Kentucky Foundation for Women, supporting feminist artists who use their art for social justice, and lives with her partner in Willisburg, Kentucky, on a small farm with three horses, two dogs and one cat.

Bob Masterson resides with his wife and daughter in Louisville, Kentucky, where he moonlights as a writer and songsmith. His song "Mister Coal and Mister Green" can be heard on the compilation disc *Rising: A Gathering of Voices for New Power* on the Nekked-Rekkedz label. Bob is also a regular contributor to *Keep Hearing Voices* on Crescent Hill Radio.

Clay Matthews lives in Bluff City, Tennessee, and teaches at Tusculum College. He is author of two poetry chapbooks and two full-length collections: *Superfecta* (Ghost Road Press) and *RUNOFF*

(BlazeVOX). His poems have appeared widely, including *The American Poetry Reivew, AGNI* (online), *Black Warrior Review, Gulf Coast, Willow Springs* and *Still: The Journal.*

Journey McAndrews is a writer, organic gardener, and freelance journalist. Her essays and articles have appeared in several newspapers, and her poetry has recently appeared in *Inscape* and *New Verse News*. She received an artist grant from the Kentucky Foundation for Women, and is the editor and publisher of *The Single Hound*, an online literary journal. She lives on a farm in Kentucky with three formerly stray cats, surrounded by wildlife, including several ancient maple trees, all of which inspire her writing.

Jay McCoy was born and raised in eastern Kentucky and now lives in Lexington. He holds BA degrees in English and Biology from Transylvania University, and an MA from The University of Akron. Jay is a member of the Poezia poetry group and has attended the Appalachian Writers Workshop.

Greta McDonough writes the popular weekly column "From This Place to That" for her hometown newspaper in Owensboro, Kentucky. She is author of *Her Troublesome Boys: The Lucy Furman Story* (MotesBooks, 2010). She teaches at Owensboro Community and Technical College.

Llewellyn McKernan has a Master's degree in creative writing from Brown University. She has been an adjunct English instructor at St. Mary's College, University of Arkansas, and Marshall University. She has four books of poetry, including her latest, *Pencil Memory*, from Finishing Line Press. Her poetry has also been published in such literary journals as *The Kenyon Review, The Antietam Review, Now & Then, Appalachian Journal, Appalachian Heritage, Southern Poetry Review* and *Still: The Journal.* She lives on a rural route in West Virginia, with a creek in front of her house and a mountain in back.

Phillip Meeks is a county Extension agent in southeastern Kentucky, where he lives with his wife and three children. When he isn't writing, he likes to backpack, garden and beekeep. This is his second publication in a *Motif* anthology.

Jim Minick is the author of the memoir, *The Blueberry Years,* a SIBA finalist for best book of the year, 2010. His poetry collections are *Her Secret Song* and *Burning Heaven*, winner of the 2008 Book of the Year Award from The Virginia College Bookstores Association. His collection of essays is *Finding a Clear Path*, and he edited *All There Is to Keep*, poems by Rita Riddle. His work has appeared in *Shenandoah, Orion, San Francisco Chronicle, The Sun, Appalachian Journal, Bay Journal* and *Wind*. He teaches literature and writing at Radford University.

Norman Minnick is author of the poetry collection *To Taste the Water* (Mid-List Press, 2007), which won the First Series Award, and editor of *Between Water & Song: New Poets for the Twenty-First Century* (White Pine Press, 2010). He earned the MFA in 2001 and was awarded an Academy of American Poets Prize that same year. He lives in Indianapolis with this wife and two young children.

Gwendolyn Joyce Mintz is a fiction writer, poet, and blogger about the writing life. Her work has appeared in various online and print journals. In other incarnations, she is an actress, a teddy bear maker and somebody's mom.

Sunny Montgomery is an essayist and spoken-word poet. Recent awards have included winning *Ace Weekly Magazine's* "Worst Summer Job" essay contest, first runner up at Kentucky Women Writers Conference Gypsy Slam and first runner up of 2009 Alltech Marc Smith Poetry Slam. Her stories have been published in *Limestone* and on *Public Republic*.

R B Morris is a poet, editor, singer, songwriter, and playwright from Knoxville, Tennessee. He is widely published as a poet and is a celebrated recording artist. His CDs include *Local Man, Take That*

Ride, Knoxville Sessions, Zeke and the Wheel and *Spies Lies and Burning Eyes.* A former Writer-in-Residence at the University of Tennessee, he also wrote the one-man play *The Man Who Lives Here Is Loony* (1992), taken from the life and work of another Knoxville writer, James Agee.

Debbie Mosley grew up near Chicago in Dyer, Indiana, started a family in Lafayette, Indiana. while finishing her Master's Degree at Purdue University, and settled in Southern Indiana near Louisville. A teacher, author, and songwriter, Debbie guides 5th graders to find their own voice through writing. She has two sons, Matthew and Travis, and a dog, Hershey.

Elaine Fowler Palencia, a native Kentuckian, is the author of four genre novels, two short story collections, and two poetry chapbooks, *Taking the Train* and *The Dailiness of It.* Her poetry has received two Pushcart Prize nominations and awards from the Illinois Arts Council, *Willow Review*, The Kentucky State Poetry Society and *Passager*. Her poetry chapbook, *The Big Woods*, is forthcoming from Pudding House Publications.

Lisa Parker received the MFA in Creative Writing from Penn State. Her work has appeared in *Southern Review, Louisville Review, Parnassus: Poetry In Review, PoetLore,* Bedford/St. Martin's *Poetry: An Introduction, 4th and 5th editions* and *Introduction to Literature, 7th and 8th editions.* Her first poetry collection, *This Gone Place* (MotesBooks), won the 2010 Weatherford Award for Poetry. Lisa grew up in rural Virginia and currently splits her time between Virginia and New York City.

Tina Parker's poetry and short stories have been published in *Appalachian Heritage, Limestone* and *New Millennium Writings*. A native of southwest Virginia, Parker now lives in Berea, Kentucky, with her husband and their two daughters.

Lynn Pattison's poems have appeared in *The Notre Dame Review, Heliotrope, Rhino, Diagram, Dunes Review, Controlled Burn* and *Poetry East*, and been anthologized in several venues. Her poetry collections are *tesla's daughter* (March Street. Press, 2005), *Walking Back the Cat* (Bright Hill Press, 2006) and *Light That Sounds Like Breaking (*Mayapple Press, 2006). A retired teacher of academically talented students, Lynn is a board member of Friends of Poetry, Inc., a nonprofit group that promotes/publishes writing/reading of poetry in the larger community.

Edwina (Eddy) Pendarvis was born in Floyd County, Kentucky, and has lived in West Virginia most of her life. Retired from Marshall University, she is currently the Book Editor for *Now & Then: The Appalachian Magazine*. Her most recently published prose is a dual-language book for Chinese college students—*Unlikely Hero: A Biography of Jean-Paul Sartre.*

David S. Pointer lives in Murfreesboro, Tennessee. In 2010 he was nominated for three Pushcart Prizes in poetry and was a winning writer in the *Empty Shoes: Poems on Homelessness and Hunger* anthology. His recent publications include *The Medulla Review, Theory Train* and *Hobo Camp Review.*

Melva Sue Priddy earned the MFA in Writing from Spalding University. She has had a long relationship with Hindman Settlement School's Appalachian Writers Workshop. Her work has been published in *ABZ, Appalachian Heritage, Foxfire's Hands On Journal, Motif*^{v2}*: Come What May* and *Standing on the Mountain: Voices of Appalachia.* Priddy lives in Winchester, Kentucky, with her husband Gene Strode. Together they share five children and 10 grandchildren.

Mary Anne Reese was born in Knoxville, Tennessee, and works as an attorney in Cincinnati, Ohio. She is a graduate student in English with a creative writing concentration at Northern Kentucky University. Her chapbook is *Raised by Water* from Finishing Line Press.

Joshua Robbins is a Ph.D. candidate in English at the University of Tennessee where he teaches literature and creative writing. His recognitions include the James Wright Poetry Award, the *New South*

Prize, selection for the *Best New Poets* anthology, and multiple Pushcart Prize nominations. His work appears in *Mid-American Review, Third Coast, Verse Daily, Copper Nickel, Southern Poetry Review* and elsewhere.

Rosemary Royston's chapbook *Splitting the Soil* is forthcoming from Redneck Press. Her poetry has been published in *The Comstock Review, Main Street Rag, Alehouse, Literal Latte, Public Republic* and *Dark Sky Magazine*. She was the recipient of the 2010 Literal Latte Food Verse Award, and she currently serves as the Program Coordinator for the North Carolina Writers Network-West. Rosemary holds an MFA in Writing from Spalding University.

anna Saini has lived many lives as a political scientist, radical activist and multi-media artist. She completed a BA and MA in Political Science from the University of Toronto and McMaster University respectively. Her writing appears in *Bitch Magazine, Diverse Voices Quarterly* and *Two-Bit Magazine*. An interview with anna appears in the book *Feminism FOR REAL: Deconstructing the Academic Industrial Complex of Feminism!*

Jane Sasser, a North Carolina native, was raised to believe in hard work. Her poetry has appeared in *The Sun, The Journal of the American Medical Association, The North American Review, Appalachian Heritage* and other publications. She has written two poetry chapbooks, *Recollecting the Snow* (March Street Press, 2008) and *Itinerant* (Finishing Line, 2009). She lives in Oak Ridge, Tennessee.

Mike Schneider lives in Pittsburgh and works as a science writer at Carnegie Mellon University. His poems have appeared in many journals, including *Notre Dame Review, Shenandoah, Hunger Mountain* and *Poetry*. His chapbook, *Rooster,* appeared in 2004.

Roberta Schultz plays guitar, sings and writes for the Kentucky women's trio, Raison D'Etre. Her songs have gained recognition in the MOVA Songwriting Festival (with Pierce Pettis judging), Mike Pinder's (Moody Blues) Song Wars, and the Great American Song Contest. Resulting songs appear on Raison D'Etre's 2009 release, *Tales from the Tall Side*. Roberta's compositions are included on five Raison D'Etre recordings, *Isn't it a Wonder*, a 2008 children's compilation, SouthernArtistry.org's first compilation in 2006 and the festival CD for Womensfest, 2007.

Anne Shelby is the author of seven books for children, most recently *The Man Who Lived in A Hollow Tree* and the award-winning *The Adventures of Molly Whuppie and Other Appalachian Folktales*. In addition to plays, songs and poems, she has written a collection of short essays published by MotesBooks. Her play, *Passing Through the Garden,* was based on the works of Belinda Ann Mason.

Savannah Sipple is a writer who lives in eastern Kentucky. She is an instructor at Hazard Community and Technical College, where she teaches English, reading, and writing. Her work has also appeared in *Appalachian Heritage* and *The Louisville Review.*

Nick Smith is an eastern Kentucky hillbilly and editor of *Wind*, who BELIEVES IN THE FREEDOM OF PRESS AND ALL SPEECH, currently adventuring before retreating to a cave to live a long, lazy life.

S. Cook Stanforth is an English professor at Thomas More College, specializing in creative writing, ethnic American literature, and folklore. Her work appears in NCTE book publications, *MELUS*, *Language and Lore*, *Indiana Review* and other journals. She regionally performs in an Appalachian folk band, studies indigenous plant remedies and raises many children.

Pamela Steele, MFA, Spalding University, is the author of the poetry collection *Paper Bird* and a recipient of the Jim Wayne Miller Poetry Prize (2004), as well as a runner-up for the James Still Award for Poetry (2005). After several trips across the Continental Divide, she lives in Oregon, where she teaches at Blue Mountain Community College. Someday, she's coming home.

Katerina Stoykova-Klemer is the author of the bilingual poetry book, *The Air around the Butterfly* (Fakel Express, 2009), which won the 2010 Pencho's Oak award, given annually to recognize literary contribution to contemporary Bulgarian culture. Her English language chapbook, *The Most* was published by Finishing Line Press in 2010 and received a Pushcart nomination. Katerina hosts "Accents"—a radio show for literature, art and culture on WRFL, 88.1 FM, Lexington, and is the founder and senior editor of Accents Publishing.

Erik Tuttle is a poet and photographer from Girdler, Kentucky. His recent work can be seen in *Cold Mountain Review, File Magazine* and *F-Stop Magazine.*

Wendy Vardaman has a Ph.D. from University of Pennsylvania. Co-editor of *Verse Wisconsin* and the author of *Obstructed View* (Fireweed Press, 2009), she works for a children's theatre, The Young Shakespeare Players, in Madison, Wisconsin.

Donna D. Vitucci has work published or forthcoming in, among others, *Natural Bridge, Hawaii Review, Gargoyle, Front Porch Journal, Chautauqua Literary Journal, Smokelong Quarterly, Storyglossia, Another Chicago Magazine, PANK* and *L. A. Review*. "Need to Know, March 1954," is excerpted from her novel, *Feed Materials*, a finalist for the 2010 Bellwether Prize.

Davi Walders' poetry and prose have appeared in journals and anthologies, including *The American Scholar, The Journal of the American Medical Association, Washington Woman, Crab Orchard Review, Seneca Review, Potomac Review, Travelers' Tales*, and elsewhere. She developed and directs the Vital Signs Writing Project at National Institutes for Health in Bethesda, Maryland, which was funded by The Witter Bynner Foundation for Poetry. A recipient of a National Endowment for the Humanities Grant, her work has been choreographed and performed in New York City and elsewhere, featured on *The Writer's Almanac*, and nominated for Pushcart Prizes.

Frank X Walker is associate professor of English at University of Kentucky and founder and editor/publisher of *PLUCK! The Journal of Affrilachian Arts and Culture.* He is the author of five poetry collections.

Amy Watkins comes from a family of carpenters—incredibly creative people, although they don't see themselves that way. Her poems have appeared in many journals and anthologies, including *Bayou, The Blue Collar Review* and *Motif*^{v2}*: Come What May*. She is co-editor and host of the weekly poetry podcast *Red Lion Square*.

Karen J. Weyant's most recent work can be seen in *5 AM, The Barn Owl Review, Copper Nickel, Cave Wall* and *the minnesota review*. Her poetry chapbook is *Stealing Dust* (Finishing Line Press, 2009). She was a 2007 Fellow in Poetry from the New York Foundation for the Arts. She lives in rural Pennsylvania, but teaches at Jamestown Community College in Jamestown, New York.

Amber Whitley served as a Peace Corps Volunteer in Kazakhstan from 2004-2006. Her writing has since appeared in several literary journals and anthologies, most recently in the *Norton Anthology of Hint Fiction* and the *Licking River Review*.

Keith S. Wilson is an Affrilachian Poet and Cave Canem Fellow living in Northern Kentucky. Some of his previous publications include *Appalachian Heritage, Kudzu, Mobius: The Journal of Social Change* and *Evergreen Review*.

Sylvia Woods lives in Oak Ridge, Tennessee, where she plies her trade as an English teacher at the local high school. Her work has appeared in the previous *Motif* anthologies as well as other publications including most recently *ALCALINES* and *The Southern Poetry Anthology, Volume III: Contemporary Appalachia*.

Jeff Worley is the author of four chapbooks, four books of poetry, and was editor of the anthology *What Comes Down to Us: 25 Contemporary Kentucky Poets* (University Press of Kentucky, 2009). His poems have appeared in *Poetry Northwest, The Georgia Review, New England Review, Shenandoah, The Southern Review* and others. Recently retired from the University of Kentucky, he enjoys spending time at his Cave Run Lake cabin, discussing world events with the deer, wild turkeys, nuthatches, cowbirds and chipmunks.

Sheri L. Wright is the author of one full-length book of poetry, *Nuns Shooting Guns*, and four chapbooks. Her poetry appears in *New Southerner, Pegasus, Leo, Out of Line, Chiron Review, Clark Street Review, Darkling and Earth's Daughters, Crucible, Kentucky Monthly Magazine* and many others. She is a regional chair for the Kentucky State Poetry society and co-chair for their adult poetry contest for 2011. Currently she is the host of *From The Inkwell*, a one-hour radio show dedicated to all things literary, on Crescent Hill Radio.

Therese Zink is a family physician who practices in a small town in Minnesota. Her stories and essays have been published in a variety of medical, lay, and literary magazines. She edited *The Country Doctor Revisited: A 21st Century Reader* (Kent State University Press, 2010), a compilation of stories, poems and essays by rural health care professionals across the United States.

About the Editor

Marianne Worthington is editor of *Motif v1: Writing by Ear, An Anthology of Writings about Music* (MotesBooks, 2009) and *Motif v2: Come What May, An Anthology of Writings about Chance* (MotesBooks, 2010). Her poetry chapbook, *Larger Bodies Than Mine* (Finishing Line Press, 2007), was included in Finishing Line's New Women's Voices Series and won the Appalachian Book of the Year Award in Poetry. She is poetry editor for *Now & Then: The Appalachian Magazine* and co-founder and poetry editor of the online literary journal *Still: The Journal*. Her poems, essays, reviews and feature articles have appeared widely and in several anthologies including *Knoxville Bound, Women. Period, Cornbread Nation 5* and The *Southern Poetry Anthology Volume III: Contemporary Appalachia*. She received the Appalachian Music Fellowship from Berea College in 2009, the Al Smith Fellowship from the Kentucky Arts Council in 2008, an Individual Artist Grant from the Kentucky Foundation for Women in 2007 and the Denny C. Plattner Award for creative nonfiction in 2007. A native of Knoxville, Tennessee, Worthington has lived in Whitley County, Kentucky, since 1990. She is associate professor of communication and journalism at University of the Cumberlands.

ACKNOWLEDGEMENTS

Many kind people and generous organizations worked hard to make this third volume in the *Motif* anthology series possible:

Erik Tuttle designed the cover of volume one of the *Motif* series, and we've carried over several of his design elements. Special thanks go to: Kate Larken, MotesBooks owner and publisher, for her support and enthusiasm and for originating this anthology series; The Haroldines for literary sustenance and camaraderie; Toby J Larkins for giving us his photograph, "Two American Workers," to use as the cover art; Jackie White Rogers for giving us her photograph, "Drugstore Lunch," to use as the back cover art; Linda Parsons Marion for her suggestion of this volume's title; friends at the Appalachian Writers Workshop, the Mountain Heritage Literary Festival and the Knoxville Writers Guild; my writing teachers who still guide me, especially Jeff Daniel Marion; finally, to my husband, daughter, mother, sister, and brother-in-law . . . *sine qua non*.

Grateful thanks to the editors, publishers and writers who granted us permission to reprint the following:

"A Clown Without Pity" by Erin Keane, copyright © 2010 by Erin Keane, published in *Death-Defying Acts* (WordFarm, 2010). Used with permission from WordFarm. "Braid" by Linda Parsons Marion appeared in *Bound* by Linda Parsons Marion, Wind Publications, 2011. Used with permission of the author. "Celestial Farmer" by Lee Howard appeared in *Harvest of Fire: New & Collected Works by Lee Howard,* edited by George Ella Lyon, MotesBooks, 2010. Used with permission of the editor and publisher. "East Avenue Gulf" by Marilyn Bates appeared in the *Pittsburgh Post-Gazette* as "Greentree Gulf" (in memory of Richard Fogel 1949-2007). Used with permission of the author. "Elegy for a Hay Rake" by Jesse Graves appeared in *Appalachian Heritage,* 38.3, 2010. Used with permission of the author. "House/Tree/Person" by Alison Kolodinsky appeared in *Since the End* by Alison Kolodinsky, MotesBooks, 2010. Used with permission of the author and publisher. "How the Heartland Works" by Mary Anne Reese appeared in *Raised by Water* by Mary Anne Reese, Finishing Line Press, 2011. Used with permission of the author. "Last Words" by Frank X Walker appeared in *black box* by Frank X Walker, Old Cove Press, 2006. Used with permission of the author. "Lightning Over Walgreens" by Joshua Robbins appeared in *Rougarou,* Spring, 2010. Used with permission of the author. "Looking for Mount Fuji in the Japanese Tea Garden" by Kit Kennedy appeared in *San Francisco Peace and Hope.* Used with permission of the author. "My Land is Calling" by Katerina Stoykova-Klemer appeared in *The Louisville Review,* 65, 2009. Used with permission of the author. "Paradiso Lost" by Jennifer Barton appeared in *Work,* 2:42, 2011. Used with permission of the author. "Silent Hope" by Bill Brown appeared in *Important Words: A Book for Poets and Writers* by Bill Brown and Malcolm Glass, Boynton/Cook Publishers, 1991. Used with permission of the author. "Song for Atlantic Avenue" appeared as the song "Atlantic Avenue" on the CD *Knoxville Sessions* by R. B. Morris and The Irregulars and as a poem in *Early Fires* by R B Morris, Iris Press, 2007. Used with permission of the author. "Starlight Shift" by Suzanne Coker appeared in *ALALITCOM*, 2007. Used with permission of the author. "The Last Woman in America to Wash Diapers" by Barbara Crooker appeared in *Ordinary Life* by Barbara Crooker, ByLine Press, 2001. Used with permission of the author. "The Stigma of the Laundry Line" by Bobbi Buchanan appeared in *New Southerner*, June, 2005. Used with permission of the author. "Virginia Green" appeared on the 1995 CD *Muddy Water* by Kate Larken. Used with permission of the Nekked Rekkedz label and Kiss Me Quick Music (ASCAP). "Waiting" by Lauren J. Bryant appeared in *Now Comes the Petitioner* by Lauren J. Bryant, Finishing Line Press, 2011. Used with permission of the author. "Work Till Jesus Comes" from the play *The Gifts of the Spirit* by Belinda Ann Mason is contained in the Belinda Mason Papers, 1997MS348, Special Collections and Digital Programs, University of Kentucky Libraries, and provided to *Motif*^{v3} by Anne Shelby. Used with permission of Stephen Carden, executor of the Literary Estate of Belinda Mason.

—mw

CPSIA information can be obtained at www.ICGtesting.com
Printed in the USA
LVOW010030281011

252316LV00004B/1/P

9 781934 894460